TOO POOR TO DIE

Fresno County Cemetery: Mass Burial—September 13, 2018. Photo by author.

TOO POOR TO DIE

THE HIDDEN REALITIES OF DYING IN THE MARGINS

AMY SHEA

Foreword by Jillian Olmsted

R

RUTGERS UNIVERSITY PRESS

New Brunswick, Camden, and Newark, New Jersey; London and Oxford

Rutgers University Press is a department of Rutgers, The State University of
New Jersey, one of the leading public research universities in the nation. By
publishing worldwide, it furthers the University's mission of dedication to
excellence in teaching, scholarship, research, and clinical care.

Library of Congress Cataloging-in-Publication Data

Names: Shea, Amy, author.
Title: Too poor to die : the hidden realities of dying in the margins / Amy Shea.
Description: New Brunswick, New Jersey : Rutgers University Press, [2025] |
Includes bibliographical references and index.
Identifiers: LCCN 2025005146 (print) | LCCN 2025005147 (ebook) |
ISBN 9781978843998 (hardcover) | ISBN 9781978843981 (paperback) |
ISBN 9781978844001 (epub)
Subjects: LCSH: Death—Social aspects. | Poor—Social aspects.
Classification: LCC HQ1073 .S485 2025 (print) | LCC HQ1073 (ebook) |
DDC 306.9086/942—dc23/eng/20250225
LC record available at https://lccn.loc.gov/2025005146
LC ebook record available at https://lccn.loc.gov/2025005147

A British Cataloging-in-Publication record for this book is available from the
British Library.

References to internet websites (URLs) were accurate at the time of writing.
Neither the author nor Rutgers University Press is responsible for URLs that
may have expired or changed since the manuscript was prepared.

♾ The paper used in this publication meets the requirements of the American
National Standard for Information Sciences—Permanence of Paper for Printed
Library Materials, ANSI Z39.48-1992.

rutgersuniversitypress.org

For anyone who has ever experienced homelessness

CONTENTS

FOREWORD

As I read the pages of *Too Poor to Die*, I find myself deeply moved by Amy's journey. Lessons of the lives and deaths of the forgotten somewhat mirror my own—marked by lessons in humility and respect, learned while witnessing the challenges and inequities faced by those in poverty. Her work reflects the values I hold close, and her stories shed light on the complex layers of dignity and justice in end-of-life care.

My experience with death and hospice care began unexpectedly when both my mother and stepfather were diagnosed with cancer within weeks of each other. In the space of a single year, both passed away, only six weeks apart. At the same time, my father was facing a second bout of colon cancer but struggling to find treatment due to his "preexisting condition" and lack of health insurance. No hospital in his tristate area would provide him with the operation he needed. Shortly thereafter, I worked with a local cancer institute who was willing to provide charity care for my father and moved him in with me. He spent a year recovering from a liver resection and endless rounds of chemo and radiation. He would have died without a caretaker and surely couldn't have done this without a roof over his head. Living through my parents' final days, experiencing hospice twice in rapid succession, I was struck by the beauty of compassionate care—a comfort that every person deserves but that many are denied.

During this challenging time, I learned about The INN Between, Utah's first nonprofit end-of-life care facility for those inadequately housed. I was confused by the community resistance to its opening. How could a community rally against something so innately humane as a dignified death for all? Dignity, it seems, is a luxury that some hesitate to extend to everyone. As this book highlights, dignity is not free.

Amy has encountered many of these same realities and contradictions in her own way. Through each experience and story that she encountered, she allowed herself to learn and expand rather than shy away from the uncomfortable. She leaned into the discomfort, allowing herself to witness the raw reality of poverty and homelessness in death and sharing her insights so that others might better understand and push for change. This journey eventually brought her to The INN Between, where I started as a volunteer shortly after they opened their doors and now proudly serve as executive director. During her visit, Amy spent meaningful time with our residents, asking thoughtful questions and listening with both empathy and purpose.

What stands out most about Amy's narrative is her unapologetically vivid descriptions that bring readers face-to-face with the neglected, those who society has decided to keep hidden away. It's easy to offer empathy or assistance to those who fit neatly within our perceptions of "respectable" need, but Amy pushes back against this. Her work highlights the biases and fears that lead people to ignore or avoid the homeless, especially in death. Some may find it difficult to confront these realities, but this book makes clear that averting our eyes does not erase the suffering of the poor.

Each chapter of this book offers perspective on the inequalities in life and death, asking us to reconsider our assumptions about who is "deserving" of dignity. The first chapter, "Remembering the Forgotten," introduces the concept of unclaimed (or, as they are often called, "indigent") burials and the ways in which physical and social boundaries separate the wealthy from the poor, even in death. Amy's recounting of the mass burial in a Fresno County cemetery shows how poverty strips people not only of their comfort in life but also of their dignity in death. The parallel Amy draws between access to services in life and end-of-life care should cause an urgent call to action to those of us who have the means and privilege to influence change. While it may seem nuanced, this also shows the importance of exposing our children to what is happening in our world and taking off the rose-colored glasses, as you never know what is going to spark their desire to advocate for change.

Amy's final chapter, "Rest in Place: Hospice for Homeless People," resonates deeply with me. It explores The INN Between's mission of offering end-of-life care for those without homes, a mission that is still met with resistance by some. When I think of those who come to The INN Between, I'm reminded that they each carry a narrative, a lifetime of experiences that brought them to our door. They are much more than the labels that society places upon them. Like the narratives in *Too Poor to Die*, their lives and deaths highlight the intersections of identity, poverty, health, and humanity. But as this book poignantly reminds us, death is universal, and so too should be the right to a peaceful and dignified transition. We all deserve compassion, no matter our circumstances. It is our responsibility to extend this compassion, to help break down the barriers that prevent the most vulnerable among us from receiving the care they need.

Amy's book is an honest and compassionate exploration of a reality that many choose to ignore. Through her extensive on-the-ground research, personal reflections, and bold storytelling, she offers readers a chance to confront the harsh truths of poverty and death—and, more importantly, to envision a world where every person's life and death are valued equally. Dignity, as she makes clear, is not a privilege but a right—one that we must fight to ensure is granted to all.

It is an honor to introduce this book and to stand alongside Amy in the pursuit of a more compassionate, equitable world. Let her words inspire you, as they have inspired me, to see and serve the dignity in every life.

Jillian Olmsted
Executive Director / CEO
The INN Between

TOO POOR TO DIE

Introduction

*T*OO POOR TO DIE: *The Hidden Realities of Dying in the Margins* explores several angles of death, dying, and inequality. It is a journey to understand what happens to someone who dies while experiencing homelessness. Through creative and critical elements woven into personal essays that are informed by research on medical care, end-of-life care, and death care for those experiencing homelessness, my aim has been to bear witness to the disparities in death and dying faced by some of society's most vulnerable and marginalized. This work seeks to engage a broad audience by utilizing the creative tools and elements provided by the essay form and structure such as narrative, scene, and dialogue while incorporating the rigor of academic research in a readable and engaging manner. It works within the space of the wider issues of funeral poverty and health-care inequalities and then zooms in on the experiences of unhoused individuals. The intention of this book is to increase awareness around the intersection of death, dying, poverty, inequities, and homelessness in order to advocate for a better quality of life and death for all, including those who are too often left behind.

In 2013, I wrote an essay titled "Pushing Up Mare's Tails," about accompanying my dad to the county cemetery (a.k.a. the potter's field) in my hometown on a visit home. At the time, I wrote this in an effort to explore my relationship with my dad, home, and the memories I associated with growing up in Fresno, California. But along the way, I realized this cemetery, one for people too poor to pay for their own burials, had a hold on me. A writing instructor once told me to "write where the heat is," and this essay was hot. It grew bigger over the years and spiderwebbed out with each new experience I encountered in what became a quest to learn more about death and dying, and ultimately, how they intersected with poverty and homelessness. Eventually, this essay about visiting a cemetery with my dad became the foundation for this book.

•

I chose the creative nonfiction essay as the modality I'd use to enter into this conversation of death, dying, and inequality. The essay is an "attempt" and, therefore, felt like the best genre for navigating such a complex, messy, and layered topic. For me, it was the most honest and authentic way to explore death, dying, and inequalities.

I had become deeply interested in death and dying and how this was experienced by unhoused people. Yet I had never experienced homelessness myself or known anyone personally who had. When people asked how I got into the topic, I struggled to find an answer that felt satisfying, that justified the passion I had. Each time I had to answer this question, I felt like a fraud or I felt like the answer fell flat. It took a while to figure it out, but the reason I felt this way was because the real answer was that there was no easy answer.

After a few years of giving the jumbled response, "Something about visiting potter's fields," when asked why and what I was writing about and struggling with what felt like an insurmountable amount of information, experience, and tangled emotions, I began to understand and accept that the journey itself was the story. I also learned to accept that what I was doing was a form of activism. Essay as activism: using my skills as a writer to question the status quo, bend a critical eye to the standards and norms being held before us, and bring to light issues that I believe need addressing. I didn't need a history that connected me to the issue to speak out against the injustices I saw. I didn't need a related personal trauma to care deeply and passionately. But I did need to be acutely aware of where I stood in relation to what I was researching and writing about. Attempting to discuss such a difficult topic "easily" was perhaps part of my problem.

In the introduction to *The Best American Essays 2017*, Leslie Jamison asks the question, "What can an essay be?" She asked this question of the reader, but she had also previously asked this question of her graduate students. From her students, she received myriad responses including, "an unfinished thought that doesn't get away . . . a tapestry, dishrag, or a plea" (xxv). It's a fascinating question, and so I, too, asked myself, what can an essay be? An essay can be a confession, a journey, a memory, a question, a thought. An essay can be a powerful tool for communicating information, expressing dissent, and stimulating imagination. Essays can be gateways into spaces where we feel compassion, where we live in someone else's shoes and hear their stories. Essays can be providers of thoughts, facts, emotions, measured commentary, and motivation to act. Essays can be windows through which we can witness familiar experiences while also being exposed to new ways of looking at the world. Jamison acknowledges the essay's solipsistic nature but explains with such eloquence how this and other aspects of the form are what make it the perfect genre to embody the political: "The essay isn't a retreat from the world but a way of encountering it. . . . [It] is politically useful . . . because of its commitment to nuance, its explorations of contingency, its spirit of unrest, its glee at overturned assumptions. . . . Essays bear witness, and they confess the subjectivity of their witnessing. They need some motivating urgency. . . . Wonder. Trauma. Mystery. Injustice. . . . This is something close to the precise ethical opposite of xenophobia or scapegoating. Essays take abstractions and make them particular" (xx).

My first ever published essay, "The Period Calendar," was about getting my period during a time when teen pregnancy dominated cultural fears and imagination. When I wrote it, I didn't think of it as being political writing; it felt more like a self-absorbed exercise in navelgazing. I couldn't imagine how others might relate to the very mundane experience of a girl getting her period. Yet as Leslie Jamison notes in her introduction to *The Best American Essays 2017*, "the personal is political. . . . I believe that it matters to narrate the particular stories of particular debts, rather than simply Debts Writ Large" (xxiii).

Years after my essay was published, I could look back and see that it had been political. Without saying it outright in the essay, I was examining the complexities of being female and having our bodies feared and policed, and how in turn we often are afraid of and police our own bodies. I would go on to write much more overtly political pieces on gun control and other issues, paving the way to my eventually writing on this issue of disparities in death and dying.

Writing the personal essay doesn't necessarily limit the writer to their own experience, and often, the best such essays are ones that find a way to use the personal to connect with the universal. I chose to position myself in the essays because my experiences and observations were how I entered into and was exposed to inequalities in death and dying. I felt the reader needed to see that in order to understand how I'd arrived at this topic and why I cared so much. On the flip side, I knew these essays could not be about me. I am a relatable figure through which the readers can enter into this world, but I have not experienced such marginalization; therefore, I felt that to be the central figure in the narrative would be to co-opt the stories and voices of those who had. This issue of inequalities in death and dying needed to be the central character and theme and the primary focus.

The voices and stories of people with lived experience are where the power of the story resides, and the essay is the perfect vehicle to hold the messiness of it all. I felt the need to share what I have witnessed, learned, and felt so that others could also see, learn, and feel and maybe be drawn to action. But to do so responsibly, I needed to cast my net wide, speak to lots of people, spend time in relevant spaces, listen, learn all I could, and then figure out how to distill it all down into an engaging, compelling narrative.

As I began following the thread of disparity in death and dying, I found myself in seemingly disparate physical places, such as Fresno, California; Phoenix, Arizona; Boston, Massachusetts; Lexington, Kentucky; and Salt Lake City, Utah. Initially, I worried about whether putting them together in the book would be problematic. Would doing so bring up questions about what each had in common and what linked them? Both Fresno and Boston are places I considered home, and from there, I was led to other places, all of them dealing with an acute and growing problem of people dying while homeless. The various locations highlighted differences in the details and specifics of how death and dying were handled in homeless populations, but more so, they showed how much overlap and similarity there was regardless of place. Ultimately, death and dying, especially when intersected with poverty and homelessness within a Western capitalist society, is messy and complicated, and so to present it neatly packaged, tidy, or structured didn't make sense. Rather, I felt it was important to embrace the organic nature of where the research led me and to lean into and embrace the disordered, connected nature of it all.

Over the years, my writing has been heavily influenced by other personal essayists who use their experiences and observations to drive the narrative on similarly complex issues. Such authors, and their books, include Leslie Jamison and her 2014 book *The Empathy Exams*, Eula Biss's 2009 *Notes from No Man's Land* and *On Immunity: An Inoculation*, as well as Rebecca Solnit's many books, including *Men Explain Things to Me* (2015) and *The Mother of All Questions* (2017). These women have addressed such topics as empathy, vaccination, race in America, sexism, and women's rights, and all have written on these topics via the self to varying degrees. Some, such as Jamison, centered personal experiences quite predominantly. In *The Empathy Exams*, Jamison's essays are centered on her personal experience. Biss does likewise in her book *On Immunity* but is noticeably absent in her essay "Time and Distance Overcome" in *Notes from No Man's Land* until the very end. Solnit utilizes her experience to open *Men Explain Things to Me*, but then she quickly widens the focus beyond that inciting incident of a man unknowingly lecturing her on a book she authored.

The more I read, the more my faith in the essay as a means to engage and inspire readers was cemented. As I've "assayed the essay," I've long held on to and frequently gone back to *The Art of the Personal Essay*, compiled by Phillip Lopate for guidance. In the introduction, Lopate writes, "The hallmark of the personal essay is its intimacy. The writer seems to be speaking directly into your ear, confiding everything from gossip to wisdom.... [They] are adept at interrogating their ignorance.

Just as often as they tell us what they know, they ask at the beginning of an exploration of a problem what it is they don't know—and why" (xxvii–xxxvii).

I understood that with the personal essay, I could utilize my own ignorance; I could question all the problems on the page and use that first-person point of view through the "I" to create a rapport and an intimacy with the reader. I could take them along with me on this exploratory journey. The essay allowed me to navigate the complicated issue of homelessness, which often created more questions than it did answers, in a way that didn't try to distill it down or oversimplify it. I could invite the reader to sit with me on the page in the presence of all the complexity and contradictions with no obligation to have all the answers.

There were other writers I looked to who spoke to not only the validity of the essay but its particular effectiveness as a genre for political activism. In the craft article, "The Braided Essay as Social Justice Action" author Nicole Walker also discusses how the entwining of the personal and political gives what might otherwise be an abstract piece of writing a shape that readers can recognize: "You take a personal story and give it syntax, grammar, language, punctuation. . . . But now you've got to give it context, associate meaning to it. So next to that personal story, you set a paragraph about apples, or condoms, or chickens, or gun violence. Suddenly, your personal story is reshaped by these new facts, and the facts of your personal story cut into the hard statistics of your paragraph about imported apples or the failure rate of condoms" (3). Additionally, Walker notes that adding the personal narrative can engage with a reader who might not be inclined to share your viewpoint—or even one who might share it too readily: "I write politically, but I have found that political writing is often shallow and ideological; in political writing I agree with, I often find nothing new, and in political writing I don't agree with, I find nothing persuasive. . . . But the braided form expands the conversation . . . stretches the choices beyond right or left, one or the other. . . . The brain resists new ways of thinking, but resistance is an important political tool. Resistance is the metaphor that will rule all other metaphors" (8).

Creative nonfiction essays are works rooted in personal truths and experiences, yet done with the creative flare of artful formatting and prose. They possess multidimensional aspects that enable them to convey expansive themes without being overbearing or insistent. The essayist places different facts alongside one another in unexpected ways, giving space for their reader to consider topics they'd never thought of before and question their own knowledge and established beliefs. When I first began writing essays, I perhaps did so selfishly. It's deceptively easy to write about yourself, the things you did, that happened to you, that you think you remember. But as I grew into the genre, as I became comfortable calling myself an "essayist," I began to understand there was nothing easy or simple about the genre. The essay demands both reader and writer to question everything, even itself. For all these reasons and more, I moved forward with the conviction that the essay as activism, particularly in its braided form, is the best space for this work to exist and thrive in.

Each experience I had, each interview I conducted, each book or article I read, and each movie I watched played a role as a step that led me on to the next piece of knowledge. I'm so glad for the natural development of the research, as it never felt forced, and I followed leads and allowed the relationships I was cultivating to direct where I went next. This allowed me to weave it all together and craft the story that I needed to tell.

◆

The first half of *Too Poor to Die* examines what happens to someone when they die homeless, indigent, or unclaimed, including what options are available for disposition (the term used for the various forms of "disposal" options for dead bodies) and the reality of how much it costs to be dead. Although a majority of the examples in this book are of people who are unhoused, one of course doesn't have to be homeless to be "too poor to die." It's simply not that clear-cut; therefore, there are examples from numerous experiences, including people who might not be homeless but have no family, or have families who are unable/unwilling to claim them, as well as people simply deemed indigent, or without resources to pay for end-of-life care and/ or disposition. Both "indigent" and "abandoned" are technical terms often used by public programs that deal with people who don't have the means for a private disposition. But there's growing awareness and discussion in the deathcare community around how problematic, and often inaccurate, these terms can be. Another term often used is "unclaimed," which refers to someone who cannot afford private disposition for any reason. I use all of these words in this book, trying to use "unclaimed" more often, as it feels less pejorative; but ultimately, these are the terms at our disposal until the community can find and agree upon more accurate, descriptive, and less marginalizing language.

This book also reviews various cultural touchstones related to death and dying, such as films, books, and cultural movements and how they influenced my research, thinking, and writing. I take the reader out into the field with me to experience different places such as cemeteries across the country, a medical respite unit in Phoenix, and a homeless shelter in Boston. The latter half of the book takes a closer look at societal, linguistic, governmental, cultural, and systemic causes that prevent people from easily getting out of chronic homelessness and how those things coincide to create disparities in health, health care, end-of-life care, and death care, which refers to services provided in relation to death, including funerals, disposition, and more.

Some of the chapters and content explored in *Too Poor to Die* include "Remembering the Forgotten: The Space That Remains," which reviews the physical separation of rich and poor in both life and death. It explores how this makes it difficult to extricate oneself from living on the streets, as well as how homeless persons are buried and memorialized. "Death by a Thousand Viewings" critically reviews the documentary *A Certain Kind of Death* and discusses how this film drove me to act and to focus my research on the indigent and unclaimed death. "Field Notes of a Tombstone Tourist" is rooted in visits to different cemeteries and explores the differences between burial places for those who have money and those who do not. "Sweet Feet" is a recounting of my experience as a foot-care assistant at a homeless day shelter. This chapter moves us from death into dying through the health dispari- ties faced by those living on the streets. "Deaths of Disparity" takes a deep dive into systemic issues around health care and end-of-life care and how homelessness is exacerbated by un- or undertreated health issues and how those health issues can lead to untimely deaths. This chapter also highlights some of the initiatives that have been designed to bridge the gap in health and end-of-life care disparities including medical respite units and Housing First.

While working and writing, I've held the belief that these essays should be accessible and engaging to a wide variety of readers. There- fore, I avoided taking the reader on too many tangential journeys that would blur the focus of the primary issues: death, dying, and inequali- ties. However, I'd like to draw attention to two implicit subjects that are woven through these essays: capitalism and respect.

Capitalism is the rubric through which many of the central issues of this book are viewed. The myth of capitalism, that it is a fair market with opportunity for all, is important to consider. Capitalistic societies function under the idea that the path to resources is one that's available for all to take should they choose it and be willing to work hard for it. The role that it plays in such concerns as chronic homelessness, access to health care, or the expense of funerals cannot be ignored. There are three primary concerns involved with capitalistic thinking that frame the core of this thematic element of the book.

The first is that inequities in end-of-life and death care stem partly from having a lack of access to resources or the lack of time to make future considerations, such as living wills or advanced directives. Even the abstract idea of "future" is problematic for someone living in chronic poverty or homelessness, where choices in life may be very limited. The idea of having any agency in death might feel immaterial to someone in those circumstances. In an economy like that of the United States, neither access to resources nor time is free.

Secondly, I argue that the idiom about how nothing is certain in life except for death and taxes should be considered within the matrix of capitalism—that for every life, money is certain to be made or spent on death and taxes. Consider the deathcare industry and the death positivity movement. Both suffer from the professionalization of death and dying, which opens the door for entrepreneurship. Where there is death, there is profit to be had, whether that be in the form of upselling coffins, offering services as a death doula (similar to a birth doula), selling death positive swag, and more.

Lastly, access to health care is also considered through the capitalist lens, including general lifetime health care and end-of-life care as they pertain to people who experience chronic homelessness. In the United States, health-care costs are inextricably linked to our economy. As the article "Health Equity and the Circle of Human Concern" notes, "Critics have pointed to [the U.S. health-care system's] siloed structure in which care is separate from public health and coverage is tied to employment" (Powell and Toppin 166). If you want to maintain a certain level of health in the United States, being gainfully employed is more or less a requirement. Social determinants are often ignored when considering the health and death of unhoused or indigent people. Issues such as systemic racism, classism, and other forms of exclusion and oppression exist within all these frameworks, including our economy, and they create marginalization, which then leads to those marginalized often being blamed for their own failings, including their perceived inability to be responsible for maintaining their health.

My exploration of this issue of capitalism and personal responsibility became intertwined with another theme, which is respect. There is often a lack of respect for those seen as less than, which is partly what allows people to become marginalized in the first place. When we don't respect someone, we don't see them as deserving of our help. When we don't respect someone, we don't see them as someone worth remembering. When we don't respect someone, we don't see their worth. When we don't respect someone, we don't see them as deserving. When we don't respect someone, we don't see their humanity. When we don't respect someone, we don't see them.

Another important point to note is how COVID-19 has altered so much for so many. In my chapter "How to Have a Good Death, or The Dead Grandma Essay," I reference sociologist Lyn Lofland, author of *The Craft of Dying*, who noted that in Westernized societies, it's not that there is a fear of talking about death as much as there is just a lack of need for it most of the time. Thanks to medical and technological advances and the professionalization of death care, many don't have to face mortality as readily as we once did. For the privileged majority of us, death has become something that's dealt with behind the scenes; therefore, we don't see it as our problem—until it is. COVID-19 brought death to the forefront, making it everyone's problem. It enveloped our world toward the final months of my research and writing of this book, and with the disease being so nascent, I was unable to go into depth regarding the pandemic. Yet it's important to note how this virus led the topic of death and dying into regular public discourse. Just as Lofland noted in her book, when the need arose we talked about it, but whether we were adequately prepared for how to deal with mass death is another matter.

Perhaps therein lies the central issue: When we are forced to deal with death, after not having to think much about it, we may find ourselves woefully unprepared to make life-altering decisions at the end of life for ourselves or our loved ones. This may leave us in positions where we can't afford final disposition options (including, but not limited to, burial or cremation) or we can't manage from a psychological standpoint.

In addition to bringing death and dying into mainstream conversation, COVID-19 also has brought up a multifaceted conversation on inequality. The pandemic didn't create these inequalities, but it absolutely pulled the curtain back to expose them and, in some cases, further exacerbated them. When we talk about how capitalism works, we only have to look at the economic destruction the pandemic wreaked on the middle class and poor.

Ultimately, the goal of this book is to motivate the reader to ruminate on all these issues: death, dying, mortality, disparities, inequalities, homelessness, capitalism, respect, deservedness, and our shared humanity in both life and death. Regardless of where we come from or where we're coming from, we all have the shared experience of being mortal. It is my hope that through this common ground, we can agree that dignity in death is something that should be afforded to everyone, not just those who can afford it.

Pushing Up Mare's Tails. Photo by author.

Remembering the Forgotten
The Space That Remains

Burying the Masses

O N SEPTEMBER 13, 2018, I stood in the county cemetery in my hometown of Fresno, California, which swam with more police officers than I could count. My dad and I parked on the street alongside Ararat Armenian Cemetery, then walked across the train tracks and onto a dirt road that led into one of three cemeteries owned by Fresno County. We'd dressed up, my dad in gray slacks and a short-sleeved button-up shirt and I in head-to-toe black. Even in a tank top, I realized that wearing black on a ninety-five-degree, sunny day might have been a bad idea, but it felt necessary. We were here to show respect.

On this day, the county was burying 740 cremated remains, known in the industry as "cremains," belonging to unclaimed people who'd died in Fresno over the last nine years. "Unclaimed" is a word used by many public agencies to refer to anyone they have to assist with disposition because they cannot afford private burial. This includes people with known next of kin, those without, and those who are unidentified. Each set of cremains was stored in a six-by-nine-inch box, labeled, and then placed into two wooden coffins.

Prior to the 2018 service, the last mass burial at Fresno County Cemetery had been in 2009. A few weeks prior to this, the sheriff's department had advertised the names of those to be buried, in the event that any family and friends wanted to claim their cremains before they were put in the ground, as once interred, cremains cannot be dug up. The ad posted on the Fresno County Sheriff's website read, "Please call (559) 600-3400 or email coroner@fresnosherrif.org. The last day to collect was September 11, 2018. Otherwise respects can be paid at 242 N. Hughes Avenue, Fresno CA 93706: Plot #s 58 and 59" (Coroner/Public Administrator).

This notice went out far too late, and with such little time before the burial, the sheriff's department pushed all the names out onto their website and offered free reclamation of cremains (which normally would cost $250) if proof could be provided that you had a connection to the person you wished to take. Only sixty sets of cremains were ultimately claimed, leaving the county with 740 to be buried.

Potter's Fields

Potter's fields are graveyards for the indigent, the unclaimed dead, or those whose families either cannot afford or don't want to bury them. The first time I saw Fresno County's potter's field was in the summer of 2010, when I accompanied my dad to the Holy Cross Cemetery on the corner of Belmont and Hughes, where my maternal great-grandparents were buried. In tracing and recording the genealogy of our family tree, my dad wanted to take pictures of their headstones so that he could upload them to the grave finding site, Findagrave.com: Facebook for the dead.

Upon retiring, my dad began working with the Fresno County Genealogical Society housed within the local library. He'd initially gotten involved with them as he worked on completing our family tree. He then became a volunteer, working on a project to map and catalog cemeteries in Fresno and those individuals buried in them so that families and others could find them if they wished.

This work eventually led him to the Fresno County cemeteries and the coroner's office, which maintained the physical records he needed to complete his mapping and database of names for the cemeteries they owned, including their last unfilled potter's field. The coroner's office had the records for the county cemetery piled up in a spare room, and with no time to deal with them, they were happy for my dad to take the files back to the library.

I had lived in Boston for a decade by this time, and while I was in Fresno visiting my parents for a couple weeks, I asked to join my dad on one of his graveyard outings. We would visit family member's graves, but I was most curious to see what a potter's field looked like. I'd never heard of such a thing until my father started his volunteer work. I'd never considered what could happen in and after death to those who died unclaimed, including those who died while homeless. To be clear, not everyone who is homeless goes unclaimed in death, and not everyone who is unclaimed is homeless. Plenty of people end up buried in potter's fields for a myriad of other reasons.

On that first visit to the Fresno County Cemetery, after visiting my great-grandparent's graves at Holy Cross Cemetery, we walked toward the back of the grounds, beyond an elaborately decorated building, with its pillars and marbled walls. This ornate structure held cremation lots. As we walked on, I wondered if that was where the phrase *one's lot in life* had come from. When we reached the chain-link fence that bordered the cemetery, my dad pointed past it: This was the potter's field. I peered through the holes in the fence, amazed at what we were looking at adjacent to the lush green lawns of Holy Cross Cemetery. On the other side of the fence lay a barren lot absent of any obvious indicators that it was a place of burial. One could drive right by and all they'd see was an empty dirt field with a handful of mare's tail in one corner. Mare's tails are notoriously nasty weeds that stand three feet tall, are thin in stature, and have needles for leaves. They look like nature's toilet scrub brushes. Weed killer has little effect on them, so they must be pulled out by their roots.[1]

As I processed the views of this neglected lot, I struggled for words and meaning. I wondered how many times throughout my life I had driven past, through the west side of Fresno, to go to the nearby cemeteries, the zoo, or to Roeding Park Playland. It appeared an empty field, land without a purpose, not land that held the bodies of thousands. My attention rested on the weeds, and all that came to mind was the old cliché: *pushing up daisies*. Or in this case, *pushing up mare's tails*.

I leaned into the fence and noticed small, unassuming numbers engraved in the thin stone strips that ran along the field every foot or so. My dad explained that these cement strips had plot numbers etched into them, indicating where the graves were. The county used to bury only one person per plot, but they long ago ran out of space, so when that happened, they began cremating everyone and burying 450 people per grave. It seemed crass to be burying so many cremains in one grave. Boxed up then buried with hundreds of others. Left for eternity to push up mare's tails.

What I discovered upon telling and retelling this story of my experience was that I wasn't alone in my ignorance. Whenever I told people about "potter's fields," I often received blank stares, which I'd then have to follow with some explanation. Others had knowledge of what they were but thought that they were an outdated concept.

But after that first visit to that Fresno County cemetery, I couldn't stop thinking about it. Each year after, when I'd come home for a visit, I felt the pull to return, just as I did other places, such as my old high school or Woodward Park—places that held memories and importance. Instead of peering through the fence from the sanctuary of Holy Cross Cemetery, as we had the first time, we eventually found out how to enter the potter's field, where we could walk among the weeds, the coyote holes, the ever-deteriorating Chinese cemetery and headstones, the piles of trash that people had dumped (which my dad would call to have removed), and the occasional piles of plastic flowers, flags, dolls, religious figurines, and candles that people had brought to pay their respects.

In doing so, we discovered the only headstone in the potter's field, made of a red marble and flush with the ground, which we would later discover was created in the early nineties by a funeral director, Jim Copner. Jim and his son made the headstone as a memorial for one of the mass burials for those who died between 1979 and 1989. In 1995, when the headstone was placed during a service for those being buried, the local newspaper, *The Fresno Bee*, covered the event and interviewed eighteen-year-old Eustolia Ramirez, who was there to remember her mother, Julia Chavez. Julia had died when Eustolia was

Fresno County Cemetery: Day. Courtesy Gene Sibley.

Fresno County Cemetery: Night. In the dark, the telephone poles look like crosses. Courtesy Gene Sibley.

five. Although not homeless nor indigent, her family couldn't come up with the money to cover the burial costs, so her mother became one of the 450 buried that day in a dirt field tucked back from the street up and adjacent to a brick wall, hidden behind all the known cemeteries (such as Ararat, Mountainview, and Holy Cross), in row 37, section S, grave number 53.

Dignity Isn't Free

By 2018, the mare's tails were gone, perhaps removed in preparation for the service, and the flurry of activity as everything was put into place for the ceremony made for a party-like atmosphere. All the big Fresno news outlets were there. Yet in the midst of the commotion, it was hard to miss the men working with the backhoe and shovel. My dad and I were surprised that the holes were just being dug. But after walking up to the two plots, it was evident that we weren't going to see the burial actually happen. They had already dug the holes, buried the coffins with the cremains, and filled them back in—they were merely bringing extra dirt to smooth over the top.

Awnings were set up with white plastic chairs placed beneath them, and a podium was carried by a couple of workers. One man handed out programs: On the front of the six-by-nine-inch folded cardstock was an angled image of an unidentified nature scene, with tall blades of bright-green grass creeping up from the bottom of the page, dotted with red and yellow flowers, a few tree branches leaning in from the left side. Set behind the grass and trees was a river undulating past.

Where was this scene meant to be? If I hadn't been standing in the vacant dirt lot that was the Fresno County Cemetery, or hadn't known the reality of the landscape of Fresno as hot, dry desert, I might have thought, *What a nice, comforting picture.* It was an image of serenity. It was a lie. One woman, who luckily had been able to rescue her brother's cremains from the mass burial that day, was quoted by the news as saying, "It's terrible . . . we have a pet cemetery that is prettier than this."

She wasn't wrong.

Underneath the awning, I stood on a patch of green turf that had been laid down with the plastic folding chairs placed on top of it for any mourners who wanted a seat. At some funerals, cemeteries lay green turf over the mounds of dirt for families who prefer not to see the land in its raw form. Sometimes, seeing the dirt is too much of a reminder that their loved one is dead. Too much of a reminder that they're burying their dad/brother/wife/daughter within that dirt. Too much of a reminder that the earth is claiming them. Too evocative of the reality of decomposition and decay. As we waited for the service to begin, I watched a county worker set up one of two large flower arrangements with white roses and a bow, and behind him, another worker walked past, shovel in hand, his helmeted head bent down past a stone wall with razor wire spiraled across the top.

A few days before the ceremony, the Fresno County Cemetery had been home to an unhoused man, which wasn't uncommon. But the sheriff's department came through and physically removed him along with his things, in order to prepare for the upcoming burial and memorial service of nearly eight hundred unclaimed individuals, some of whom, like him, may have been unhoused when they died. That he was cleared out so the rest of us could come and pay our respects to those like him felt wrong, hypocritical. Would it be too stark a reminder of how as a society, we have failed too many to actually see an embodiment of who we were memorializing? Many of those buried that day may not have been homeless, but they were living in that tenuous margin of being too poor to have agency in where and how they were buried.

Dignity isn't free.

The path that leads someone to use a cemetery as a home or to having a potter's field become their final resting place is a complex, layered, messy one. Actually, there isn't just one path, but many, often beginning long before the deathbed, that may lead to the same dismal end. Many who are homeless have the trimorbidity of poor physical, poor mental health, and drug or alcohol dependencies, which may lead them down a path where, even in death, as is evidenced by the potter's field, they are forced to the far reaches of "wasted" space: the only space that remains.

In 2015, a woman appeared around the corner from my parents' house, standing on the sidewalk adjacent to a neighbor's backyard fence. A shopping cart full of her things was parked on the street curb nearby. She stood there for three days. During that time, my mom periodically went out for walks to confirm whether she was still there.

It was autumn, and I was staying with my parents while I was teaching at a local community college. One afternoon, as I drove past the corner near where this woman stood, I wondered why she'd chosen that spot. It seemed that she might have been trying to obey city loitering laws to avoid getting moved along; she was in a residential area, not in front of any shop, and she was on the side of the house, so out of view from windows and not obstructing doorways or walkways. As a woman, I could also imagine that the neighborhood sidewalk might be a safer option than other spots in the city. If she were to be attacked there, in a quiet neighborhood at night, possibly people would hear her screams; someone might notice a struggle and be able to intervene.

It was also notable that she never sat while she was there. Someone once told me that this was because if she didn't lean or sit, the police couldn't make her move, yet I was unable to verify whether this was an actual law on the books in Fresno or anywhere else at the time. For those three days, she remained on that sidewalk corner, minus any time, I have to assume, when she may have left to go sit down for a bit, sleep, piss, shit, and generally be a living person.

When she finally left, I could only guess why she chose to move when she did. It certainly wasn't a permanent solution of any kind, but maybe she'd found somewhere better to go, maybe someone finally came along and asked her to move, or perhaps she just decided to give up her position as a living statue, the endless standing becoming too much.

Growing up in Fresno during the 1980s and 1990s, I don't recall homelessness being the ubiquitous thing it is now. One obvious reason for this is that it wasn't until the 1980s that the United States really saw a substantial jump in homelessness. At this time, shrinking

economic opportunities coincided with decreased safety-net protec-
tions (Padgett et al. 3). Bigger cities were hit the hardest.

It wasn't until 2004, when homeless encampments in Fresno
such as Tent City (located on the west side of town under Highway 180) started gaining traction, which was a few years after I'd moved
away to Boston. The Poverello House (a homeless service charity in
Fresno) upgraded tents that sat on wood pallets, which they'd been
using for temporary housing, by moving people into a neighborhood
of individual-sized toolsheds that they named the Village of Hope
(Rhodes). Yet hope wasn't enough, and soon after the 2008 recession,
things got worse. With five thousand people calling it home by 2013,
Tent City had grown large enough to draw attention from academics
who wrote theses on it (Speer) and journalists from news outlets and
publications, including NPR and GQ, who came to write articles on its
inhabitants and their lives there.

This is when Fresno officially disbanded Tent City, possibly due to
some of the negative attention it had received, requiring the encampment's residents to find other places to shelter throughout the city.
With few options, some, like the woman on the corner near my parents' house, moved north to camp in various residential neighborhoods. Many found their way to live along the banks of the myriad of
irrigation canals that snake their way through Fresno. Others wound
up breaking into abandoned homes in West or Central Fresno, a left-
over consequence of the 2008 housing market collapse. Sometimes
the illegal inhabitants of these abandoned homes would accidentally
start fires, often in an effort to keep warm, to have light, or to cook,
and sometimes those fires would get out of control and burn the
houses down.

For years, my dad has awoken each morning before sunrise and
walked four miles along the embankments of the canals, one of which
passes right behind his and my mom's home. On one visit, I decided
to accompany him, which was how I found myself walking in semi-
darkness at 5:00 a.m. along the canal. My dad carried a walking stick
with him, not for support, but to beat away one of the many packs of
stray dogs that might pass by him and become aggressive. Only a few

Fresno County Cemetery: Plots 58 and 59, Mass Burial, 2018. Photo by author.

minutes into our walk, and just houses down from my parents' place, the dark air began mingling with a stringent, toxic smell. I put my hand to my face to try to protect myself from the burning I felt in my nostrils.

"The neighbor's burning trash in his backyard again," my dad replied to my actions and the horrified look on my face. I responded by shouting about how disgusting that was, and he quickly shushed me, not wanting to draw attention from the people doing the burning. As we moved farther along, we passed by large piles of what appeared to be heaps of garbage, and on the end of one heap sat a man surrounded by his belongings. When I first saw him, I thought he was a child's doll—moonlight hitting a porcelain face staring out from a sleeping bag—but as I stared back, the eyes blinked.

By this point, people in Fresno were calling for something to be done about the rise in homelessness. But the reality was less about a large spike in numbers and more about a slight growth in numbers combined with the displacement of the people who'd previously resided in Tent City and other encampments but now were living unhoused directly alongside the housed.

As my dad and I returned home that morning, I was grateful for the sun rising and to no longer be out on the canal banks in the dark. It seemed to me that the homeless were the least scary thing we'd encountered on our walk—compared to the person illicitly burning trash in their yard and polluting the air with toxins, the threat of stray dog attacks, and the piles of garbage that were mostly being dumped by homeowners in the area. Yet none of those things seemed to arouse as much passion or bring out the pitchforks quite like the threat of the homeless "infestation." In Fresno, as with many other places, the fight over public space was beginning to heat up.

Right of Access: Private Property—Get Off My Lawn

Who has the right to exist, to be visible, in public spaces? After living in Boston for some years, I couldn't help but see how some of its public spaces had asked these questions of citizens over the course of history. Boston has been negotiating in regard to the Boston Common since its inception. The Common is the oldest public park in the United States. Established in 1634, it's been used for grazing livestock; Puritanical punishments, including a whipping post, pillory, and stocks; hanging people; a redcoat encampment during the Revolutionary War; public oratory, discourse, and public gatherings, including a rally led by Martin Luther King Jr. in 1963; protests against the Vietnam War; the 2017 Women's March; general entertainment and recreation, including picnics, walks, sitting on park benches, and tai chi; and organized activities such as baseball games in summer and ice-skating on Frog Pond in winter.

The Freedom Trail Foundation, a tourist website, notes in their page for "Boston Common" that "Boston Common is open for all to enjoy." But this is not so. In 2018, when I volunteered at a foot-care clinic in Boston's Chinatown area, one man told me of how the city was clearing out the homeless for the summer, so that tourists wouldn't see them, by making sleeping in the Boston Common park a fineable offense. He went on to claim that the government was responsible for all the opioid deaths inflicting swaths of the homeless population across the country. His gaze bored into mine as he spoke: "How else do you explain how fentanyl so quickly replaced heroin, huh? They're trying to get rid of us." It would come out a few years later that much of the opioid crisis was tied to the pharmaceutical industry's push for profit amid a display of capitalism at its finest. Of course, there wasn't any covert operation by the U.S. government to kill off the homeless, but he wasn't wrong in that they did want them out of sight. It seems that as homelessness grew, or at least became more visible between 2010 and 2020, the fight over public space intensified in cities all across the United States and the world.

In 2017, Fresno passed the Unhealthy and Hazardous Camping Act in response to the rising voices demanding something be done about the visible homeless problem. This made camping in tents or lean-to shelters on both public and private property illegal across Fresno.

In 2019, in San Francisco, residents of the Mission District paid for and installed twelve large boulders on the sidewalks in their neighborhood to deter "what they described as a year of flagrant drug-dealing and unpredictable behavior. Housing advocates and other civically minded critics were quick to call the boulders out as anti-homeless architecture" (Ho). This continues to be a recurring narrative that plays out across the Bay Area.

Even six thousand miles away from California's struggle, in Hungary, the social affairs state secretary bluntly stated that legislation in the form of antihomelessness laws seemed to be designed to dictate use of space for the homeless versus the citizen. In other words, if one is homeless, then for all intents and purposes they are considered stateless noncitizens.

When calls for reducing homelessness and political war-waging over public access reach a crescendo, as they have in recent years, the government seems to have two primary tools for dealing with it, sequestration/corralling or criminalization: Either cordon off the offending groups or try to police its way out of the problem, with reducing the visibility of homeless people at the core of both options. In one photo I came across, a man stands alongside a tent beside the fence of an abandoned property somewhere in the countryside of California with a handwritten sign that reads, "If not here, then where?" (Policy Advocacy Clinic).

Modern-Day Hoovervilles

In 1939, John Steinbeck wrote in *The Grapes of Wrath,*

> And then the raids—the swoop of armed deputies on the squatters' camps. Get out. Department of Health orders. This camp is a menace to health.
>   Where we gonna go?
> That's none of our business. We got orders to get you out of here. . . .
> [And] the tractors moved in and pushed the tenants out. (237)

I guess some things never change. In spite of many state and federal rulings that supposedly protect the rights of unhoused people to camp in public places if there is no place for them to be housed, the reality is much more complex, and regular sequestration and criminalization of unhoused people still occurs. In 2025, new laws are increasingly being enacted within cities that make camping illegal. With regard to corralling and sequestering groups of people experiencing chronic homelessness—tent cities are the most obvious way of doing this. Usually set in parts of town where there's little commerce and therefore not much public activity, these locations can be out of sight and out of mind. An NPR article notes how the growing encampments in California "evoke shantytown 'Hoovervilles,' where hundreds of thousands of destitute Americans lived during the Great Depression. The encampments are . . . fueling a debate over poverty and inequality in one of the nation's wealthiest states" (Westervelt).

One of the most infamous encampments is Skid Row in Los Angeles, California, which began to take shape in 1976, when the city established it as an unofficial "containment zone." As *Los Angeles Times* reporter Steve Lopez notes of Skid Row, "[It] smells like the death of hope" ("City of Angels"). But for decades now, Los Angeles has tolerated Skid Row's existence because its fifty square blocks have acted as a sort of barrier, penning in and containing a large mass of people in homelessness. But as the homeless crisis and the number of people on the streets have grown in California, the borders of places like Skid Row have begun to creep out or dissolve completely. There isn't enough space for everyone, and the poorest of the poor are beginning to commingle with the richest of the rich, resulting in conflict.

Venice Beach, an exclusive neighborhood in Los Angeles, is one such battle site where housed people who live there have fought over the public spaces with those who are homeless and who are also using those spaces. In response to these issues, Los Angeles residents voted to increase their taxes to raise money for affordable housing. Yet when the city tried to use the money to build the affordable housing, neighborhood after neighborhood, including Venice Beach, fought against it being built near them ("City of Angels").

As encampments grow too large and spill into actively used space, such as shopping and business districts or residential neighborhoods, as seen with Skid Row in LA and Tent City in Fresno, the homeless are no longer seen as being successfully corralled. But being relegated to certain areas of town can produce unwanted consequences for those experiencing chronic homelessness, whether in shelters or encampments. Shelters and affordable housing are also often only allowed and placed in lower-income areas or on the outskirts of town, making them inconvenient for accessing needed social and health services, and they are often too far away to commute for work.

I'm struck by how loud what isn't being said can be heard, like a dog whistle of mutual exclusivity being sung: us versus them, quality versus mediocrity, morality versus immorality, citizen versus homeless person. Without affordable housing, homeless encampments can be the safest and most preferred place of shelter for some. They don't operate under the same auspices of governmental control that shelters might, which means there's potential for more drug use and criminal activity. Yet on the flip side, they also give the people who live there the opportunity to govern themselves. They can better create trusted communities, maintain some semblance of control over how they live, and possibly avoid or reduce their level of institutionalization.

As anthropologist Robert Desjarlais writes in his 1997 book, *Shelter Blues: Sanity and Selfhood Among the Homeless*: "The homeless can be felt too much. Those living on the streets and in shelters are disturbing because they threaten assumed paradigms of meaning. . . . It is thus fitting that . . . shelters [be] set up . . . out of sight and beyond the reach of most social and economic commerce. . . . [And] the most valued sites are policed in such a way that the poor and others are forcefully kept away. We maintain and control the resources, the knowledge, the means of production and visibility" (33, 65, 103). The criminalization of poor and homeless people is not a modern invention. Under the guise of quality-of-life laws, the homeless are pushed out and driven away. This practice stems from a long history of sweeping the undesirable along. The United Kingdom's "Vagrancy Act of 1824" states that "every person wandering abroad and lodging in any barn or outhouse, or in any deserted or unoccupied building, or in the open air, or under a tent, or in any cart or wagon, [not having any visible means of subsistence] and not giving a good account of himself or herself" can be forcibly moved.

American colonists developed vagrancy laws, stemming from the English Poor Laws, which were not directed at homeless people, yet which seem to be an early version of what modern-day loitering laws were modeled after. Coming into the nineteenth century, some cities and states created "ugly laws" that tried to ban people who were diseased, deformed, maimed, or mutilated. In the late 1800s, there were "sundown towns" in the Southern United States that banned African Americans from being out on the streets after dark. Cities in California did the same to Mexicans, Native Americans, and Chinese Americans. After the Dust Bowl and Great Depression drove people from Oklahoma and other states into California looking for work, California tried to outlaw these "Okies" from coming into the state (Policy Advocacy Clinic).

As instances across the world have shown, finding a solution to homeless encampments and their visibility is desired, but many don't want that solution to land in their proverbial backyards. When people have nowhere to sleep, sit, or perform basic bodily functions privately, they are forced to do these things in public spaces meant to be shared with all in the community. They're then penalized through citations, jailing, and other means that push them further into the system in ways that only perpetuate their state of homelessness and poverty, and the cycle repeats. Is the "choice" to live in a tent under a highway or on a canal really a choice?

Public health concerns exist and need to be taken into consideration, but that means public health for everyone. Community members cite fears over tent cities including fire risk, violence, and disease (Barry-Jester), yet often the ones most at risk are not them but those in the camps. Although encampments are not up to public health standards, that doesn't necessarily mean it's safer for people to be moved out of them. The consequences of being moved on without being placed in housing are also very serious. Numerous studies and organizations have shown that each time someone is moved from an encampment, they run the risk of losing so much:

personal property
medications
identification
shoes
medical and legal documents
blankets
tents
family photos
any sense of stability and safety

These are things that hold meaning—tools to survive, small comforts, all being expeditiously gathered. People take what they can before the highway crews come through to clear out the area, what the campers in California refer to as the "Caltrans shuffle" (Barry-Jester). It can be difficult, if not impossible, to imagine what it must feel like to frantically have to pack and move everything you own every few days or weeks. What's not difficult to understand, though, is how in the midst of such moves, crucial items, such as walkers, identification cards, and prescriptions, are lost—and how devastating that could be (Herring).

Each time someone is cited for not moving on or for some other activity that falls within the purview of antihomelessness laws, this creates a knock-on effect of misery and frustration: *A fine is issued that they can't afford to pay → a bench warrant is issued → with no fixed address, they may miss any notices to appear in court and hearing dates → they get arrested → miss crucial appointments required for receiving benefits → the likelihood of remaining on the streets increases, as well as engendering a further distrust of and disenfranchisement from the system* (paraphrasing Barry-Jester, Desjarlais, Herring, Hodge et al., Padgett et al., and National Coalition for the Homeless). Often, when sanitation crews come through, people are prevented from collecting any of the belongings of those who aren't there at the time, which means that people are sometimes too afraid to leave camp, resulting in many unintended consequences. Sociologist, Chris Herring provides a haunting scene in his 2019 article, "Complaint-Oriented Policing: Regulating Homelessness in Public Space," that exemplifies such consequences: "The threat of property destruction [and loss] resulted in homeless people avoiding the hospital, missing social service appointments, and being unable to hold a job. . . . One of the elderly men who lost his property while hospitalized had called my cell phone before calling 911, as he lay paralyzed on a city sidewalk during a stroke, in hopes I could get to camp to watch his property before he was taken to the ER" (772).

Who Is Grievable?

Historically, across the centuries and the world, people have been and will continue to be buried in mass graves. Some of them have been lost to epidemic or natural disaster, others to the horrors of war or the evils of mass murders in the name of politics or ethnic cleansing. These graves have often been impermanent places, abandoned after an epidemic, when full, or when the money for upkeep has run out.

In the blog post, "Precariousness and Grievability—When Is Life Grievable?" Judith Butler writes, "Only under conditions in which the loss would matter does the value of the life appear. Thus, grievability is a presupposition for the life that matters."

We grieve people who fought and died in wars and those who died from famine, disease, or tragedy. We make the moral judgment that they were not perpetrators of their own demise and therefore are worthy of our grief. There are military cemeteries and war memorials dedicated to those who have died in battle. There are the locations of horrific tragedy and violence that become museums and sites of pilgrimage and tourism: the concentration camps of Germany and Austria, the Hiroshima Peace Memorial Museum. We name to remember, and in instances when we don't have names, we have something like the Tomb of the Unknown Soldier, an important stand-in for soldiers whose bodies may have never been identified or found, for soldiers who never made it home.

In the United States, individuality is revered. It's a nation born of rugged individualism, inextricably linked to our personhoods, to our identities. Dying anonymous becomes not so much a choice as a social stigma for having been connected to a life seen as less than. In such a society, not being named is shameful.

Each year in the United States, the names of all 2,753 people killed in the September 11 attacks are read in totality within the memorial, which has the name of every victim etched into the panels surrounding the reflecting pools that now stand where both towers of the World Trade Center once stood. It's painful, beautiful, necessary.

That day in Fresno, when we memorialized the nearly eight hundred people who had died in poverty, homelessness, or without friends or family, both the Catholic priest and the Unitarian minister spoke of naming. The priest impressed upon us that God would remember the names of those we didn't know in life. The minister recited a poem on the importance of naming. Yet no names were read or printed on the program that day. It would have taken too long, taken up too much space. People are busy.

The Space That Remains

We change the physical space through which we move via the erection or eradication of barriers: fences that keep people out, sidewalks and crosswalks that keep pedestrians contained, laws saying where your body can exist and where it cannot. Where do we have the right to be? Where do we belong? The more spaces someone is barred from existing in, the more marginalized their existence becomes. All this warring over space can lead to the social injustice of health disparities, which may lead people down a path in which, even in death, as is evidenced by the potter's field, they are forced to the far reaches of "wasted" space: the only space that remains.

The regular public witnessing of this mass burial ceremony may serve as a necessary impetus for communities and leaders to begin actively exploring how poverty, income and health disparities, and ultimately, homelessness can be solved instead of merely hidden. Time and again, it seems that when those experiencing homelessness are seen, it is only in the form of a blight: something to be weeded out.

As my dad and I left the cemetery after the ceremony on that hot September day, we dragged the bottoms of our shoes along the dirt-paved road, trying to remove all of the burrs stuck to our soles. We were quiet, our spirits low. We both agreed that a lackluster service was better than none, yet something about it had left me feeling hollow.

Perhaps my feelings were rooted internally. I didn't want to be a tourist, a gawker, who simply ticked the box of "concerned citizen." I wanted to be a witness to something powerful, but more so, I wanted to work toward a solution that afforded dignity in death to all.

When we got to the car, I took my flats off and tipped them upside down, watching the sand pour out of them. A crescent-shaped layer of dirt had caked onto the tops of my feet, which carried the stark reminder of the disparity between the rich and poor, the beloved and the forgotten. The potter's field had no tree-lined paved roads winding

through avenues that housed gothic reminders of opulence, no perfectly manicured lawns with benches to sit and contemplate loved ones
gone. Once the circus of the day died down, the party disbanded, and
each of us headed back home, all that would remain would be a dirt
field scored with strips of cement. Trash would be dumped; someone
might bed down there for a night, a week, or longer; coyotes would
come back and re-dig their holes. Mare's tails would grow once more,
standing tall to watch over those who rested in this place.

Postscript

An email from my dad on October 12, 2018: "Taken yesterday, the only
indication of the remains of 740 people."

What Remains. Courtesy Gene Sibley.

Postscript 2025

Since 2018, Fresno County has changed its process for handling unclaimed
and indigent decedents. They no longer will bury the cremains in
Fresno or do a memorial service. Cremains are now shipped to Marin
County and disposed of at sea.

Final Resting Place. Photo by author.

Assaying

On the Anxiety of Positionality

Over the years, while living in Somerville, I couldn't help but notice a man I'd come to think of as Somerville Mike. Living in Metro Boston, I regularly took mass transit, and over time, I'd come to recognize him as someone who occasionally got on the bus along the route I took down Somerville Avenue. He was always slightly hunched over, his close-shaved hair beginning to bald in the front, and he was missing a handful of teeth, which could be seen when he would smile. Sometimes he liked to wave and yell, "Hello!"—to both children and adults. Most times the adults looked right through him; some made eye contact or smiled, as I often did. But no one ever waved back. Other times Mike would get on the bus and begin shouting loudly, seemingly distressed, his words unintelligible, garbled. Again, most took no notice.

I mostly saw him on the bus, but I'd also occasionally catch glimpses of him walking around town, seeming to stick to a one-mile radius. He was never stemming (begging for spare change), usually I'd just see him wandering around or sitting on the sidewalk or a bench somewhere along Somerville Avenue. Sometimes talking to himself, sometimes just staring ahead, always alone. He usually wore sweat pants that would be falling down, the crack of his butt sticking out, and he never carried any belongings with him and never seemed much dressed against the cold or heat one way or the other. Based on his behavior, I assumed he had a mental disability of some kind. I also assumed that he was being looked after, possibly in a group home. I was wrong.

One night, we were sitting in our local pub when Mike came in—he was yelling at the bartender, Matt, asking him for money for cigarettes. Matt shook his head, "Mike you can't stay in here." "One dollar!?" Mike asked/shouted back. Matt shook his head again then gently placed his hands onto Mike's shoulders and guided him out, "You can bum one of my cigarettes," he said as they walked out the door together, with Mike repeating, "One dollar?" as they went. When Matt came back in I asked, "Does he live in a group home nearby?" Matt laughed, "No, he's homeless." I felt a fool for not knowing this. Matt went on to explain that Mike was the way he was because he was beaten severely as a baby and child, which had left him brain damaged. That story was heartbreaking enough but was made worse for the same reason I didn't assume he was homeless—I just couldn't believe someone who'd been so mentally disabled for most of his life had been left on his own.

At this point, the focus of my research and writing was on general attitudes on death and dying, such as exploring how to die well, how to talk more openly about end-of-life wishes, or how to have a more environmentally friendly burial. But seeing Mike's situation brought up so many questions for me and problematized the research and assumptions I'd held around death and dying. What happened if Mike got sick or injured? Would he get medical care? Would that care be consistent? Did his inability to readily communicate and his combative nature isolate and alienate him from services? Would he ultimately be one of those who die on the street and end up buried, nameless, in a potter's field like the ones I'd seen in Fresno that had initially sent me on this death-and-dying knowledge quest? Mike is an extreme example, yet the image of him burrowed under my skin, and I couldn't forget him.

I'd been thinking about the inequities faced by people living on the streets for years before I encountered Somerville Mike. But it was only just before that I'd begun thinking about those inequities within the framework of the U.S. health-care system and what such disparity meant for someone approaching the end of their lives.

Death is supposed to be the great equalizer. The thing we all experience regardless of our class, race, or any other identities we've held or experiences we've had in life. Yet not all deaths are created equal. Not everyone has a good or dignified death or is treated with respect and dignity once dead.

◆

How could I research and write about inequality, homelessness, death, and dying and do it justice while not taking on the role of benevolent outsider? I could witness a handful of Somerville Mike's very public moments, yet I couldn't know what he thought or felt when he was alone or what he went through the other twenty-three hours of the day. I could only imagine. The worry threatened to stonewall me before the words could even escape. I worried that not unlike many of those who drove the death positive movement, I was just a white, housed, middle-class woman and that my privileged position would prevent me from seeing and hearing people's stories.

In the essay "The Book of the Dead," Catherine Venable Moore writes about the Hawk's Nest Tunnel tragedy in 1930s West Virginia. More than seven hundred workers died as a result of digging up silica that left them stricken with terminal silicosis. It might be considered one of the worst disasters in the country if it hadn't been covered up or if its victims weren't mostly poor African Americans. Moore is neither poor nor Black, but she's from West Virginia, and she felt the pull to investigate this story. In doing so, she uncovered unmarked graves and untold stories, as well as records and files from the company responsible, which included the names of the victims—something thought to be long lost. Halfway through the essay, she writes, "Yet none of this suffering was mine, was it? 'Mine.' I feared I was reinforcing some kind of savior narrative I had about my own white self—a middle-class woman who just wanted to 'do the right thing,' not embarrass anybody, most especially herself. I worried that, instead of resurrecting, I had desecrated the resting dead—ghosts who had never elected me their spokesperson" (153). In "Professions for Women," the first essay in a collection titled *Killing the Angel in the House,* Virginia Woolf discusses the difficulties of being a woman writer during her time, including external expectations and the voices that threatened to derail her ability to write. She describes this about the angel in the house:

> It was she who used to come between me and my paper when I was writing reviews. . . . I took my pen in my hand to review that novel by a famous man, she slipped behind me and whispered: "My dear, you are a young woman. You are writing about a book that has been written by a man. . . . Never let anybody guess you have a mind of your own." . . . I turned upon her and caught her by the throat. . . . Had I not killed her she would have killed me. She would have plucked the heart out of my writing. (3–4)

Although that essay was written in 1931, it still resonated with me nearly a century later. I'd seen men interact with the topic of homelessness, engage in ethnography and research, live among people on the streets, and write about those experiences with seeming impunity. They appeared unconcerned about writing on this topic regardless of how they identified their race, gender, class, or housing status. If they had given any thought to these things, it generally seemed to be absent from the page. For me, that didn't feel like an option. Perhaps this concern, in part, was gendered, driven by cultural and societal expectations of women. I'm not sure. I wasn't sure about how I felt with regard to the whole notion of positionality, but I felt it necessary to carefully consider it openly.

In her essay, Virginia Woolf discusses herself as someone writing from a disadvantaged position (a woman trying to engage in a patriarchal cultural system), whereas Catherine Venable Moore in "The Book of the Dead" writes from a place of privilege (a white woman writing about a Black experience). For Woolf, that internal editor was a hindrance; for Venable Moore, it was a valuable reminder of her position. Ultimately, I was able to draw from both of these writers to come to my own conclusions about how to approach such a difficult topic.

"Killing the angel" didn't mean I was choosing to ignore my white-ness or my middle classness; it meant I wasn't going to let those facts para-lyze me from speaking up about the injustices I saw. Those facts instead guided me through deciding what to read, who to speak to, what to write about. I knew for certain that my insecurities and worries would get in my way if I didn't address them head-on. Killing the angel in the room meant that I had to set my fears and insecurities aside, armed with the knowledge of my identity in relation to those I was writing about, so that I could continue to guide my writing by thoughtful, careful consideration of the intended and unintended consequences that writing might have.

◆

I knew if I was going to write responsibly and in depth on this topic, I needed to be "on the ground," and that part of my research had to include fieldwork. It was imperative that I share spaces and conver-sations with people living a life on the streets. It wouldn't replace the lived experience, but it would allow me to hear stories and to deepen my understanding. So I jumped at the opportunity to travel to central and northern England to visit some medical facilities and temporary housing organizations that worked with the homeless communities in the area. I'd be given tours, and I'd speak with and interview staff and possibly interact with some patients and guests. In the weeks leading up to my trip, I decided that I needed to consider what to wear. That's how I came to be standing over a pile of clothes that had begun as a few sweater options but ended up almost waist-high.

It seemed I had pulled out half my wardrobe in an effort to strike the right balance: professional but not fancy, casual but not informal. The thought entered my mind: *Don't wear any cashmere.* It seemed so asinine, but telling. I didn't want to be needlessly insensitive. I didn't want to send the wrong message. I didn't want to alienate. I didn't want to try to be something I wasn't. In the weeks leading up to this trip, I worried myself into a frenzy. It hadn't come out of nowhere though. From the moment I took on this project, I had felt excitement and a sense that I was working on something important. I was speaking up when I saw social injustice, and I wanted to use my privilege to pay it back, as well as pay it forward. But coupled with that excitement was a deep-seated fear. People who are or have experienced homelessness don't need me to tell them what it's like; they don't need me to tell them about the physical realities and dangers.

I could hear the question being asked: "Who are you?" Who was I to be writing on this subject? As is sometimes said, *just because you can doesn't mean you should*. I didn't have a personal experience with homelessness, no relatable lived trauma, no connection to someone who had.

What would happen if I said something stupid, insensitive, privileged? No, not *what if*. What would I do *when* I said something stupid, insensitive, privileged? I was fearful that I would sound like a condescending academic, that I would ask stupid things that would be obvious to anyone who'd ever been homeless, or that I'd ask things that were irrelevant or insensitive. Could I ask what hobbies they enjoyed? Could I ask about favorite foods, or was that just cruel? *Well, I love lasagna, but can't cook that up in an alleyway, can you?* I was concerned about just dropping into places for a day, of parachuting in, of being transitory and transient, of being a tourist in a world where people were already filled with so much instability and loss. Simply caring about the issue of homelessness and what happens to those who experience it in health, sickness, and death didn't seem like a good enough reason to write about it. Of course, I then worried that people would ask why I *did* care so much. What was I, some we-are-the-fucking-world, Miss America, I-want-to-save-the-world bleeding heart? I hated the fact that I was worrying about such trivial things in the face of speaking with people who have very real, immediate, life-or-death concerns.

I'd gone on previous research trips in the States the summer before. I'd had similar worries, such as not wearing black to a medical respite unit in the event that any hospice patients were there. It had turned out fine, and my clothes hadn't been an issue. In those instances, everyone had been so accommodating and generous, happy to speak about and share their experiences. Some staff members expressed excitement over and hope about my attempts to be a link to the general public by bringing this often-hidden world where homelessness, death, and dying intersect within the medical community to a larger audience. Yet the worry set in later, as I became concerned that in the process of my research and learning about what these health-care workers did, I was also an albatross clinging to them, gawking and weighing them down, if only for the day or a few hours, preventing them from getting on with their work. Had I wasted their and their patients' precious time, especially the patients I had the opportunity to speak with who were both dying and in hospice? Even if those conversations were only twenty minutes, I was taking from them, asking something of them: *Give me.* I fantasized about having some kind of meaningful interaction, some positive impact. I wanted to feel closeness, a shared humanity with the people I was speaking with. But did they need that from me? And how ridiculous was I to think that I could create such a bond when I was dropping in and out? I knew that wasn't realistic. I knew that the only way I could do that would be through sustained, regular, consistent contact. Even the three months I spent volunteering at the foot-care clinic felt too short, and I worried that it was too self-serving—serving my own interests and needs.

As fearful as I was about my own actions, I had never feared any of the homeless people I encountered during my visits. Yet there had been one incident that occurred while I was in San Francisco that made me realize that I could not ignore my position in relation to those I was writing about. It was 9:00 p.m. as I got off the Bay Area Rapid Transit (BART), which I'd taken from the airport. I began walking to the hotel where my husband was. In my head were the stories he'd told me of roving bands of homeless people on the streets of San Francisco, attacking people, snatching phones from their hands. I walked down Embarcadero and saw a group of homeless people standing around taking up most of the sidewalk, some near the street, some near the building, with a hole between them large enough for me to walk through. I was putting my own words in response to such stories, that homeless people generally are not dangerous, to the test.

In that moment, I didn't believe myself. I was a woman walk-ing alone at night in a city that does sleep, where residents disperse from the downtown area, leaving only those without homes or sense to wander the grid. I tried not to look scared, although no one really seemed to take notice. There were drugs being taken and shared; I was inconsequential. I turned left, rounding the corner, as I walked up the street that Google Maps told me to take: a dark, wide street dwarfed by tall buildings and closed storefronts. A skinny man who looked to be in his fifties walked toward me, shouting and swinging a hair dryer around like a lasso by its cord. I was following Google, but I did not want to go this way. I called my husband, and he suggested that I just keep walking. "Uh-uh," I replied, frozen, trying to decide if I should cross the street or go back toward the drug party on Embarcadero. The man with the hair dryer made the choice for me and crossed into the middle of the road, still mumbling, screaming, but past me now and moving on. As I walked on, eventually meeting up with my hus-band who'd come out to find me, I repeated my mantra to myself, "Homeless people generally are not dangerous," and in that moment, I felt like an utter hypocrite. But I also had to realize that being fearful didn't mean being a hypocrite. I needed to interrogate where the fear was coming from and understand that personal safety, especially as a woman, is something that should always be kept in mind, particularly when walking down an empty city street at night.

◆

Positionality refers to the social and political context of how a person identifies in terms of race, gender, sexuality, and ability and to how researchers' identities are positioned in comparison to those they research as well as the potential to affect influence, bias, and under-standing regarding those they're working with or researching.

In the essay "The Problem of Speaking for Others," Linda Martin Alcoff discusses the complexities around speaking or writing out-side of your own experience. Her essay refuses to take a side or solve the problem; rather, it examines different angles and the pros and cons of speaking for others, leaving the reader to come to their own conclusions. I held closely one idea in particular as I moved through my work: "In both the practice of speaking for as well as the practice of speaking about others, I am engaging in the act of representing the other's needs, goals, situation, and in fact, who they are based on my own situated interpretation" (5). Alcoff also heeds a prudent warning: "[Some] speakers offer up in the spirit of 'honesty' autobiographical information about themselves . . . meant to acknowledge their understanding that they are speaking from a specified, embodied location without pretense to transcendental truth. . . . Such an act serves no good end when it is used as a disclaimer against one's ignorance or errors and is made without critical interrogation of the bearing of such an autobiography on what is about to be said" (18).

Anthropologists have a lot to say about the topic of positionality as well. Thirty years ago, anthropology turned to "reflexivity," or what essayists have been doing for ages, which is bringing themselves into the writing. In the article "Against Reflexivity as an Academic Virtue and Source of Privileged Knowledge," Michael Lynch explains, "Reflexive analysis is often said to reveal forgotten choices, expose hidden alternatives, lay bare epistemological limits and empower voices which had been subjugated by objective discourse" (36). This was done to correct issues with previous ethnographic writing that often ignored the researcher/narrator and did not address the effect that their presence had on those they were researching, and vice versa (Robertson). Since then, some critiques have arisen in response to the use of positionality within ethnographic reflexive writing. In "Reflexivity Redux: A Pithy Polemic on 'Positionality,'" Jennifer Robertson notes, "Anthropologists today often begin a manuscript with the words, 'writing as a [name the category].' . . . These categories are the 'ready to wear' products of an identity politics that has been especially endemic to American universities. Wearing these categories as self-evident does not reveal but can instead actually obscure one's unique personal history" (788). Robertson goes on to argue that these "ready to wear" categories—such as white, female, straight, and so on—create more problems than they solve. They obscure the complexities of individuals and erase their histories, and they assume that the relationships within the research "*could only have been defined* by unequal power plays" (789). She posits that it also can become a form of self-stereotyping, and it assumes that the only response capable of those being researched is reacting to the researcher, thereby minimizing their abilities and agency. It may be that the academic's exercise of identifying their positionality in relation to those they are researching does the opposite of what's intended.

As Lynch notes, I see the intention being to empower the voices of those marginalized (36). Yet the possible danger in thinking and acting on this may set up the same power structures and barriers to access that already exist. Such thoughts and actions risk minimizing the skills, knowledge, and abilities of the research participants by assuming that the only knowledge to be gained on this matter is through the researcher identifying and naming those positions. As I previously noted, those experiencing homelessness know that they are marginalized and vulnerable. Does stating my privilege in relation to that change or enhance that knowledge in any way? Is it just a selfish exercise in proving that I am aware, or worse, as Alcoff warns against, a way to indemnify myself for any misguided things I might say or do?

These arguments tapped into my own concerns that by parachuting into shelters, I was committing an act of unintentional violence. The connections I made with people were brief, and some asked if I'd be coming back. I had to explain that I was only there for the day. The reality of my being a transient visitor in their lives couldn't be avoided, and I was acutely aware of how this could affect them or make them feel used, othered, or abandoned. In one instance, I stopped by a food bank in Manchester, England, and as I was talking to one of the men who often came by to pick up some food, he asked if I'd be back next week. His face fell when I explained I was just there for the day, and it felt like a gut punch. It wasn't the lack of my specific future presence he was disappointed by but rather the lack of consistency, of regularity. The staff working in these places were there day in and day out. It required such consistency and time to build trust and relationships among their patients and guests. Was I inflicting violence by parachuting in? Was I turning people's lives into specimens by observing?

Consider It is a current affairs program created by Vox Media. In one particular video on allyship, there was a panel of women speaking on the issues of inclusivity for women of color or different abilities and other marginalized voices in the context of feminism and the ongoing fight for women's rights. The advice of the women in the video was to "show up and shut up," and as one put it: "Take the time to learn, but don't post selfies of your learning and think you're better than others because you've learned. . . . Don't assume you're trying for other communities makes you a hero, and realize those communities are already trying to help themselves" ("Consider It").

Another example comes from Rebecca Solnit, who writes in *The Mother of All Questions* about silences and the ways in which people are silenced or engage in silences to keep up certain societal norms. She speaks of this in regard to gender inequality. But the same theory and types of silence also occur with class inequality. The poor and homeless are silenced through poverty and the inability to meet the most basic of needs. Silenced by hunger, lack of safety, exposure to the elements, and perpetual threats of violence, harm, and death. Silenced by the way some who are housed ignore them or look down upon their dirtied, smelly, wild bodies and the way some blame them for not having the bootstraps to pull themselves up with. Silenced by both the assumptions and the effects of drug or alcohol addiction and mental health.

Assuming that unhoused people are helpless isn't any more productive than assuming that they're all dependent on drugs or alcohol, mentally ill, or violent. Not all people who experience homelessness are dangerous—nor are they all innocent. But assuming that someone on the streets can only be a victim of society and never be a perpetrator of evil or poor decision-making also misses the point. All these assumptions serve only to further silence people, robbing them of the very agency, choice, and personal responsibility an individual deserves.

Of course, silence can work both ways. By silencing others, we enact a violence on them, but we can do the same by silencing ourselves. I regularly see signs around my Oakland neighborhood that read, "White Silence Is White Violence." Claudia Rankine so eloquently writes on this issue of white silence in *Citizen: An American Lyric*, "The man at the cash register wants to know if you think your card will work. If this is his routine, he didn't use it on the friend who went before you. As she picks up her bag, she looks to see what you will say. She says nothing. You want her to say something—both as a witness and as a friend. She is not you; her silence says so." This is a reminder to myself that ultimately, it comes down to context and knowing when you need to listen versus when you need to speak up. It's important to listen to others and their stories. Also, being in a position of power (including one of privilege) carries a sense of responsibility to speak up when witnessing an injustice. In this case, as a writer, educator, and member of the death positive community, I feel a duty to write about the disparities that exist within end-of-life and death care.

◆

In the essay "The Girl in the Surf: Exploitation vs. Documentation" B. J. Hollars discusses the ethics of reporting on the tragedy of strangers. He concludes that writers, particularly of nonfiction, can write ethically about tragedies that afflict people we don't know, but it needs to be done in the service of spurring action. It may not be possible to know in advance the consequence my writing might produce, but that could be said of any action taken. Hollars quotes Lou Hodges, a professor of journalism: "Reporters . . . should strive to present 'an accurate image of that world, not one sanitized. . . . Where the world is bloody . . . it is dishonest and deceptive to hide blood from readers.'" As I navigated my way through my research and writing, I had to accept that I would make some missteps, commit some errors. I shouldn't try to explain those away by shifting the focus to my identity and positionality. Rather, I felt that I should use the knowledge of where I was positioned as a guide, not a hindrance, to move with care and to keep other's best interests in mind. Before I could write and add my voice to the mix, I first needed to listen, to "show up and shut up."

By the time I headed out for my trip to England, after weeks of planning and fretting, I realized that the mountain of clothes on the bedroom floor certainly caused stress, but it had also become something of a salvation. If this was a physical manifestation of my anxiety, then I could sit down with it; dismantle it; make separate piles of sweaters, trousers, and dresses; systematically assess the setting I'd be in each day of my trip (a hospital, a group home, a walking tour), puzzle together the appropriate outfit, and maybe find a way out of the tunnel of worry. The process didn't alleviate my anxiety completely, but it kept me from buckling under its weight. And when I finally went on my trip, I knew that I was as prepared as I could be. Of course, it didn't stop me from asking the occasional stupid question, such as when a man I was chatting with told me he signed up for a creative writing workshop, and I asked him how long it went for. His reply was to shrug and say, "I don't know. It was just something to do." With my life organized and run by spreadsheets and calendars, I had mistakenly tried to apply that same logic to someone just getting by on a day-to-day basis. But it also wasn't the worst, and in return for my patience and listening, he recited to me one of the many poems he'd written while living on the streets. I couldn't ignore that I lived in a society where something like home-lessness was so ubiquitous that it was easy to become inured to. Yet that's where things went wrong (or right) for me, as I had never been able to get used to it, and so pen to paper felt necessary in its face. It wasn't lost on me that in doing this, I needed to remain vigilant against my own biases and worldview, which may obscure my intention, and I also needed confidence that I wasn't that which I feared.

I ultimately was unable to kill the angel in the house, but we learned to coexist. I took comfort in the words and actions of others who are in a similar position, such as Catherine Venable Moore and Rebecca Solnit. Vijay Gupta was another, a musician in the Los Angeles Phil-harmonic who works to bring classical and all sorts of music to the homeless on Skid Row in LA. He was highlighted in a *Dateline* epi-sode called "City of Angels." In it, Gupta responds to critiques from people who questioned the relevancy of bringing music to the home-less when homes are what they needed: "Our role as artists is to be the bridge that changes the narrative. And to start the conversation." Leaning on Woolf, Moore, Solnit, and Gupta, as well as the other art-ists and writers out there standing up and speaking out, I gathered that needed confidence. Forging ahead, I repeated the mantra "Bridge the gap, change the narrative, start conversations."

I have spent the better part of a decade ruminating on the intersection of death, dying, mortality, disparities, inequalities, homelessness, capitalism, respect, deservedness, and our shared humanity in both life and death. Regardless of where we come from, we all have the shared experience of being mortal, and through this common ground, we should agree that dignity in death is something that should be afforded to everyone, not just those who can afford it.

I think about Somerville Mike even more now postpandemic. The bar he came into that night didn't survive, and the neighborhood has grown exponentially. I hope he survived COVID and the further gentrification of Somerville. I worry that there is no longer space for him there, and I worry that he's been pushed out and further into the margins. Mike is just one person, but the issues his story embodies are issues that impact many unhoused people. These issues also circle around the questions of mortality, which is something that affects us all.

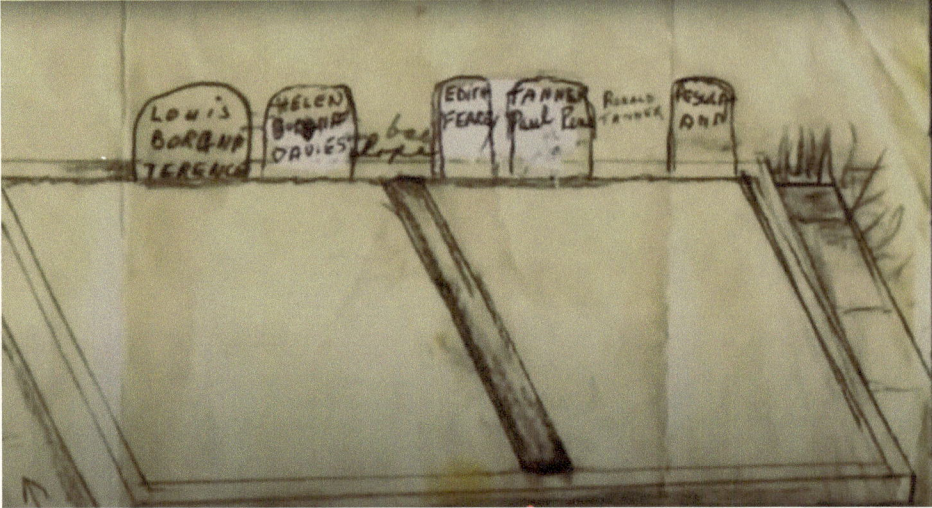

Screenshot of *A Certain Kind of Death*. Photo by author.

Death by a Thousand Viewings

A CERTAIN KIND OF DEATH, a documentary film released in 2003, opens with a close-up shot of a street sign for Crenshaw Boulevard, a street in Los Angeles notorious for its gang violence and poverty. The documentary then cuts to a man standing in a doorway wearing medical gloves while taking a Polaroid of something not immediately seen by the viewer. We're not left guessing for long, as the film cuts again to reveal the legs of a man who has died on his toilet. While the camera pans to a motionless fan, a small TV that's on, and uneaten food on a plate that the flies have gotten to, we hear the investigator's voice noting that the man is "very dried out, and you can see the insect activity taking place . . . The maggots have completely taken away his face." Then we see what the investigator sees—the whole body of this man slumped against the wall, whose eaten face looks like a solid black leather mask. The investigator talks to a police officer guarding the door and says that it looked like he'd been dead at least three weeks. This all plays out in the first forty-eight seconds of the film, and it is immediately clear what kind of deaths we'll be examining here.

The film, directed by Grover Babcock and Blue Hadeagh, follows the journey of three men who have died in ways Western society would consider to be abject. Ronald Eugene Tanner dies alone in his modest apartment, found on his bedroom floor six days later only when a neighbor began to smell his decomposing body and the landlord investigates. Donald Wight, an unhoused man, is found dead and naked in the shower of the motel room he rented for the night, the water still running. And Tommy Albertson is found covered in roaches in his small boardinghouse room. Babcock and Hadaegh show the discovery of each body and the trajectory each takes through the various governmental processes that ultimately lead to the way their remains will be handled, often referred to in the deathcare industry as their "final disposition": Ronald in a previously bought cemetery plot and Donald and Tommy in the potter's field, a fate known simply as "county dispo."

Each of these men could be described as indigent. But being poor doesn't automatically relegate you to the same fate as them; the status of being indigent involves more than just being in need. There's a ladder within poverty, like with anything else, and perhaps at the very bottom rung is where you'll find those deemed "indigent"—forgotten about by those around them until the stench of their rotting bodies invades and can no longer be ignored. In his essay "Indigent Disposition," Christopher Notarnicola explains the notion of an indigent person best: "a body in need, a body lacking, deficient, wanting . . . a poor body, an impecunious, penniless, down-and-out, derelict, bum body" (176).

A Certain Kind of Death was filmed in Los Angeles in 2003, and since California is now home to a quarter of the country's homeless, it's a fitting locale for such a documentary. The death rate of those dying while experiencing homelessness in Los Angeles doubled between 2013 and 2018; in those same five years, the average death rate overall for Los Angeles only grew by 7 percent. In 2017, Los Angeles alone had 831 people die while experiencing homelessness, and in 2018, deaths rose to 1,047. In September 2019, the number of those who died on the streets neared 1,000 people. In 2022, the number of people who died while homeless in Los Angeles County doubled to 2,000.

◆

What happens to someone who dies unclaimed? This is the question for which Babcock and Hadaegh seek an answer in this film that braids together the story of the forgotten dead with the story of the living whose job it is to deal with those deaths. Individuals in both groups seem bound together by society's ignorance and/or indifference to the existence of both. The viewer is shown a side of society that many have little to no knowledge of via the shadowing of people tasked with

cleaning up the unclaimed dead: death investigators, coroners, sher-
iffs, public administrators, movers, and cleaners.

I have watched *A Certain Kind of Death* more than twenty times.
The hour-long movie, which I first learned of from an online list of
"best death movies to watch," wasn't the first documentary on death I
saw, but it was the one that left the biggest impression, the one that was
instrumental in changing my perspective on what dying can look like,
particularly for those who are marginalized. Just like its subjects, this
film also feels on the fringe, viewable primarily on YouTube, creating a
feeling that it's hidden in plain sight.

Documentary makers may operate in the realm of fact, but just like
the essayist, the directors of a documentary will have an editorial perspective, wanting the viewer to walk away from their film with a specific feeling, belief, understanding, or conviction. They want to impart
knowledge, answer questions, shape opinions, make a statement. The
same thing that makes for powerful writing makes for powerful film:
vivid details placed alongside one another to create a stark, unforget-
table impression. These details create a sense of reality and sadness
without becoming sentimental or sappy. The message I took away
from Babcock and Hadaegh's documentary was indignation at how
our society treats certain people in death—if you are not economically
valuable in life or if you are seen as deviant in some way, then you are
not worthy of being treated with value in death either. The injustice
of it all is so explicit; these are people forgotten about, discarded, left
for the bugs to feast on until the smell of their decaying bodies inter-
rupts the lives of those around them and the county is left to claim
them, clean up after them, record and process them, and then file them
away. For me, the sadness I experienced from that first viewing grew
and morphed into anger.

After the initial scene of the dead man on the toilet, viewers are
transported to the county crematorium, a foreshadowing of our final
destination, both in life and in the film. The film weaves back and forth
between the dead and the living who handle the dead, until we end up
in the crematorium and then finally at the mass grave inside the Los
Angeles County Crematorium Cemetery, via county dispo. The film

spans about six months, beginning in summer and ending with Christmas upon us. The passing of the seasons seems significant, but it is left to viewers to reach their own conclusions. Perhaps it shows how long the process of piecing a life together takes, or maybe we end at Christmastime as a way to juxtapose the association of being with family and friends to the reality of the lives and deaths of the film's subjects.

◆

Scenes in the film are stitched together in a few obvious ways, the first being street signs, which place us physically around Los Angeles. Following these, we are led into the building where a body has been found. Another segue between scenes is via the telephone book. The camera scrolls over sections and then zooms in on words such as "morgue," "Department of Coroner—Personal Property Section," or "Crematory." These are followed by overheard dialogue spoken by someone from that department or organization who is working on a case, maybe talking on the phone or to a coworker, or speaking to someone (presumably one of the directors) off camera to explain their job or how some process has been completed. There is no other dialogue, which places the audience in the position of interviewer or the one shadowing an employee; we are there to observe and listen. No additional commentary is given—we see what we see and hear what we hear and then come to our own conclusions.

The third and less obvious transitional tool Babcock and Hadaegh use is the wall clock. It's always a black-and-white clock, like those that hang on the walls of many school and office buildings: unassuming, uninteresting, bureaucratic. The first time we see the clock is early in the film, and it's just coming up on 9:00 a.m. It's obviously morning, as it's office hours, and a woman at the coroner's office is taking calls: one from the eye bank looking for eyes to harvest from the recently dead, another caller looking for a missing juvenile who hadn't come home the night before. All this is portrayed as a normal workday.

In a review of the film, Eric Klinenberg homes in on this choice by the directors to highlight such daily tasks, including an employee of the coroner's office discussing lunch options with her colleagues.

Klinenberg writes, "She wants to know what they are going to eat. Those of us who do not ordinarily deal with the dead do not" (417). He uses this as an example of how the staff experience such "extraordinary and sad" deaths as "ordinary and unremarkable." When I first watched the movie, I, too, had a similar thought, but then I realized the filmmakers weren't commenting on these individuals; they were commenting on the systems and culture of which they are a part—the things that necessitate such work to be done. In fact, in the directors' commentary on the DVD, Babcock and Hadaegh note, "We tried to include explanatory comments about the process but left out their feelings, or opinions about how 'society' should feel. The workers featured could easily have functioned as authority figures and short-circuited a person's chance to judge things for themselves." This is something I'm aware of regarding the choices I make in my own work. My intention, much like Babcock and Hadaegh's, is to draw the reader in and pull the curtain back on an issue they may have not known or thought little about. Through a series of decisions including the utilization of literary devices and craft elements, I invite the reader in to consider the facts I present and to judge things for themselves.

The directors also noted that when they approached the county for permission to make this film, people who worked for the county were interested in them doing so because such work was considered "low profile" and the staff felt that some awareness might lead some to plan ahead for their end-of-life needs. Contrary to not caring, these people cared very much; nevertheless, there was a job that needed doing.

Shortly into the film, we see a man in the coroner's office take a call for a pickup request for a body found during a welfare check due to noticeable odor. We hear the one-sided conversation, the camera focused in on one side of his office: "Ah, OK . . . real decomp." He laughs. "I don't mean to laugh; you just don't sound like you want to go back in there very bad." From here, we will soon meet the first of our three men, Ronald E. Tanner.

The film then cuts to a shot of another street sign, this time Fountain Avenue. Then to an apartment, where a naked man, partially covered by a bath towel, lies dead on his side with his mouth agape on his bedroom floor, just past the bathroom door. An investigator from the coroner's department stands above him, taking notes. The shot jumps back and forth between the scene in the apartment and the investigator in his office as he reads from his notes: "The decedent was found unresponsive lying on the bedroom floor of the premises on his left side. His face was resting on a comforter blanket while his right side is covered with a blue towel. Several dark stains appearing to be blood and/or fecal matter were observed on the carpeting below the decedent's buttock area. Dark staining was also observed on the floor leading into the bathroom, as well as on the box-spring mattress." Ronald's apartment and belongings become the lens through which his character is revealed. The investigator describes his place as "unclean." We are shown what he means, as the camera focuses on the stripped mattress covered in blood, piles of clothes on the couch, dirty dishes piled up in the sink, folded towels in a laundry basket waiting to be put away, jars and cans of food sitting on the kitchen counter, a box of unopened fish sticks sitting in the freezer. In one shot, we see what looks like a handwritten restaurant ticket; the camera zooms in, and we see the words written "1 Alfredo, 1 cheesecake, milk."

In the essay "Lost Boys," Leslie Jamison describes the case and documentary of the West Memphis Three—three teenage boys convicted (then later absolved) of the murder of three young boys in Tennessee. Jamison notes that one of the most effective, saddening moments of the documentary *Paradise Lost* was when one of the arrested teenagers eats a Snickers bar while giving an interview: "To think of how these treats are nothing, in the face of everything, but still the only things he got to choose all day. Empathy is easier when it comes to concrete particulars. I can't imagine being in prison, but I can imagine choosing a snack" (166).

It seems this was the intention of the directors of *A Certain Kind of Death* as well. I may not know what it's like to have the kind of life where someone wouldn't know I'd been dead for a week, but the empathy comes in the form of the familiar. I know what it's like having a pile of folded laundry to put away, and I know what food is in my freezer that would be left behind for people to find. I can imagine Ronald ordering his Alfredo, cheesecake, and milk.

Through the pile of papers that Ronald has left out on the table, we're also able to piece together a life. He'd left bank account statements, his funeral home papers, and other potentially important documents out on the table for someone to find. His mother died when he was young, he'd had a younger brother who committed suicide in 1963, his dad died in 1991, and his stepmom died in 1999, but prior to her death, she had pushed him to set up a pre-need of his own, and when she died, she left him $60,000. We also learn that he was gay and that his partner, James (only ever referred to in the film as a friend), died of AIDS ten years earlier, and Ronald had buried him in a plot he'd bought in Forest Lawn Cemetery in Hollywood.

In complete silence, we're shown a series of still shots of old family photos: a black-and-white headshot, school photos where he's circled himself in the photo, vacation pictures of him and James, an image of James's headstone that reads, "My Loving Companion." The scene feels voyeuristic, as though we're surreptitiously flipping through someone's private photo album. We're being shown that this is someone who had loved and been loved, who had been a part of the world.

We're left to wonder how and why this sixty-three-year-old man, who knew he was dying, did so alone. He'd sketched a picture of the family plot up in Fort Bragg, California, over five hundred miles away from his home in Los Angeles, with a headstone drawn in for himself. There had been no family left for him to share this information with, but I found myself wondering why he had no friends to tell, why he had not gone into a hospital or a nursing home, why he hadn't asked for help.

My list of questions felt endless. Did he have an illness that could have been treated, or was it terminal? Did he know the money his stepmom left him would cover funeral expenses? In fact, he paid for not only his funeral but also his embalming. Was it that he didn't want to die in a hospital or nursing home, or had he come to lack trust in others? Was he a shut-in? Did he know that it might be days before he was found and that it would be county officials who would find him? Had he nothing left to live for anyway, since all those he'd loved had already died? Had he simply come to accept that he was dying and wasn't afraid to die alone? Had he known there'd be few people there to mourn his passing, or had he expected any at all? There's such ambiguity in Ronald's story as well as so much that's familiar. In many ways, Ronald wasn't truly indigent, yet he still died in a very hidden way, and because there was no one left to advocate for him when he died, the location of his burial was not what he had envisioned.

Of the three men highlighted, it was the vulnerable body of Ronald Eugene Tanner that was the main focus of the film, and his was the story that felt most relatable. He'd had a life, loved ones, a job, yet he had no children and no extended family, so he ended up the last one standing. At first, I thought he just stood out to *me* because I'd chosen to connect with him. Yet on closer examination, it became obvious that that feeling of connection was by design. The filmmakers chose to spend the most time with Ronald and to develop his character, perhaps using his ordinariness as a conduit for our empathy; therefore, the audience feels they know him best.

The film leaves Ronald behind for the time being, and the camera pans to the clock as it approaches 11:10 a.m. A woman from the public administrator's office looks past the camera and explains the overall trajectory of what happens if you're not as fortunate or fortuitous as Ronald: if there is no next of kin, no burial arrangements already made, or not enough funds for private burial, your deathcare fate may head down a very different path, where the coroner will send your body to the Los Angeles County morgue. From there, the morgue then transports your body to the Los Angeles County crematorium, where you will be cremated and your ashes later buried in the county cemetery.

We recognize that we're now moving on to a new story, a new death in a new location, when we see the street sign for Sunset Boulevard before entering the hotel room where Donald White has been found dead. Homeless, he's managed to get a room for the night, and it's determined that he likely fell or suffered some kind of medical event while in the shower, causing him to hit his head and die of blunt-force trauma. This is all determined by the investigator on scene at the motel room. It's rare for someone who has died homeless to be brought in to the coroner to be autopsied if the cause of death is obvious from a visual examination.

Lastly, we meet Tommy Albertson in his tiny room in a boarding-house. The camera scans the room, showing a calendar, an employee ID badge, and a bag of oatmeal that is held up for the camera by a man who seems to be the landlord or building owner while those there to clean up and sort through his things make comments on the smell of body odor in the room and the cockroaches that are crawling all over everything. We learn from Tommy's mail that he was receiving weekly paychecks of $271 and that he was donating half of that check each week to a local homeless mission. Babcock and Hadaegh seem to be attempting to show us multiple sides of this man so that viewers can understand that poverty does not make you a one-dimensional character; being financially poor does not equate to being morally bankrupt. Yes, he may have been a former convict, likely had been homeless at one point, and lived in what seemed to be deplorable conditions, yet he was giving most of his money to charity.

A large part of the reality of such deaths as those highlighted in this film is a lack of money. Where they end up buried depends on how much money there is. Part of this includes going through the decedent's belongings and determining whether there is anything of value that can be sold at auction to pay for the disposition of their body, especially if there were no funeral arrangements paid for in advance. The county's job is to determine and collect the final value of all items and any cash in accounts. If there's enough money, then a private burial is paid for, and any remaining money is held by the county in the event that friends or family ever come forward.

For Tommy, it was determined that he had $3,700 in total assets, which included what he had in his bank and after the sale of his tools (the only thing of financial value that he owned). The cost for his disposition in 2003 came to over $2,000: $750 for public administrator fees, $40 for two death certificates, $600 for the movers and cleaners, $207 for coroner fees, $541 for county cremation fees. The rest went to rent reimbursement, so Tommy's cremains would be buried via county dispo.

As of 2019, the cost for Los Angeles County direct cremation has gone down slightly to between $350 and $470. But even with minimum wage in California now being $16.50 an hour, if a person works part-time at just under forty hours a week, their take-home pay after taxes would only be marginally more than Tommy's $271 a week. According to the Los Angeles County cremation log forms, between 2012 and 2015, almost seven thousand people were cremated through their county cremation program.

For Donald, it appears he owned even less. A woman from the personal property division of the coroner's department lists off the belongings found in his possession: a black wallet, an ID, miscellaneous papers, farmers market nutritional program food coupons, and $290 cash. She notes, "The public administration office had no interest in the case because it was nothing of value, just miscellaneous items in a wallet." These items would be held for ninety days, then disposed of carefully and confidentially through shredding and being placed in red hazardous material bags, then picked up by a special collection company. While she explains this process, we're shown still shots of each piece of paper that was in Donald's wallet: a dry cleaner's receipt, a pamphlet from Hollywood United Methodist Church, a clothing store business card, and farmers market coupons. As with Ronald Tanner, Donald's story is told through the items he's left behind. In his case, his life is reduced to a few papers of no value to anyone else, and this is where Donald's story ends. As Tommy's story also wraps up, and the camera slowly zooms in on the only photo they found of him, in the background we hear one of the cleaners singing, "Dada dada dee, dada dada da . . . and the beat goes on . . ."

We crave narrative because we want a story to follow. It allows us to connect with one another and humanize and familiarize experiences different from our own. With someone like Ronald Tanner, all we're left with are artifacts—documents and objects from which we're left to piece together a story that may only ever be partial and not necessarily accurate. This type of storytelling seems to be a desire of the media, which is reflective of society. In a *New York Times* article, "The Lonely Death of George Bell," N. R. Kleinfeld details the story of a man very similar to Ronald, found dead in his apartment with no next of kin. The New York City investigators, and Kleinfeld, create a story about who George Bell was from papers and belongings and by talking with a few people who interacted with him at the local bar. Kleinfeld taps into what is at the heart of why we crave these stories: "*George Bell*—a simple name, two syllables, the minimum. There were no obvious answers as to who he was or what shape his life had taken. What worries weighed on him. Whom he loved and who loved him."

The media often portrays dying alone as "a 'worst case scenario' . . . associated with personal failure on the part of the deceased individual, or with social decline" (Turner and Caswell) and "as undesirable, creating the perception that when someone does die alone, their death may be termed a failure of 'emotional accompaniment'" (Caswell and O'Connor, "I've No Fear"). Yet some studies on dying alone suggest that there are people who do not hold the view of a good death as one that is "pain-free and peaceful and occurs at the end of a long life, in the individual's home, surrounded by family and friends" (Turner and Caswell). But rather, "A number of people who live alone make the decision to withdraw from social contact with others and thus enter a self-imposed period of social death prior to their biological deaths. In doing so, they are exhibiting agency and creating identities for themselves that are based on personal choice" (Caswell and O'Connor, "Agency"). Such people may choose to continue living alone in spite of the risk of dying alone and may do so because they do not care nor are they concerned with having such a death. As Glenys Caswell and Morna O'Connor note in their study, "Agency in the Context of Social Death," such deaths may be interpreted as a societal failure, yet such interpretation "negates the individual's agency and power they held to make their own decisions, casting them as victims of life and loneliness; but it is not the case that all those who are alone are necessarily lonely" (18).

We can't really know who George Bell or Ronald Tanner were; we can only guess. We can take those items left behind and impose meaning on them through our own life experiences and worldview. In trying to humanize them, it feels like we run the risk of creating a caricature or stereotype—someone to be pitied. With Ronald, the directors skate close to this, perhaps on occasion stumbling into that trap. But there is ultimately some hope, since he does get a proper burial. Even if it's only cemetery and funeral home staff who attend the ceremony, he's still buried in the family cemetery. Some dignity has been restored, and Ronald has made it home.

This is possibly another reason why the movie spends more time on Ronald's story. It can be seen as a sad or bad death, yet there's redemption and remembrance in a way that Donald and Tommy's stories don't have. It bridges a gap, because we might all be able to recognize something of ourselves in Ronald (someone who was once loved and who loved, someone who had a place in a world we can recognize) and so his experience allows us to enter into this otherwise hidden world. Or maybe it was simply that there was more left behind from which to create a story.

A gay man, a former convict, and a transient . . .

By 2004, being gay wasn't seen as being "deviant" by most. But it would have been so in the 1950s, the 1960s, and even the 1970s. In addition, having a partner die of AIDS would have brought its own hardship. Becoming a felon or homeless is often seen as being due to social deviance or moral bankruptcy—a failure of the individual or society. I believe that Babcock and Hadaegh chose these three men because they represented the most outcast of the outcast and to give credence to the clichéd yet true quote from William Gladstone, "Show me the manner in which a society cares for its dead, and I will measure with mathematical exactness, the tender mercy of its people" (AZ Quotes). We can see that none of these men was living the ephemeral American dream, and none died in a way we would call dignified or "good." Tommy and Donald's deaths seem to have been accidental or at least unexpected, though the experiences of prison, poverty, and homelessness made such deaths far from surprising.

Fifty minutes into the film, we're back to the wall clock, now at 10:30 p.m. All three men's bodies have been collected, their possessions dealt with, their fates determined. It's dark out, and we're in what looks like a warehouse, presumably part of the morgue. The scene is overwhelmed with the sound of a forklift, which we watch pick up bagged bodies in cold storage. The forklift stops, jerks forward, and we hear a squish as it butts up against the visible arm of a body inside one of the bags. Cut to two gurneys, each laden with three bodies bagged in clear plastic. A man, perhaps the coroner, walks into the shot, wearing a surgical gown over his clothes, heavy-duty yellow plastic gloves up to midforearm, and a face mask. With one hand, he shifts and quickly examines each body. In his other he holds a knife with a long, skinny blade, maybe a bone or carving knife meant to deal with large pieces of meat. He then begins making strategic jabs and slices into the bagged bodies. The camera pans down beneath the gurney, and we see bodily fluids and blood dripping onto the ground below.

As this scene closes, a second man comes into view with an industrial-sized hose; we hear the sound of the water as he cleans the blood off the floor, and then the camera follows it to the drain it is all circling toward. Throughout the film, there are close-up shots of bodies, the faces of the deceased, filing cabinets, the time on the clock, excessive decomposition, blood, the water fountain in the office, piles of papers. It all creates a dual, conflicting sense of understanding the necessity for such systems, processes, and jobs to handle these kinds of deaths as well as heavy feelings of emptiness, futileness, and sadness. We're left with a sense of uneasiness, a sense of the unfairness and injustice that anyone should have to die and be treated in such a way in death—unceremoniously and in obscurity.

In the 1998 ethnographic study, "Contemporary Hospice Care: The Sequestration of the Unbounded Body and 'Dirty Dying,'" anthropologist Julia Lawton theorizes about Western society's repulsion of bodies ravaged by disease and illness that present in dirty ways. By "dirty," Lawton means bodies that leak, seep, and project bodily fluids, blood, excrement, and such through the likes of wounds, incontinence, or vomiting: bodies that are disintegrating in front of our eyes. Why do we fear such "unbounded" bodies, as Lawton describes them? She suggests that "Western constructions of the body as a 'peculiarly

intimate and private thing' [develop] in the form of self controls—
of a whole series of taboos and precepts regulating such things as
bodily functions and bodily exposure. As a consequence, a number
of 'natural functions' such as defecating, urinating and spitting which
had previously been public acts were eliminated from social life and
displaced 'behind the scenes'" (15). Because bodily control is tied to
social acceptance as well as to selfhood, identity, and independence,
those who die in such "unbounded" and "dirty" ways may lose their
sense of self or place in society. They may suffer a social death (a
removal from society by themselves or others) before the physical one
occurs. In Lawton's article, she focuses on hospice as a place where
people who have unmanageable symptoms, including nonstop incontinence or bleeding, are sequestered from the public gaze so as not to
offend. In Babcock and Hadaegh's film, we see something similar happen to the dead who are alone and left to decompose far beyond what
is considered normal or acceptable. They are hidden and sequestered
by the nature of how they are found, dealt with, and removed, all of
which happens in very sanitized and subversive ways so that the public
is often unaware of their very existence.

Is this part of the reason why Babcock and Hadaegh don't look away
from the grotesqueness of advanced decomposition? Is this why I'm
drawn to the visceral imagery and sounds of this film? In the face of
bodily degradation (whether that be dying a dirty death or being the
dirty dead), those who have such privilege as to not regularly witness
such forms of death may fail to see such bodies as human ones. So
unremarkable are these deaths that they threaten to offend our sense
of justice. It's not the way I hope for my body to be treated in death: an
anonymous piece of flesh, collected by an anonymous van taking me
to be cremated and anonymously buried in a mix of ash. In Los Angeles, how many of those 831 people who died homeless in 2017 and the
nearly 1,000 who died in 2019 did so in such anonymity?

◆

I'm not sure if it was something I noticed the first time I watched *A
Certain Kind of Death*, but on subsequent viewings, it occurred to me

that there is no music at all in the film except for the last three minutes. To choose not to have music in a film is a bold decision, as music can be a strong filmic device for giving the viewer emotional cues. Yet it seems there is no music appropriate to the background of a life that goes unnoticed in the end.

Instead, the filmmakers use synchronous sounds—noise the camera happens to pick up, from the banal to the visceral: cars driving by, bodies thumping onto metal gurneys, the slicing and squishing of flesh being cut, bone fragments being ground up, checkbooks being ripped, coins being counted, bugs getting caught in the zapper inside the cold storage, metal tins clanking as cremains are dumped into the ground, keyboards typing, paperwork being shuffled, phones ringing. As Babcock and Hadaegh note in the film's commentary, they had originally considered various jazz and blues songs, but they decided against it: "We wanted each viewer to have a clean opportunity to react to the images and scenes and think about their meanings. Specific music might tip a viewer too easily. Worse, it might seem too sentimental." This decision creates an unedited feeling of being in scene, which transports us into these shared moments. We are here to witness.

At the end of Ronald's story, after he's been buried and after the movers have left with his belongings, the camera homes in on the discolored wall where pictures had hung previously. We hear the haunting music-box jingle of an ice-cream truck passing by, along with shouting neighbors and the hum of cars whirring past, that parallel universe that coexists with the one we are currently inhabiting in Ronald's now empty apartment. The hubbub of the living, with places to go and people to see, juxtaposed against the quietness of death, of a life now erased, of a man who will be forgotten, who it seems was barely noticed in the first place. That noise we now hear, and presumably that Ronald would have heard while living there, perhaps suggests an outside world unaware of the death that has occurred as much as the life that once existed.

The last time we see the clock, it's 4:00 a.m. We're back with the man from the crematory with whom we began this journey. He's at the morgue to pick up the bodies we saw earlier on the gurneys. We follow him from the relative quiet of the front desk of the morgue to the roaring sound of the retorts in the crematorium as bodies are burned. The camera focuses in on a skull that is fracturing from the heat of the hot orange flames. Then the film cuts to outside, where it's light out, daytime upon us. Smoke quietly plumes out of the stacks with an unassuming hum, the only hint as to what's happening inside. We follow the crematory workers, who are covered in head-to-toe white paper suits and face masks, to the county cemetery. They stand above a large hole in the ground and begin opening six-by-nine-inch metal boxes one at a time, tipping out the cremains of box after box, metal clinking on metal.

◆

Art allows us to momentarily inhabit the lives of others and experience someplace wholly different from anything we've known or experienced ourselves. In the textbook *Introduction to Documentary*, Bill Nichols writes, "The value of nonfiction films lies in how they give visual and audible representation to topics for which our written language gives us concepts. Photographic images do not present concepts; they embody them." *A Certain Kind of Death* allowed me to cross the threshold; it was that first glimpse inside an existence unlike anything I'd known, an unflinching embodiment of what happens to the poor, penniless, and destitute body and the lives that once belonged to those bodies.

When I first saw this film, just as when I first visited the potter's fields, my perspective on death and dying became more entwined in the social injustice I had been exposed to, which I could not and did not want to look away from. It gave me a concrete example of what happens to those pushed to the farthest margins of our society, as we see in the film. I wouldn't be able to just walk away and forget this film; it had burrowed into me and demanded action. This documentary wasn't the only knowledge I was gathering about such inequalities, but it seemed to emulsify something I was coming to understand: Death might be the great equalizer, but not all deaths are created equal.

In the final three minutes of *A Certain Kind of Death,* the silence and background noises that dominated the film until this point are overcome by the haunting instrumental melody of the song "Greensleeves." This accompanies a montage of scenes: grave markers in the county dispo cemetery, with only the year stamped on them to indicate when the cremains were buried; the words "Merry Xmas" scrawled on a window in the coroner's office; tags on the walls identifying the locations for "regular crypts" and "overweight cases," with the merriment of Christmas lights hanging above. Eventually, the screen fades to black while the credits roll and the song plays out. Life has moved on, more bodies have arrived, and the process will be repeated indefinitely.

Grandma Rago. Photo by author.

How to Have a Good Death, or
The Dead Grandma Essay

M Y GRANDMOTHER WAS dying for twenty years.

No, she wasn't in extremis for twenty years, but she would remind us of her impending doom on the regular. When she did finally die, as with many who die of old age or a protracted illness, there were a series of incidents leading up to it that seemed to accelerate in frequency and build upon one another until it became clear that the end was upon us.

While visiting my parents in the summer of 2012, my mom and I came home to my grandmother Carmella calling. She was having trouble getting the microwave to work and could we come over and take a look? We arrived at my mother's childhood home and entered through the back door into the kitchen, as we always did. The house was sweltering. My grandmother slowly emerged from her bedroom, pushing her walker along the carpet of the narrow hallway, dressed in a thin floral nightgown with snap buttons up the front. She moved to the microwave and explained how she'd been trying to heat something up earlier but couldn't get it to turn on. The problem was that she'd been pushing the Stop button rather than Start.

With the microwave sorted out, she sat down on one of the chairs at the Formica-topped table, which was covered with vitamins of differing colors, sizes, and shapes; half-empty pill bottles; balled-up used tissues; an old radio; and sticky bits of spilled food that had been left to dry on the surface.

"So did you want something heated up then?" my mom asked her.

"No, maybe just some bread with butter," my grandmother replied.

My mom pulled a piece of bread from the bag and a small container of margarine that sat on the kitchen countertop, just out of reach.

"Grandma, aren't you hot? Don't you have a fan?" I asked.

She didn't respond, just stared off toward the dining room.

"She likes the heat," my mom said to me.

We waited another ten minutes to see if she would eat any more of the buttered bread, occasionally commenting on the weather or some other topic that didn't beg much of a conversational response from my grandmother. We spoke loudly, in part to make sure she could hear but mostly to fill the soundless void that seemed to have settled into the kitchen, along with the suffocating heat. I went to turn on the water in the sink in order to clean the stack of dirty dishes that had piled up. When it was evident she was not going to eat anything else and there was no more small talk to be had, we started cleaning up.

After getting her back into bed, I picked up a sponge, squeezed some dish soap onto it, and washed the dishes. My mom threw away the used tissues and wiped down the kitchen table. I went into the living room and turned on a lamp, which illuminated my grandmother's collection of praying hands displayed on a three-tiered pedestal: figurines of disembodied hands all made with a variety of materials including ceramic, glass, wood, and metals. We then walked past the wall railing my dad had installed and out the back door. The night air tingled upon my skin, the sweat started to dry off, and once again, I could breathe. Three months later, my grandmother would be dead. Even though I didn't know that at the time, I could still sense the shift caused by the pallor of death that had moved in.

A few days later, my grandmother fell for the last time. This final fall put her in the hospital, where a lump of fluid was discovered in her lungs, which turned out to be caused by lingering pneumonia. She was also dehydrated and had low blood pressure. The afternoon before I was set to fly back to Boston, I went with my dad to the hospital to say goodbye. She appeared depressed and tired, and she slept most of the visit.

We stayed for about half an hour and watched her. I spoke to the room, to her, to my dad, about how I was heading back to Boston that day and that my cat, Bella, would be happy to see me. She opened her eyes when I mentioned Bella and told us a story of her youngest son—my uncle Peter, who had died almost twelve years earlier of AIDS—and how he'd once adopted a cat. When he moved from Fresno to Seattle, he had taken the cat with him. His apartment was on the third floor, and one day, he forgot to close the screen door to the balcony, and when he came home, the cat was gone. Every time I heard this story, I imagined a cat falling to the ground, and with a broken leg, crawling away into a bush and dying, never to be found. When she finished the story, she closed her eyes. Unsure if she was listening, or what to say, I chose the benign topic of weather, noting it was a bit cooler back east but quite humid, and that hopefully this heat wave in Fresno would ease up a bit. My dad reminded me that she loved the heat and didn't find it uncomfortable.

Before we left, my grandmother bemoaned the fact that I had to see her in this state. She said she was going to die there. Although she never said so, I took this to mean that dying in the hospital was not her ideal death. I responded by telling her that wasn't true, that she'd get better, as though aging was an illness one could bounce back from. When I went to hug her goodbye, I stood awkwardly over her shrunken body, placed one arm over her chest, and patted her shoulder, fearful of breaking her. I was afraid of tripping on a tube and crushing her, or squeezing out of her what air was left if I hugged her too tightly. I left feeling like a jerk. I'd pretended I didn't know she was approaching the end of her life, and our last conversation would end up being about dead cats and the fucking weather.

Carmella was my maternal grandmother, but my dad was the one who ushered her through her final years. So he was the one who went to the nursing home on the morning of the day she died, which was a five-minute walk around the corner from my parents' house. As he watched her lying there unresponsive, her breathing becoming shallow, sometimes stopping then starting again, like an engine trying to sputter on, he knew she was coming to the end. He went home to quickly refresh his clothes and take care of a few quick house chores—the things any of us would do when being a caregiver—taking a brief moment of respite, but he asked the nurse to call if anything changed or if it appeared she was actively in extremis.

The nurse checked on her and the others under his care over the course of the day. But while he was on a break, she died. For just a moment, she may have woken fully, ripped from sleep, no one around, fear flashing through her, then nothing. Maybe. Or perhaps she sensed she was finally alone and chose that moment to let go. Or maybe she remained in a dream-like state, floating away from life without effort.

With my grandma's decline and death came the realization that mortality was very real. If I went by age and general statistics, my parents would be next. Time was moving, things were changing, and our family was entering a new phase. Until then, death had been a very abstract thing for me. Although I'd experienced the deaths of all my other grandparents, I'd either been too young or not close enough to them to be much affected. It seemed ridiculous that at the age of thirty-two, death seemed to be news to me, and that grief was unfamiliar.

In some MFA programs, there is a joke about the "dead grandparent essay." Some young people who come into an MFA in creative writing haven't had much experience with loss or grief, and when looking for something profound to write about, they may choose the death of a grandparent. It's not to say the loss of a grandparent isn't important or grief-worthy; the joke is more of a commentary on the overwrought prose of the inexperienced writer. It's less about death than it is about writing quality. Yet I always took part of that joke to heart. I found it even more interesting that I too was writing about a dead grandparent in an MFA program, yet I was doing it at the age of thirty-two, not twenty-two. The fact that I'd experienced such a dearth of loss in my life said nothing of my writing but spoke loads about my privilege.

I had initially been angry with the nurse for not being there to see that my grandmother was dying and for not calling my parents. But then I looked at my family and thought, *What is wrong with us?* Why hadn't we rallied around her if we knew the end was so imminent? Why hadn't we had a proper death watch, one where we sat there with her and took turns keeping vigil, telling stories and remembering with her? Why had we not known if she wanted to die alone or whether she'd have wanted to die at home if possible? I felt guilty that she might have been scared and felt alone in those final moments with no one there to comfort her. Had we emotionally abandoned her long ago and then again failed to be there for her in those final moments?

Even with a support system, even with financial resources, it felt like we didn't do as well as we could have for my grandmother at the end. It's hard to ignore that someone without some or any of the same resources potentially has an even bleaker end to look forward to.

The Art of Dying

Ars moriendi, or the "art of dying," is a body of fifteenth-century Christian literature that provides guidance for the dying and those attending to them: a how-to-do-death of sorts in the form of illustrated block books.

This desire to die well, to have a good death, has persisted throughout the ages. After all, no one wants to die "poorly." Yet the understanding of what constitutes a good death is not universal among cultures, or even within a single culture, nor has it remained consistent over time. Periodically, societies, cultures, and generations have had to learn a new way of dying: each time having to decide for themselves what it means to die well.

The phrase *good death* has a couple of derivations, but one in particular most aligns with the way it's thought of in contemporary Westernized cultures, which is from the Greek term *kalos thanatos* (which means, "dying beautifully" or in an ideal way). This is often seen as a death that is positive and has meaning to many people within a community.

But what about people without a community? Those who are homeless, poor, mentally ill, familyless and friendless, or anyone on the fringes of society who struggles to access the most basic of resources needed to live a healthy, happy life? How are you supposed to prepare for a good death, one that is both positive and meaningful, when you're working multiple jobs or struggling to find work, or when you're worrying about where you'll sleep that night, or when you don't fluently speak the native language, or when you're fighting demons in your head that force you to behave in socially unacceptable ways, or when you're just struggling to survive in the first place? Unlike my grandmother, they won't be prebuying their own flowers for their wake, choosing their headstone, or having family take them to appointments and plan the eventually needed memorial service.

If you struggle to live well, how are you meant to die well?

Being Positively Happy About the Inevitable

In the 1970s, a small movement cropped up in the United States called the happy death movement. The name was coined by sociologist Lyn Lofland and given context in her 1978 book, *The Craft of Dying*. The happy death movement was trying to find a new way to "be dying," or in other words, how a person should act "*en route* to the grave."

This idea that the end of one's life needed to be rediscovered during this period of time stemmed from the belief that Westernized societies had become estranged from the realities of death. A lot of that can be attributed to advancements in medicine and medical technology that came about during WWII and have since continued to flourish. New technologies such as ventilators and intravenous feeding methods provided the ability to keep people alive artificially, creating the ability to extend and save lives in ways previously out of reach. But they also complicated the dying process. Some of the advances have made it less clear when someone should be considered dead, as we now have to consider brain activity as well as whether someone's heart has stopped beating or lungs have stopped breathing. New technologies and advances in medicine have also led to a prolonging of the dying experience. As Lofland aptly notes, "Many humans are currently dying who fifty years ago would already be dead" (19). This complication of the dying process and death itself has professionalized something that had previously been dealt with primarily in the home by friends, family, and community members, leading to a disassociation and a loss of understanding about how to deal with death or the dying.

In response to these trends, Lofland described the "happy death" movement as a disparate group of individuals, groups, and organizations involved in activities promoting a societal/cultural change in how we "do death," including emotional, legal, and normative practices related to death and dying. Her ideas about preparing for the end of life were instrumental in making some concrete changes to the way we deal with death and dying, including bringing the living will and the advanced directive into the purview of many in Western culture. We now commonly accept the importance of such documents in preparing ourselves and our families for our eventual demise. Additionally, in 1982, Congress approved the Tax Equity and Fiscal Responsibility Act (TEFRA), which made Medicare available for hospice coverage and solidified hospice as a common service offered to the dying in the United States (Lofland 90).

By the 1980s, though, the happy death movement had petered out, at least visibly, and eventually, Lofland's book went out of print. But in 2018, a fortieth anniversary edition of *The Craft of Dying* was reprinted because, by then, a new kid was in town and there was a thirst for content. The death positivity movement, which took up the torch from the happy death movement, developed sometime in the early 2010s. The beginnings of the death positivity movement can be attributed to The Order of the Good Death, an organization founded by the mortician and author Caitlin Doughty, which promotes, "making death a part of your life." Doughty also coined the phrase *death positivity*, which she describes as having come to accidentally. It began with a tweet where she noted that movements such as body positivity and sex positivity existed, so why couldn't mortality fall under that same umbrella of forward-thinking?

The death positivity movement is uncanny in its duplication of the happy death movement format. Some of the most robust similarities include the push for death education and death talk, pursuing and successfully creating legislative change, and the insistence upon a positive or happy spin, offering (as Lofland put it in the 1970s) the "possibility that death itself and what ensues will be pleasurable" (79). But why has such an interest in dying well been revived now? In both eras, there has been a need for a new way of experiencing dying in Western society. Today that includes issues such as a desire to bring death back to the family home, or considering the environment when we bury our dead. Some reasons for this resurgence may also include the fact that the large population of baby boomers are aging, and Gen Xers and millennials are charged with caring for them. As Lofland notes, "Once that group [for whom death is salient] reaches a sufficient size . . . it becomes aware of itself as a group [and] . . . the emergence of death and dying as fad, fashion, and social movement begins" (25). Additionally, medical technologies have continued to advance since the 1970s, further affecting how, where, and how long it takes us to die, and more people have begun moving away from religion and the grounded traditions around death that those may have provided. All this has left us in need of finding our footing with the old, yet new, territory of death and dying.

Some of the more pragmatic desired outcomes of the death positivity movement include being able to discuss your end-of-life and disposition wishes with family, thinking more deeply about what dying well looks like for you, being a savvier and greener consumer of funeral products, and understanding your legal rights around dying and disposition. There are lots of organizations and individuals doing varied work within the space of death positivity, including Death Cafe, which promotes pop-up-style cafés where tea, coffee, and cakes are provided as a way to ease attendees through open-ended discussions about death and dying. There's the U.K.-based organization Dying Matters, which promotes death awareness partly through an annual Death Awareness Week. The Funeral Consumer Alliance in the United States works to keep people apprised of their legal rights around disposition, changes in laws or pricing, and updates in funeral technology, such as green burials. There are even nurses in California working to promote advanced directives and living wills for the poor and homeless.

As it was with the happy death movement, the death positivity movement has managed some legislative wins as well. The Funeral

Consumer Alliance has been lobbying for transparent pricing in the funeral industry. There have been developments in laws on assisted suicide and the right to die, as well as greener, more climate-friendly disposition options. For instance, The Order of the Good Death promoted lobbying efforts in alkaline hydrolysis (water cremation) in California. There has also been a larger nationwide push for "human composting." The official name of this is Natural Organic Reduction (NOR). NOR uses the principles of nature, combining microbes, oxygen, and plant matter to gently transform human remains into soil. Six states have legalized human composting. Washington was the first. Colorado and Oregon legalized it in 2021, Vermont and California in 2022, New York in 2023, and in mid-2023, legislation was drafted for human composting in Massachusetts.

Not all these efforts are the same, of course, and it's important not to conflate them all with the death positivity movement. However, regardless of whether they're directly associated or not, all these efforts represent death positivity in action, and they are responding to the needs of death and dying within their communities. And intentionally or not, their collective efforts have effected real change.

This desire to find new ways to die, educate people, and change laws so that people might die well and experience better death practices all come from a place of good intentions. But of course, it all also comes from a place of privilege. As Lofland writes about the happy death movement, which also rings true for death positivity, "Undoubtedly, within this ferment . . . there are elements of fad and fashion—a thanatological 'chic' as it were, having approximately the same level of import as organic gardening, or home canning"—or human composting?—"among the rich" (2).

Lofland also offers this haunting sentiment: "Not 'getting off' on death may become as déclassé as sexual unresponsiveness. Then, perhaps, a 'dismal death' movement will arise to wipe the smile from the face of death and restore the 'Grim Reaper' to his historic place of honor" (86). I sometimes worry about this with the death positivity movement—that it may be too out of touch, too white, too middle class, too "thanatologically chic."

I thought this for sure in the midst of the pandemic, when we also experienced a necessary resurgence of the Black Lives Matter movement. With the death of George Floyd at the hands of the Minneapolis Police Department, perhaps for the first time (in significant numbers), white Americans were waking up to the reality of Black Americans and how they face death with far more regularity due to systemic racism. Floyd's death, along with the deaths of Breonna Taylor and countless others, pushed this into public discourse.

And so did COVID. Everyone was facing the uncertainty of an unfamiliar disease. Yet as months went by, the data was showing Black Americans were much more likely to die from the disease than their white counterparts due to generations being deprived of necessary resources such as quality health care, income and housing equality, and other systemic factors.

Systemic racism is also inextricably linked to inequality and homelessness. In the video "Homelessness Is a Symptom of Racism," Jeff Olivet and Marc Dones from the Center for Social Innovation discuss the institutional racism that has led to homelessness in the States disproportionately affecting Black Americans. Dones notes in the interview that 45 percent to 50 percent of people in American homeless shelters are Black, whereas only 13 percent of the American population are Black. When asked about solutions, Olivet and Dones said it perfectly: "Stop being racist. We can solve racism, and [that will] solve homelessness." Something about webs tangling and weaving comes to mind.

Yet there are voices that are gaining traction in the death positivity movement, advocating for inclusive good deaths. This includes the Collective of Radical Death Studies, whose mission is to decolonize death; or Wake, a nonprofit in New Orleans that crowdsources funds for funerals and dispositions. There's the Human Prison Hospice Project, advocating for another very hidden population, people who die while incarcerated. And my own fledgling group, the Equitable Disposition Alliance, works to advocate for accessible disposition for all.

I'm not advocating for a less disparate way of operating. It's not really feasible for all these different organizations and individuals to operate beneath a more structured umbrella, and it's also not really necessary. What's most important is that these are the voices that become larger, louder, more present, which drives the death positivity movement toward the vision of more equitable and accessible death practices in a capitalist-centric society.

Now "positive" is not how I, nor most people who know me, would describe my personality; therefore, the irony was not lost on me when I found myself being drawn into the death positivity movement. Four years after my grandmother died, I was still haunted by the way in which we'd managed it as a family, questioning what we'd done right, what we'd done wrong, and wondering if we really knew how to deal with our dying loved ones and how that would play out with my parents' death—and with my own.

As a sociologist, Lofland lent a critical eye to the happy death movement of the seventies in real time, asserting there were two primary tools used by this movement: nostalgia and taboo. The death taboo is the idea that, culturally, Westerners are afraid to talk about death and that this is at the root of our problems associated with not dying well or in ways we might prefer to die (such as at home vs. in the hospital).

When I stumbled upon the death positivity movement, they, like the happy death movement, were touting the death taboo as one of the biggest concerns for modern-day death and our seeming inability to do it well. This spoke to my feelings of inadequacy and unpreparedness, and it presented a place to channel, and take owner-ship of, my grief. I read all the books, including canonical titles like *The Denial of Death* by Ernest Becker; Philippe Aries's, *The Hour of Our Death*; *The American Way of Death* by Jessica Mitford; Irvin D. Yalom's psychological exploration of the fear of death, *Staring at the Sun: Overcoming the Dread of Death*; and *Being Mortal*, Dr. Atul Gawa-nde's account of how the medical profession can help patients die bet-ter. I watched Doughty's YouTube channel, *Ask a Mortician*, as well as a myriad of other death and dying films. I even attended a couple of Death Cafes; the first I went to had a cake with the words written in frosting, "We talked about death and it didn't kill us."

In 2016, as I wallowed in all things death positivity and wholly bought into the death taboo, I came across a blog post on a website called Death Rookie. In this post, the unnamed author of the blog writes about the politics of death positivity and insists that we need to consider where these ideas are coming from: wealthy countries, privileged (white) folks, and those who possibly haven't experienced trauma or significant loss. When I first read this, it felt like the blog was speaking to me directly, holding up a less-than-flattering mirror. It might not have had such an effect on me, being that this was an anonymous source writing on the internet, if it wasn't for the fact that I knew deep down this person was right. It also might have not been so impactful if I hadn't begun to see that same sentiment mirrored in more substantial places such as organizations like the Collective of Radical Death Studies or in news articles noting the large numbers of people who were becoming homeless over the age of fifty, or being aware of the plain facts of how expensive it was to have any sort of burial or cremation, let alone the exorbitant costs of green burial or other modern disposition options.

I could no longer ignore that my own concerns regarding the good death stood in stark contrast to what is faced in death by someone dying on the streets. In *Stories from the Shadows: Reflections of a Street Doctor*, Dr. James O'Connell, founder of Boston Health Care for the Homeless, writes, "Death lurks steadfastly on the streets and in the shelters. The causes are legion and complex: exposure to the extremes of weather and temperature, the spread of communicable diseases such as tuberculosis and pneumonia in crowded shelters with inadequate ventilation, neglected chronic illnesses, horrifying violence, co-occurring medical and psychiatric illnesses amidst the ravages of substance abuse, and inadequate nutrition, to name only a few" (50). It seems so obvious, and yet, due to the hidden and often misunderstood nature of homelessness, it isn't something that's at the forefront of many people's minds. Of course, it's absurd to expect someone in such difficult circumstances to have the time or resources to make a will, complete a do not resuscitate (DNR), consider alternative disposition options, or spend evenings chatting over coffee and cake about the existential crisis of whether there is an afterlife.

The Dirty Death

Resources are the biggest obstacle to accessing a good death and dignity in death care for someone dying on the streets or someone simply too poor to die well.

In Lofland's efforts to examine how people in the seventies were learning to die well, she outlined three case studies in *The Craft of Dying*. Of those highlighted, one person achieved their ideal death, one had what could be described as a pretty good death, and the third person unfortunately suffered what, for them, was a bad death.

The story of this third person, Mrs. Abel, jumped off the page. Lofland writes, "Mrs. Abel spent quite a bit of time weeping off and on. She was very frightened of the pain . . . [yet, when she] put her buzzer on, no one would come" (48).

The two men who had better death experiences were able to shape their endings due to having sufficient resources. As Lofland points out, financial resources were of course necessary. But Mrs. Abel also importantly lacked personal and social connections. She had no one to advocate for her or help her navigate the state-run hospital she spent her final days in. The nature of capitalism makes such scenarios a reality.

Yet I'm convinced there is an additional underlying reason as to why there is sometimes a disparity in death. I'm not convinced we're necessarily a culture fearful of death, but I do think we may be a culture that is afraid of the dirty death. Afraid of witnessing and experiencing the sometimes painful, visceral, and gruesome realities of dying.

Nostalgia has been one of the two tools used by both the happy death and the death positivity movements. One example that has stood out in particular for me in regard to the visual, tactile, and olfactory realities of death that are fairly hidden in our modern ways of dying is found in Caitlin Doughty's first book, *Smoke Gets in Your Eyes*. She writes of the need to confront the physicality of the decaying body as a best practice for dispensing with the fear of talking about death, "If decomposing bodies have disappeared from culture (which they have), but those same decomposing bodies are needed to alleviate the fear of death (which they are), what happens to a culture where all decomposition is removed?" (165).

Doughty's beliefs were likely in part inspired by Phillipe Aries's *The Hour of Our Death,* one of the most well-known scholarly works on death practices in the Westernized world from the Middle Ages to modern times. In his discussion of late twentieth-century death practices, Aries writes,

> Death no longer inspires fear solely because of its absolute negativity; it also turns the stomach, like any nauseating spectacle. It becomes improper, like the biological acts of man, the secretions of the human body. It is indecent to let someone die in public. It is no longer acceptable for strangers to come into a room that smells of urine, sweat, and gangrene, and where the sheets are soiled. Access to this room must be forbidden, except to a few intimates capable of overcoming their disgust, or to those indispensable persons who provide certain services. A new image of death is forming: the ugly and hidden death, hidden because it is ugly and dirty. (569)

Although Aries is writing explicitly about the dying body, if you ignore this for a moment, you can almost believe he's talking about the homeless body (dying or not). How often are news stories about the "crisis of homelessness" sprinkled with words such as *ugly, dirty, blight, mess, unclean, filthy, disgusting, an eyesore*? Something to be hidden away, to be cleaned up, to be moved on, to only be dealt with by the "few . . . capable of overcoming their disgust, or to those indispensable persons who provide certain services."

In Julia Lawton's 1998 sociological study "Contemporary Hospice Care: The Sequestration of the Unbounded Body and 'Dirty Dying,'" she addresses this modern practice of hiding away the dirtiness and messiness that accompanies some deaths via hospice. In the article,

Lawton relays the story of Annie, a sixty-seven-year-old woman with terminal cancer. In the late stages of her disease, Annie developed a recto-vaginal fistula, which resulted in urine and feces expelling from the same passageway. It began taking her an hour to clean up after using the toilet, and as she developed periodic bouts of diarrhea, she became humiliated at being unable to hide her dirtiness from her family. So she checked herself into hospice.

Lawton writes of the modern hospice, "Contemporary hospices [are able to] set a particular type of bodily deterioration, demise, and decay apart from mainstream society. In so doing [they] enable certain ideas about 'living,' personhood and the hygienic, somatically bounded body to be symbolically enforced and maintained" (123).

Annie exemplified this. Following her admittance to hospice, the fistula enlarged, and each time she stood to get out of bed, diarrhea would pour out of her. The staff would sometimes find her in bed, covered to her shoulders in piss and shit.

This is what Lawton refers to as the "unbounded" body, a body that no longer is able to contain its various fluids, including "incontinence of urine and feces, uncontrolled vomiting (including fecal vomit), coughing up large amounts of blood, fungating tumors (the rotting away of a tumor site on the surface of the skin) and weeping limbs (limbs that swell to such an extent that the skin bursts and lymph fluid consistently seeps out)" (128). A body that modern society deems unacceptable and in need of being hidden away.

Eventually, Annie was sedated and moved into a further secluded area of the hospice, at which time her family stopped visiting. None of them were present when she died, six weeks after she'd admitted herself.

Lawton's study ultimately found there to be an inextricable link between the Westerner's personhood and having a physically bounded body. She may have been speaking of dying hospice patients, but her writing echoes that of another realm. I'm fascinated as to how this links so much to the way society views homeless individuals or determines whether someone falls into the category of homelessness based on their bodily boundedness or unboundedness. How perceived dirtiness and ugliness often lead to unhoused people being further hidden from societal view.

Such an aversion to the unbounded body in death and its relation to how homeless people are sometimes viewed or described is dealt with explicitly in the 1997 book *Shelter Blues: Sanity and Selfhood Among the Homeless*. In his book, sociologist Robert Desjarlais writes about how homeless people are often portrayed in the media as "those who fail to restrain their bodies from an outpouring of scat, urine, words, or outstretched arms; they offend a spectator's sensory faculties" (3). Desjarlais notes one particular *Boston Globe* article on compassion fatigue, where the writer identifies a homeless man in a café, "partly on the basis of the limp and wailing he bodies forth; in contrast to the hunched forms of the pastry eaters, his flesh exudes blood, mucus, tears. What matters most are the bodily and social transgressions involved" (3).

Dignity, choice, and agency shouldn't be dictated based on the containment or the cleanliness of your body, which is something that, as Lawton's article illustrates well, is often beyond our control. Certainly, these things become even harder to keep "bound" when one is living in shelters or on the streets.

One of the memories of my grandmother's death that has stayed with me was her wake. My grandmother had requested to be buried in a blue dress. It fell to my mom to find one that was suitable. I wondered what it had been like for her. She had broken down at the funeral, but prior to and immediately after, she pushed it all to a deeper place, where it wasn't visible, and it was clear it became a subject she felt was no longer in need of discussion. I didn't ask all the questions that plagued me. Had she been upset by having to sort through her mother's dresses to find one to bury her in? Or had she approached it as a job to be done, something that didn't require, or have room, for emotion? Did she pick one quickly, or pull two or three out and compare them? Did she picture her mother in the coffin, something she ultimately wouldn't see?

My mom refused to go to the wake the day before the funeral. But my dad and I went and saw the dress she'd picked out. It was a soft blue one, almost lilac. Not too light, not too dark. A part of me wanted to touch it, to feel what fabric was used. Then a thought passed in my head of what was happening inside my grandmother's body as it lay there. In the back of my mind, I feared I would look over and see her sitting up, like some farcical comedy sketch.

She looked good: lifelike. Is that what one was meant to say? My dad looked at her hands folded over one another, with two of her rosaries entwined in her fingers—something I'd never seen in life, but perhaps I had failed to understand how important her faith had been to her.

"Her nails look good," he said.

"What do you mean?" I asked.

"They cleaned them up really well. Underneath the tips of her nails were pretty dirty. Looks like they were able to get most of it."

"Why were they like that?"

He explained how in the weeks leading up to her death, she had become too weak to lift a fork from the plate. Instead, she began using her hands to eat. Over time, the food got further buried under her fingernails, the way a child might get dirt under their nails after playing in the sand.

In the weeks leading up to my grandmother's death, my dad sent out regular emails to both immediate and extended family as her condition deteriorated. On September 22, 2012, the day before she died, my dad sent one final email:

Carmella ate only a small breakfast. I don't know about lunch. She had no dinner. When I got there at five pm, she was having labored breathing. Respiration between thirty and forty breaths per minute, and a gurgling in the back of the throat. The nurse suctioned her twice in two minutes, then gave her extra pain meds. After that she gave her a breathing treatment, then suctioned again. Still a lot of gurgling, but we couldn't get her to cough or clear her throat to bring the material to the front of the mouth to suction it out. Finally, I had the CNA [certi-fied nursing assistant] help me turn her on her side to get her off the bedsore. That helped relax her and bring the respiration down to under thirty min. The nurse said she would try suctioning again after she had rested some. When I left at seven pm, I told the nurse to call me imme-diately, no matter the time, if she got any worse.

I can still see her hands, those fingernails, today, and I imagine what it must have felt like to need nourishment, to need sustenance in the face of such weakness. In death, there is still life. Both life and death are messy no matter how much you try to contain and silo them.

The visceral nature of imagining the dirt under my grandmoth-er's fingernails was minor in comparison to the unbounded bod-ies described in Lawton's and Desjarlais's writing, yet, this is what I believe Caitlin Doughty is trying to get at when she harkens back to days past: "When the bubonic plague swept through Europe in the 1300s, bodies of the victims would lie in the street in full view of the public, sometimes for days. Eventually the death carts would col-lect the dead and take them to the edge of town, where tranches were dug for mass graves" (Doughty, *Smoke* 49). This passage almost exudes a longing for this very daily, public, and visual confrontation with death. In her version of fourteenth-century Europe, bodies are pres-ent, witnessed, and through this, death is brought closer and is with us every day. If it's all the same, I'd rather not go back to the days of dead bodies piling up on streets and death carts. We came close enough to a modern-day version of this in the early days of COVID, when sto-ries were circulating about bodies piling up in overwhelmed hospital morgues. But I do agree that seeing and smelling more of death—more of the body living, dying, and dead—might help challenge the way we judge the unbounded body of someone living on the streets or make us think more about how hard it might be to meet modern society's standards of cleanliness while living on the streets, and in turn how hard it can be to stay healthy. Maybe getting a little dirty would help us all be a bit more empathetic to the realities of our living, dying, decay-ing, disintegrating, mortal bodies.

Perhaps the art of dying in modern-day times needs to include unlearning our sanitized way of dealing with bodies and death, and our queasiness and repulsion with "unbounded" bodies. Regardless of how well we "control" our bodies, we all deserve dignity and respect.

Can Death Positivity Be Synonymous with Equity and Accessibility to Dying Well?

We are definitely in the midst of relearning "how to do death" in our particular moment in history, but it remains complicated and messy in spite of our attempts to sanitize it (both literally and figuratively). These things are all felt more so when someone dies while on the streets, with all the complexities and messiness that such an existence can embody. Over time, between new technologies and world events, humans will likely continue to need to periodically consider how to do death differently.

As I learn more about the art of dying in its modern iteration, I can't help but think of a picture of my cousin Damon; his dad, my uncle Tony; and my mom flanking my grandmother's hospital bed. The picture is dated September 2, about twenty days before she died. Damon leans in toward her on the left, and my mom and brother stand side by side on her right, all with smiles on their faces. My grandmother's bed is propped up, her head leaning slightly to the right, and she has a nasal oxygen cannula that rests across her face beneath her nose. Her eyes are closed. Damon wears a black beaded bracelet, which he'd mentioned to me at the funeral. When they'd been at the hospital with her that day, she had reached for the bracelet and began fingering each bead, the way one would with a rosary. My grandmother had grown up in a very traditional Italian Catholic home, and although neither Damon nor I could recall ever seeing her with rosary beads, he marveled at how that simple motion of feeling each bead between her fingers had seemed so natural and had given her comfort in that moment.

In thinking back on that conversation with my cousin, I wonder if maybe we did give my grandmother a death watch of sorts. We had all managed to spend some time with her before she passed, and that was something, seeing as Tony was up in Washington, Damon down in Los Angeles, and myself out in Boston. Perhaps my notion of the death watch where we all sat there waiting until the exact moment of death wasn't realistic, at least not for a family spread out like ours. I've also considered that she got the death she wanted. There are some who believe that some people don't want to die in the presence of others, and even when they are seemingly unresponsive, they may be aware enough to sense when everyone has left the room, and they choose to let go in those moments in between.

My grandmother would have scoffed at the idea of death positivity or even the idea of dying well. People you know and love die. You die. But *kalos thanatos* (dying beautifully), whatever that may look like for each individual, shouldn't be reserved for only the privileged in our society.

Fairview Cemetery—Boston, Massachusetts. Photo by author.

The Department of Transitional Assistance

Burial Unit

THE NATIONAL FUNERAL Directors Association (NFDA) notes that the median cost for a burial is around $8,000, and a cremation with a service and viewing is more than $6,000. According to their website, the average "nondeclinable basic service fee" is $2,100. Then there are the optional cost averages, including the removal of the body to the funeral home ($395), embalming ($845), other body preparation ($200), use of facilities/staff for a viewing ($425), use of facilities/staff for a funeral ceremony ($500), hearse ($350), service van/car ($150), basic printed memorial package ($180), metal casket ($2,400), urn ($295), and cremation casket ($1,300). And if you want, or if the cemetery requires it, a vault for burial (which is a large cement box that goes around the coffin to keep the grounds even for maintenance but which is sometimes sold as a way to keep excess water off grandma in her coffin) will cost on average an extra $1,300.

What happens to those who can't afford $6,000 to be dead? In some of California's most highly populated areas, I knew they cremated people and buried them in mass graves. But at the time I had begun my research, I'd been living in Massachusetts for over a decade. Although I assumed that what was being done in California was standard practice across the country, I wanted to know for sure. This had become an obsession for me. I'd been exposed to the fact that a different kind of death than the ones discussed within death positive circles was the reality for far too many people. I needed to know more, which included understanding the process in Massachusetts, and I felt part of that understanding needed to take shape through visiting potter's fields in Boston, where I lived, where I called home.

I turned first to an online search, trying different keywords such as *potter's field*, *county cemetery*, and *indigent burial*, but time and again, the only thing I got back that resembled mass graves or potter's fields were historic ones from the late 1800s. This wasn't what I was after. I wanted to know what happened now. How were people who died indigent today in Massachusetts being treated, and where were they being buried? I spent hours scouring Boston's Parks and Recreation websites for the various cemeteries they were responsible for maintaining, trying to locate maps that might indicate burial plots for potter's fields or indigent burials. The business of what happens to those who are poor, destitute, and homeless in death seemed to be shrouded in misdirection, legalese, and mystery.

I then turned to look for county or coroner information for Boston. I figured that if coroner departments in Fresno and Los Angeles Counties in California were the ones that dealt with indigent deaths, then the same should be true of Massachusetts. This is where I first learned of the Department of Transitional Assistance (DTA), the government arm that deals with indigent deaths in the state of Massachusetts. I didn't know whether to be outraged, to laugh, or feel both. The name sounded cold and bureaucratic, like something from a dystopian novel. I could imagine the faceless government workers processing the recently departed with no means to bury themselves: Welcome to the Department of Transitional Assistance, the Department of Transient Assistance, the Department of Liminal Transitions.

I would later come to learn that the DTA was responsible for assisting people's transitions through various points in their lives, with only one of those being that final transition through a program they called "funeral and burial payment assistance." Yet I couldn't locate much more than this basic information, and it was beginning to seem futile, like a dead end. I found forms on this site that were meant to be filled in to request the funeral and burial assistance, which I assumed were completed by funeral homes, nursing homes, or the coroner. Beyond that, I couldn't find any information that went into depth about the process that came before or after these forms or who was responsible for finding and storing the bodies of the indigent dead.

I knew that I needed to talk to a person; searching online wasn't going to be good enough. But I didn't know who to call. For a time, I considered calling the Boston coroner's office, but I could never muster up the courage. They had to be incredibly busy. Besides, I had no idea who to ask for, what I would say, or how I would explain who I was, why I wanted this information, or why I felt I even had any right to it. So I didn't call anyone and instead lamented over my lack of inner resources and gumption.

◆

In the midst of my sulking, serendipity intervened when in December, a local news station noted that there would be a memorial service for those who died homeless that year, happening on December 20 at Church on the Hill in Boston's historic Beacon Hill neighborhood. I knew that I needed to attend this service. It felt important for the work I was doing to get involved, even if that meant simply being there to physically show my support. My presence wouldn't change how those people had died or do anything to stop others from dying similarly, but it would at least be a seeing, a witnessing, a start to doing more than nothing.

When I arrived that morning, I was worried that I was an interloper. Being a professed atheist, church wasn't somewhere I had spent much time. I didn't know anyone in attendance (housed or unhoused), and I had never been unhoused myself. I quietly sat down and waited for the service to start and gradually began to feel more at ease. A man named Walter sat down next to me. He was an imposing figure, a large man, well over six feet tall. He had a big scraggly gray beard, and now, years later, I picture him all in gray, his clothes obviously old and worn and a strong musk of body odor emanating from him. I soon discovered—as the priest, the organizers of the service, and a few others came by and said their hellos to him—that he was a regular who came in for the church services and the free meals after.

As we waited for the service to begin, Walter told me how he and his wife had at one time worked for the Boston Symphony Orchestra, where he'd been head chef. He didn't go into what had happened to lead to them being on the streets, but fifteen years prior, his wife died while they were unhoused. At various moments during the service, he would whisper additional bits of information in my ear. He said higher education was a way of creating class structures (those in college were part of the problem) and that each college student who came to Boston was taking a potential home from those who were homeless. I struggled to believe this was true, as I had been one of those college students myself. I ignorantly dismissed what he was saying as the angry rants of a man who'd been chronically homeless. But only weeks later, the mayor of Boston, Marty Walsh, who was actively working to end chronic homelessness in Boston, addressed this very issue. The fact that universities were buying up buildings and land not only was taking valuable space that could be allotted to affordable housing but also was driving the housing prices up overall in the city. Meanwhile, there I sat feeling complicit and guilty in a church only steps from my alma mater, Suffolk University, where, a decade earlier, I had encountered many homeless people during that time on my way between home and class.

The memorial service included reading the names of those who had died while homeless in Massachusetts in 2017, which they did in between songs, prayers, and various sermons led by an imam, a rabbi, a priest, a nun, and a reverend. The singing was primarily being done by the MANNA singers, a program started by the ministry of the Cathedral Church of St. Paul in Boston. I later learned the name stood for "Many Angels Needed Now and Always."

The audience consisted of the housed and the unhoused, friends and family of the dead (some visibly mourning), church members, and other community members such as myself, all there to show support and bear witness. We sang "Amazing Grace" at the end, the words of which were printed on the back of the program they'd handed out. Then a candle was lit as each name was read out. We stood and held hands with those next to us, creating a chain throughout the church. I held Walter's hand as we all chanted, "Amen, salam, shalom," accompanied by a piano and guitar in the background.

At the end of the service, the reverend said that all of Boston should have been there on that day. Being the shortest day of the year, it was also the hardest one to be without a home, and that's why they held the memorial at this time each year. Although not all of Boston was there with us, it was important to the roughly sixty people who did attend to memorialize those who'd died unhoused that year.

With the service over, I thanked the reverend, quickly explained my research to him, and asked about how I might obtain the list of names that had been read. He pointed me to a man with curly gray hair who had directed the program/service. When I asked him, he simply handed me his handwritten list of names. He explained that there were sixty-two names missing because the city refused to give them for some unknown reason. I wondered why the city decided these additional sixty-two people would not be named in death.

The reverend also introduced me to the guitarist, Jeff Olivet, who was also the CEO of the Center for Social Innovation (CS4I), a nonprofit that created training materials for people who work with those who are homeless. I couldn't believe that by simply asking, I had been given so much. I had worried that my request would be met with claims of inaccessibility due to bureaucratic red tape and that what I was doing would come off as exploitative, but neither happened.

This experience only reinforced the fact it was impossible to ignore the fact I could no longer in good conscience espouse alongside other white, housed women about the need to die well, a need to have dignity and choice in death, when that conversation didn't include the dying poor, the dying homeless, or the disadvantaged dying.

A couple of months after the memorial service, I spoke with Jeff Olivet again. I had hoped that because of his experience working with people dealing with homelessness that he would know where those who died unclaimed or indigent were buried, but he didn't. However, he was able to point me to Boston Health Care for the Homeless Program (BHCHP) and its founder, Dr. Jim O'Connell. Dr. O'Connell had written a book about being a street doctor called *Stories from the Shadows: Reflections of a Street Doctor*. Here, I found a clue about Boston's potter's fields: Up until a couple of years prior, there had been a shelter on an island off Boston called Long Island. The bridge had gone into disrepair, and the city decided to move everyone off the island. Then they tore the bridge down. On Long Island was an old potter's field where some of those who had lived and died at the shelter had been buried. I wanted to visit, but with the destruction of the bridge, there was no easy way to get there. Surely this couldn't be the only potter's field in Boston. There were plenty of people who were homeless in the rest of Boston, in the rest of the state. There were those who'd never visited a shelter and those who'd never been homeless but were merely too poor to bury themselves. Boston certainly had no dearth of homeless and poor people living within its borders, so where were they being buried? I was missing something, and that was preventing me from figuring out how Massachusetts handled the deaths of those who could not afford their own burials.

After speaking with Jeff, I set off on a concerted search, determined to finally find the potter's fields in Massachusetts. I asked a friend who was an archivist for a genealogy library in Boston, and I also went to my local library, but I immediately hit a roadblock when both my friend and the librarian responded similarly: Did I mean historic cemeteries? As I stood before the stymied librarian who was shaking her head and I tried to describe what I was looking for, it occurred to me that what she was *really* asking was this: Potter's fields don't exist anymore, do they? When I told friends about the potter's fields in Fresno, they would respond similarly—they didn't think this was something that was still done.

The librarian found some possible databases and organizations to follow up with, but they weren't the solid leads I'd hoped for. In my growing frustration, I started to wonder, Was this something done only in California? But logic dictated that there must be indigent deaths in a place with 649,000 unhoused individuals in shelters and on the streets on any given night (Baggett et al. 189).

◆

There is no standard operating procedure for the burial of indigent and unclaimed people across the country. It is all a disconnected jumble, different not only state by state but also county by county. One could spend a lifetime just cataloging the various processes that each county undertakes for dealing with indigent and unclaimed deaths.

One of the most famous mass grave sites, or potter's fields, resides in New York City, underneath Washington Square. It was used after the Revolutionary War as a place to bury poor people who had died from yellow fever. This is a potter's field that is clearly no longer in use—today it's covered by sidewalk—and it may be the only potter's field a small number of people have ever heard of. Perhaps this limited knowledge of such grave sites is one reason why there is a misconception that burial in a potter's field is a historical practice, something done only in our less evolved past. Yet fewer than twenty miles from downtown Manhattan is another potter's field in New York City that is still very much in use: Hart Island. Hart Island is a 101-acre potter's field that sits on an "uninhabited strip of land off the coast of the Bronx in Long Island Sound." It's forever home to the bodies of over a million people. To this day, twice a week, a ferry ushers the dead to the island, along with prison inmates who are paid fifty cents an hour to bury them. The irony isn't lost on some of these inmates, who realize they may in essence be digging their own future graves (Bernstein).

In 2016, journalist Nina Bernstein of *The New York Times* wrote an exposé on Hart Island. She discovered that, disturbingly, the public was not allowed onto the island, not even with the clout of *The New York Times*. In response, the paper hired a drone and were able to capture images of this island that for so long has been a forced home for the outcast and unwanted in various capacities. During the Civil War, it was used as a prison for Confederate soldiers, and in 1868, it was purchased by the Department of Charities and Corrections as a boy's reform school. The island is still dotted with crumbling ruins, including a "lunatic" asylum and a tuberculosis hospital. In between those ruins are razed tracks of land with long trenches dug where the indigent dead are buried three deep. Bernstein combines images of this desolate, hidden place, along with extensive research that uncovered stories of the often complex and undignified journeys that led individuals to be buried there. In her article she writes, "Throughout human history, archaeologists say, the treatment of dead bodies has been a key indicator of status differences in a society; the 'unworthy' poor become the unworthy dead" ("Unearthing").

When someone is in the disadvantaged state of experiencing homelessness, they become particularly vulnerable to exploitation and undignified circumstances, even after death. Bernstein notes this in consideration of the effects of the invisibility of Hart Island: "It obscures systemic failings, ones that stack the odds against people too poor, too old, or too isolated to defend themselves. In the face of an end-of-life industry that can drain the resources of the most prudent, these people are especially vulnerable" ("Unearthing").

Such sentiment has been evidenced historically. Raphael Hulkower notes in "From Sacrilege to Privilege: The Tale of Body Procurement for Anatomical Dissection in the United States," that "Massachusetts was the first state to enact laws, in 1830 and 1833, allowing unclaimed bodies to be used for dissection. . . . Other states followed suit, legislating that unclaimed bodies of people who died in hospitals, asylums, and prisons would be allocated to . . . medical schools for the purpose of anatomical dissection" (25). By the late nineteenth century, some states passed laws requiring various institutions that dealt with the indigent and poor to provide corpses to medical schools to avoid burial that would otherwise be a public expense (Halperin).

The collected stories of Hart Island's operations today provide an example of how the undignified practices of dealing with the bodies of the indigent dead are not relegated to history. The poor are still disproportionately adversely affected. Even as late as 2014, in Los Angeles, California, there were still instances of unhoused bodies being used for embalming practice in mortuary schools (Doughty, *Smoke* 203). As Bernstein writes, "A pauper's grave and the specter of dismemberment never lost their horror as a final humiliation." She continues, "The street homeless and other casualties of rough living are generally not wanted by medical schools." This is due to their bodies potentially being ravaged by the effects of drug use or disease or being exposed to outdoor elements.

The indignity of Hart Island and the business of the unclaimed, indigent dead made the news again in 2020, when in the midst of a global pandemic, New York City decided to hold unclaimed bodies for only two weeks in order to make room for all those people in the morgue who had died of COVID-19 and who would be claimed. Those who died indigent during the pandemic, people already potentially lost to friends and family, would have even less chance of escaping Hart Island.

◆

It was becoming obvious that there was no national process and that cities and states were left to their own devices to decide how to manage unclaimed bodies. Yet as fascinating as all this bureaucracy was, it still wasn't answering my question as to what happened in Massachusetts. While I futilely searched online, I finally got my answer when I found a person to speak to: a former *Boston Globe* reporter. I explained my search and expressed my frustration over not being able to find the potter's fields in the state. She didn't know for sure either, but she pointed me to a two-article series: "Who Buries Massachusetts' Poor? State Pays So Little Only a Couple of Funeral Homes Will Take Them" and "Abandoned Bodies: Massachusetts' Poor and Unwanted Are Spending Months Waiting for Burial," published in 2018 by *MassLive* reporters Melissa Hanson and Phil Demers on this very subject. This finally unlocked the piece of information I'd been searching for.

In "Abandoned Bodies," Demers writes about one particular instance, in August 2016, when Stephen Ledoux, a fifty-three-year-old homeless man died while staying at a friend's apartment in Brockton. His cause of death was ruled as chronic obstructive pulmonary disease. The closest thing to family the police could find was an ex-wife who did not want to or could not take responsibility for Stephen's body. The coroner declined to take the body, as no autopsy was required. The police waited at the house for nine hours while they searched for a funeral home that would take him. Of the thousands of funeral homes in Massachusetts, only a few are left that will do this. The reason for their reluctance to take an indigent body is the cost that would be incurred for everything from transporting to preparing to ultimately burying the body (Demers).

If we go back to the figures from the National Funeral Directors Association, at a minimum, the cost is $2,100 for either burial or cremation. In Massachusetts, it's illegal to cremate a body without prior written consent by the decedent or a sign-off by their families. The Department of Transitional Assistance offers up to $1,100 in reimbursement through their funeral and burial assistance program. Any assets the DTA finds belonging to the decedent, no matter how small the amount, are deducted from that $1,100. In one case, they found $4.52, so they deducted that from the reimbursement to the funeral home (Hanson). In addition, the DTA has another caveat to paying out that $1,100 of assistance: The total disposition expenses must be capped at $3,500. If the cost goes above that, no monies at all will be provided by the DTA.

But the math from the DTA doesn't quite work. There's the base cost of $2,100. One could argue that the "optional" costs are just that, but it doesn't eliminate them entirely. Legally, in most states, you can transport the body of a family member to the funeral home yourself, which would require having a vehicle that's big enough. Of course, in the case of indigent bodies, the funeral home would be the one transporting the body anyway—for $335. Embalming a body is not required, so that can be forgone, and presumably no other body preparations would be needed, so both those costs can be zeroed out. There wouldn't be a need for a viewing or ceremony, so those, too, could be cut. We could skip the hearse and go with the cheaper option of a service van for $150 to transport the body from the funeral home to the cemetery. No need for a memorial package for someone who isn't going to be memorialized. Instead of a metal casket, noted on the NFDA's list as $2,500, a basic wood casket would come in at around $500.

If you've been keeping track, our bare-bones burial would cost around $3,085. If we went the way of cremation and replaced the $500 wood casket with a $350 third-party cremation fee plus a cremation casket for $275, we end up with a total of $3,210. Forget the urn, as these cremains will stay in a labeled box and will be filed away for possible collection by a family member someday, maybe. Either option, cremation or burial, leaves us dangerously close to the DTA's $3,500 limit.

But we still haven't accounted for the cemetery fees. In Massachusetts, all cemeteries are required to reserve space for indigent burials, or what the state calls "welfare burials." But the hitch is that there is no maximum cost enforced; they can charge customers whatever they want for a plot (Demers). According to Demers, he identified three cemeteries that willingly took welfare burials: two in Worcester (Hope Cemetery, which is public, and St. Peter's, which is private) and one in Boston, the public Fairview Cemetery, which has a dedicated potter's field, referred to as the City Poor Lot. The two cemeteries in Worcester charged around $700 for a welfare burial while Fairview Cemetery in Boston charges $276. But Fairview refuses to bury anyone not considered a resident of Boston.

If we add the $3,085 from the funeral home costs to the $700 cemetery cost, the total exceeds the DTA's $3,500 cap in order to be eligible for the $1,100 reimbursement. The few funeral homes in Massachusetts willing to do welfare burials do them out of a sense of moral obligation, and they deflate the costs on the DTA paperwork so that the expenses stay below the limit. But regardless, even with the $1,100 given back to them, they still end up paying out of pocket.

My first reaction to what happens to those buried as indigent dead back in California had been horror. It seemed so undignified to be cremated and then have your ashes buried in a mass grave without consent or a choice on the matter. Yet as the Massachusetts method unfolded before me, California's efforts seemed reasonable by comparison. At least in California, indigent bodies weren't passed around like hot potatoes.

In her book, *The Submerged State: How Invisible Government Policies Undermine American Democracy*, political scientist Suzanne Mettler writes about how much of governmental policy can be invisible to the general public due to the overwhelming size of government. She explains, "The policies of the submerged state [which are] a dense thicket of long-established public policies . . . obscure government's role from the view of the general public . . . leaving citizens unaware of how power operates, unable to form meaningful opinions, and incapable, therefore, of voicing their views accordingly" (4–6). In some instances, the lack of knowledge of processes means people lack the capacity to understand how government policies are actually helping them. But in cases such as how someone's body is treated in death when the government is left to manage it, the opaqueness around that process obfuscates and erases any public understanding of it, therefore rendering any change to it unlikely. Does it have to do with the shame of how we treat the marginalized in our society, or is it simply that society at large doesn't give it much thought? Within the submerged policy on indigent deaths, the marginalized are pushed further out of public view. When someone dies who is homeless, in poverty, disenfranchised from society, or without family or friends, there isn't necessarily an easy route to resting in peace. Marginalized and poor bodies are vulnerable bodies and include indigent bodies, homeless bodies, Black bodies, poor bodies, female bodies, marginalized bodies, forgotten bodies, unknown bodies, unclaimed bodies, and unwanted bodies.

•

Part of the issue, of course, is that no single unclaimed death is the same: Some people have no money but have living relatives happy to sort out the burial; others have homes with furniture and a prepurchased burial plot but no friends or family left in their lives at the time of death; some died alone with only what they had on their person, maybe including an ID, a few hundred dollars to their name, and no family. The reality of illness, death, and dying for the marginalized in our society is that it's messy, chaotic, and filled with gut-wrenching decisions.

Before my visit to Fairview, I studied the cemetery's online map, trying to work out where the City Poor Lot was, but to no avail. But I had also found an article in *The Boston Globe* about local-area high school students who served as pallbearers and held services for some of the welfare burials at Fairview that confirmed I was on the right track. I would now be able to walk those grounds, be in that physical space.

I didn't know what I would get or feel from it, or even what I was looking for exactly. But it felt important, necessary even, for my body to
be in the same place in order to properly bear witness.

So in the spring of 2018, while searching for potter's fields in Massachusetts, I was first led to one of the most well-known cemeteries in
New England: Mount Auburn Cemetery. A local librarian suggested
that I go there and ask the staff about potter's fields in the Boston area.
Mount Auburn itself wouldn't have any indigent burial plots, but the
staff might be familiar with the history and previous burial practices of
the area and other nearby cemeteries. It seemed as good a place to start
as any.

Mount Auburn is a historic cemetery, visited as much for its trees,
flowers, and wildlife (including turtles, turkeys, owls, and squirrels)
as for its beauty and serenity, including ponds, many winding paths,
and the notable people buried there, including Henry Wadsworth
Longfellow. It's a tourist site, just as London's Highgate Cemetery,
Paris's Père Lachaise Cemetery, or the Glasgow Necropolis are. Mount
Auburn was founded in 1831 and ushered in the era of the rural cemetery movement. This was when the word *cemetery* came into regular
use, rather than *graveyard* or *burial grounds,* as they'd previously been
referred to. The word *cemetery* is derived from the ancient Greek word
kometeterion, meaning "sleeping place." The language itself illustrates
the shift in the way people thought of death and that final "resting"
place from the dark, gloomy church graveyard to a way to come back
to nature, as it were. The transcendentalists were instrumental in this
"cult of cemeteries as 'schools of life.'" In fact, at the opening of another
New England rural cemetery, Sleepy Hollow, Ralph Waldo Emerson
delivered the dedication speech (Wills 64).

Although Mount Auburn wasn't the sort of cemetery I had originally intended to spend time in, one gorgeous spring day in Boston, I
headed out to it to take the opportunity to explore the parklike ambi-
ance and to be a true taphophile: someone who enjoys touring and
spending time in cemeteries and graveyards. I was apprehensive as I
walked onto the grounds. I felt like I was trespassing, as I wasn't there
to mourn. This was only made worse when I realized that a funeral was

about to begin in the chapel, which, according to the sign outside, also housed information services. I decided that I'd walk through the cemetery and wait for the memorial service to end. I didn't have the dollar in cash I needed for the cemetery map, and as I dropped only the fifty cents in change I had into the metal box, the shame of each kerplunk of a coin reverberated. I grabbed a map and made for the comfort of the tombstones and willow trees.

Not knowing where to begin and worrying about getting in the way of the funeral, I sat down on an engraved stone bench to study my map and noticed that I was close to Longfellow's grave. It seemed a good place to start—a writer visiting another writer's gravesite. It felt like a purpose for being there, as though my actual purpose wasn't sufficient. I followed the map toward Indian Path, where I wandered about and eventually found Longfellow's grave, which had a large foreboding headstone that you could walk up to. I took photos, wound down paths with names like Elm and Walnut Avenue, encountered a family of turtles, was nearly chased by a male turkey, and passed over ponds framed with blooming shrubs and trees via quaint bridges.

Alongside these ponds were imposing, ornate, gorgeous tombs, some with squirrels sitting on the front steps. They looked like mansions in miniature. A status of wealth permanently fixed—this was the Rodeo Drive of eternal resting places. Tombs may be out of fashion these days, but these relics still oozed a sense of class that had a look-but-don't-touch vibe about them. The tombs commanded attention in the space, but they weren't the only ones that imbued a sense of privilege. There were family plots littered about as well, many of which had black wrought-iron fencing around them, keeping those inside safe from the prying hands of the living. Of course, back when Mount Auburn was established, there would have still been concerns over grave robbing, and fences and tombs both served as practical safeguards. *The Secret Cemetery*, an ethnographic study of cemeteries, notes that moving from the churchyard gravesite to the private cemetery "provided the middle classes with membership in a new democracy of the dead and a 'symbolic geography' for a new community of the living" (Francis et al. 32). Years later, that same privilege still

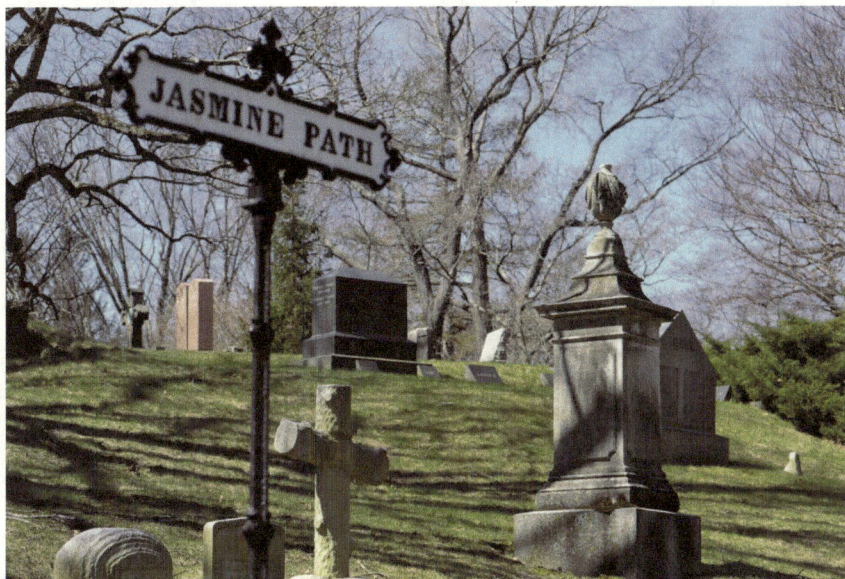

Mount Auburn Cemetery—Cambridge, Massachusetts. Photo by author.

existed. And now, as then, they send the same message: If you're not one of us, you don't belong here.

After spending nearly two hours wandering around the cemetery, I made my way back to the chapel, which now sat empty, the mourners gone. No one working for the cemetery was inside, but I encountered a friendly groundskeeper outside who told me to check in the office around the corner. There, I was greeted by an older gentleman, smartly dressed in a suit and tie, who asked how he could help. I explained that I was a doctoral student working on a book, that I was trying to find potter's fields in the Boston area, and that a librarian told me I might get help at Mount Auburn. He flashed a plastered-on, condescending smile as he replied, "Well, this is a private cemetery . . . Plots are quite expensive here." He seemed to think I was asking if there were any indigent plots in Mount Auburn Cemetery. I couldn't tell if he just hadn't listened or if I'd just done a terrible job of explaining myself. But I didn't bother to explain that that wasn't what I was trying to ask. Instead, I let him puff his chest up as he then went on to say that there might be a handful of unmarked graves of infants on the grounds. He told the story of a woman who'd learned of an ancestor who had been buried as a pauper at the cemetery, and how, when she came and saw the location, asked if she could put a headstone in. He had to deny her request because she hadn't paid for the burial or plot location—but at least she had some solace in knowing where the body was buried. He then suggested that I try the Cambridge City Cemetery just up the road.[1]

◆

I could have chalked the day up to a failure as I slunk out of there, feeling as much like I didn't belong as when I had first entered. But shortly after visiting Mount Auburn Cemetery, I finally found a pot-ter's field in Massachusetts: the City Poor Lot inside Boston's Fairview Cemetery. Fairview Cemetery rests within a beautiful neighborhood between Roslindale and Dedham, close to the Blue Hills of Boston. The day I arrived, I was apprehensive, as I had been at Mount Auburn, but this time, I knew I was in the right place. The office was open, and the friendly cemetery director inside helped point me toward the City Poor Lot. There were five sections to it, each with nature-inspired names: Goldenrod Grove, Riverview, Beech Avenue, Hillcrest, and Birch Avenue.

These five lots huddled together between the standard paying-customer lots within the wider cemetery. In a section that sat just up the hill, the headstone of the recently deceased former mayor of Bos-ton, Tomas Menino, looked down over the poor lot. He was Boston's longest-serving mayor, from 1993 to 2014, dying only nine months after leaving office. Was it ironic or fitting that in his death he now watched over the city's deceased homeless, poor, and destitute? In *The Secret Cemetery*, the authors discuss the historic placement of pauper's graves: "In the social geography of the cemetery, pauper interments and cremated remains were situated far from the prestigious chapels and main avenues that were lined with ornate monuments" (Francis et al. 143). This wasn't the case in Fairview, but I doubted that it had less to do with the democratization of burials among social classes and more to do with where there were spaces left in the cemetery to bury the indigent.

Fairview is an attractive cemetery with lots of trees, including cypress trees, the traditional cemetery tree. The Romans used to carry cypress branches as a sign of respect, as they represent hope because they point toward the heavens. Although there were many large and elaborate headstones, there weren't the ponds or twisting paths hidden by overgrown shrubs like at Mount Auburn. This was less gothic Victorian and more modern. The City Poor Lot sections weren't cast off into obscurity or barren fields of dirt like the potter's fields I'd been to in Fresno. But in spite of this, once you stepped into these sections of the cemetery, it became impossible not to see the disparities between the private and the paid sections.

Immediately noticeable was how uneven the ground was, which required careful stepping so as not to trip. Stretched across the irregular ground were long slabs of concrete with large numbers etched into them. It looked as if the numbers were handwritten with a stick, not stamped in. There were a handful of mini memorials scattered about: a few angel and religious white ceramic figurines, some upright, some toppled over. One concrete slab had a series of twigs lined up with a couple of tiny toys next to them; it looked like something a child had done. Another slab had a painted black rock with the words "Brother Love" written on it. As I made my way up the small hill to the top corner of this first lot, I noticed a pile of fake flowers and children's toys: a memorial to all the babies, who were always buried in the top rows of each lot.

Next, I walked through the Birch Avenue section of the City Poor Lot. At the end of one of the long cement rows, nestled in the grass, I came across a large photograph. It was roughly twenty-four-by-thirty-six inches and encased in a faded wood frame. A smattering of spots slightly obscured the image inside the frame from where water had found its way underneath the glass. A Latina woman smiled out from the picture; she looked to be in her twenties or thirties. Her ebony hair was styled in big curls, and she wore a short-sleeved olive-green button-up shirt with belted high-waisted blue jeans. Behind her was

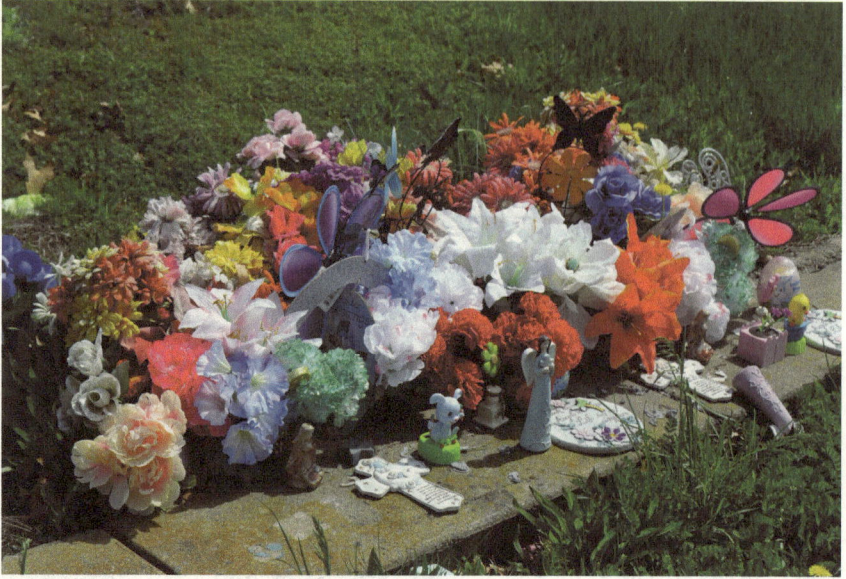

Infant Section in Boston's City Poor Lot. Photo by author.

a mantel with small figurines, one of a dog, and one of a dark-haired girl, and a landscape picture hung on the wall above. She leaned casually toward a dog that looked like a collie, her hand resting on its head. Something about the style of her clothes and hair, or maybe the painting behind her, made me think the picture had been taken in the 1970s or perhaps the early 1980s. How long had the photo been there? Who was she? Was this someone's mom, sister, daughter? Which of the unmarked graves belonged to her?

I continued my search and managed to find all the lots except Goldenrod Grove. I decided to wander to a different part of Fairview, where the cemetery director had noted the old City Poor Lot was; it had been used in the 1940s and 1950s. (During the 1960s and 1970s, indigent people were buried in unmarked graves at the nearby Mount Hope Cemetery rather than Fairview.) The ground in the older lot was even worse than the newer poor lots, having had more time to settle. It was uneven, with divots and holes; an orange cone covered one particularly dangerous hole. I had to avoid falling and injuring myself, as

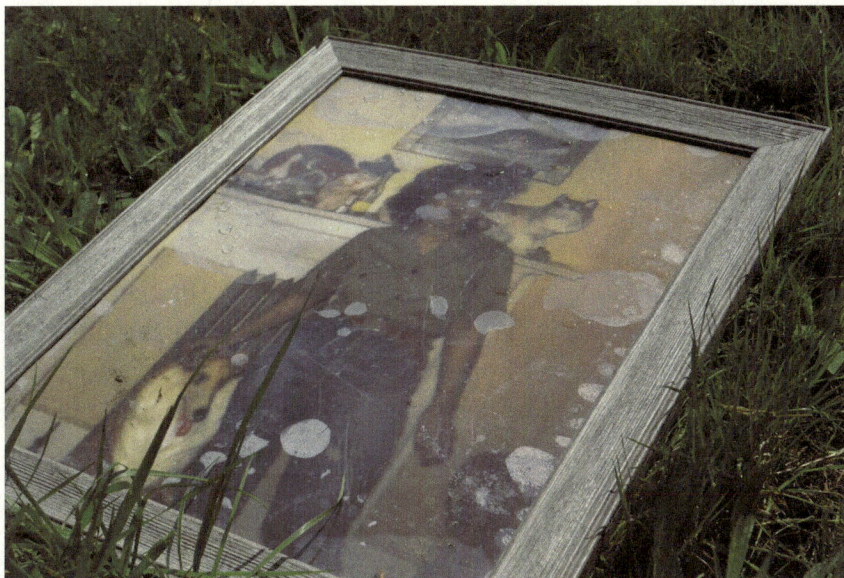

The Birch Avenue Section of the City Poor Lot. Photo by author.

walking became even more treacherous than in the newer poor lots. There were no markers in the old poor lot, nothing to indicate people were buried there except for the fact that it aligned with the area marked on the map.

◆

As I became a seasoned cemetery tourist, I learned that you need to talk to the groundskeepers if you want the good stuff: the in-depth and behind-the-scenes information. Many have been there for years and have an intimacy and familiarity with the grounds that the office staff simply doesn't. The grounds staff can also dispense with any of the formalities that those in the office have to keep up for dealing with mourning family members.

As I walked back to the road from the old lot, a maintenance truck driving by stopped. I initially worried that he was going to question or scold me for being in this no-man's-land, but when I explained what I was doing and that I still hadn't found Goldenrod Grove, Bobby suggested that I hop in his truck so that he could show me where it was. While we drove over, I noted how much better the City Poor Lots looked compared to the ones in Fresno. Because the poor lots were located within the larger Fairview Cemetery, which is owned by the city's parks department, regular maintenance could be performed. Bobby took pride in it: This was his cemetery, and he did what he could to maintain the appearance of it all.

Bobby had worked for the city parks department and at Fairview Cemetery for thirty years. I kept apologizing for taking up his time, but he assured me that he was more than happy to talk. We drove around and stood outside the truck while he told me stories and we talked about my research. He felt, like others, that there was a real need for legislation to allow the state to cremate when they can't find family to sign off on the process. He said the Goldenrod Grove lot was it, and after that, they'd be out of space. Of course, all that meant for him was that he'd have to find space somewhere in Fairview. Up until recently, they'd been burying people in single graves, but to stave off the inevitable point when they'd run out of room, he started burying two deep (one on top of the other) in Goldenrod Grove. In the old City Poor Lot, they were burying people three deep, but he wasn't willing to do that. As Bobby put it so perfunctorily, the state won't consider legislation right now because it's not an emergency, at least for the "right" person—until the bodies start stacking up; then maybe something will change.

The cost at Fairview for a City Poor Lot burial was $267 for everything ($50 for babies), which wasn't much more than the $250 Fresno County charges for cremation. This price included the opening and closing of the grave and the lowering of the coffin. Headstones weren't allowed, but on rare occasions, Bobby put their initials next to the number on the cement marker. Wooden coffins were supplied by the funeral homes that prepared the body, which would usually be wrapped in a simple cloth within the coffin. Part of what kept the cemetery costs down was a lack of vaults or liners in the grave and also that they lowered the coffin manually into the ground with the help of four to six ground crew and straps. Of course, this is why the ground was so uneven: No vaults mean that when the wood coffins rot, the dirt settles down around them, leaving holes. Following that, animals such as voles or groundhogs then come burrow and dig, exacerbating the issue. Bobby occasionally tried to fill in the holes or spots that were sinking, but it often was a losing battle. Because the cost was so minimal, families were discouraged from attending the burial. The cemetery also didn't want family there because they lowered the coffins into the ground with rope instead of a traditional casket-lowering device, which lowers it down slowly by releasing mechanical gears. This meant there'd be more chance for something to go wrong that you wouldn't want the family witnessing, like a rope slipping or breaking or the coffin falling into the grave. Also, a normal burial at Fairview costs almost $4,000, which includes a graveside service. That trendy disposition option in death positive circles, the green (natural) burial touted by middle-class and well-to-do folks as the best way to continue to care for the earth in perpetuity, is something that people are willing to pay far more than $267 for. If a family pays only $267 for a county burial, then it might stand to reason that a lot of things would be cut out. Of course, that's to assume that the people buried there in the poor lot had family or friends to miss and mourn them to begin with. Some did, but plenty did not.

River Valley Cemetery: Homemade in Louisville, Kentucky.
Photo by author.

River Valley Cemetery: Homemade in Louisville, Kentucky.
Photo by author.

Field Notes of a Tombstone Tourist

W E BURY OUR dead in cemeteries, resting places, lands of repose, gardens of remembrance. These spaces embody our social mores and reflect changing ethos over the decades and centuries. Cemeteries are a necessity in the disposal of the dead, but they are primarily designed with the living in mind.

According to the authors of the 2005 book *The Secret Cemetery*, in the eighteenth century churches were the primary guardians of indigent burials (Francis et al. 30). In some cases, charitable and fraternal organizations stepped in to purchase burial plots for marginalized community members (Sloane 2, 97). Many such places are meant for sitting, walking, and talking with and remembering our dead. But there's another type of cemetery, where there is only function, no form. Where there are dead bodies buried rather than people laid to rest. Places no one would ever refer to as "gardens of remembrance." Places that feel more like fields for forgetting.

As we progress with technology and a deeper understanding of how all our actions, including burying our dead, affect the environment, newer, innovative disposition options are being developed and tested. Some of those new ideas include green/natural burial, mushroom suits (suits encased with mushroom spores meant to grow and help degrade the body after burial), human composting (where bodies are placed in vessels with organic mulch and then composted until they become soil that can be returned to the earth), alkaline hydrolysis (also known as liquid cremation—a greener cremation not requiring burning or smoke), and more. Not all will become common practice, but one thing that seems to have remained a relative constant in the ever-changing landscape of the disposition of our dead is what to do with the bodies of indigent people: those who are poor, marginalized, disenfranchised. As I thought more about death, dying, inequity, and homelessness, I knew I needed to go back to where my journey began. I needed to go back to the cemetery.

In the spring and early summer of 2018, my cemetery jaunts were solo journeys in New England. But as the summer days grew long, I made my way out to California and met up with my original tombstone touring partner: my dad. I'd asked him if he knew of or could find any other potter's fields beyond the two in Fresno County that we'd already been to numerous times, and he found two more. One was in the small farming town of Hanford, about thirty miles southwest off Highway 99, and the other was in the city of Madera, just north of Fresno. We decided to tackle both on the same day—Hanford in the morning, with a stop back in downtown Fresno for necessary refreshment at Triangle Burger, and then north to Madera in the afternoon.

Pioneer Cemeteries was the home of those who died alone or penniless in the Hanford area between 1893 and 1959. We both had the same thought as we approached the large, maybe seven-foot or higher headstone with the simple title of *Potter's Field* at the top: Where did they bury them after 1959? It was a reasonable question. Before 1893, there was likely less of a need (or no need) for potter's fields in this area: People had family farms to be buried on or family plots. Back then, homelessness (a big contribution to many a potter's field or a poor lot) was also a nascent issue and often took a different form. Death and burial still often fell within the family's purview, and it wasn't the pricey privatized, corporate enterprise it became after World War II. But none of these things had gotten better after 1960; they had all become worse. It would only be logical that if small towns such as Hanford had a need for a potter's field then, they'd have it now. Where was it? I wondered out loud if the town perhaps had some arrangement with Fresno County, but if it was going to contract with a larger government body, it would more likely be Kings County, which it is a part of. Or did it mean that Harford simply had switched to cremation or mass burial after 1960, the same way Fresno had?

I was struck by the beauty of the potter's field section and how well they'd kept it up, with a plot of green grass and flowers and trees. This side of the street was clearly the part of the cemetery that was full up. The nearby headstones all had older dates on them, from the 1800s and early 1900s, and stood tall, the way the fashion of the day would have dictated. The cemetery office was located across the street, and behind it was the wide, expansive cemetery with the flush headstones seen today, meant primarily for uniformity and ease of maintenance. While we were there, in fact, the grounds crew was mowing the old cemetery, their mowers moving quickly in wide swaths over the minimal stone markings. To get to the large potter's field headstone, you had to walk down a long, paved path of pristine white cement, surrounded on both sides by green grass (something not seen much anymore in these parts). At the end of the path was a neat square of pavement with the headstone in the middle so that you could walk freely around it. This was lined with rows of small flowers and bushes.

This headstone was so large for a reason—the names of all those buried there were engraved on both sides. I suppose in some ways that this was understandable with only sixty-six years to account for instead of over a hundred in Fresno. Although I didn't count the number of names, there were clearly far fewer buried here in Hanford. The dignity of being named, memorialized, and landscaped in such a way made it look almost like a war memorial. These people were being honored and remembered. Also hard to miss was the fact that the Chinese cemetery was positioned alongside the potter's field, something Hanford had in common with Fresno. In Fresno's case, in 1913, the city had insisted that burials of Chinese people be segregated: separate but certainly not equal.

Yet this place didn't imbue a sense of sadness in the same way that other potter's fields I'd seen had. Sure, the names were all lumped together on one headstone rather than having names put with individual plots, but I didn't see a single John or Jane Doe (perhaps this was due to Hanford being such a small town where it was less likely to be an unknown), and it seemed that this place had been a true community undertaking that said to passersby, "Even those without money still have value."

Later the same day, my dad and I arrived at Arbor Vitae, a public cemetery for Madera County. When we asked one of the office employees at Arbor Vitae for directions to the potter's field, she called one of the maintenance guys to show us over to the area. I wanted to insist that such effort wasn't necessary, but when Ronnie showed up with his maintenance truck, we got in our car and followed him the hundred feet to the potter's field section (labeled as "County Burials"). I was ready to thank him for his time and wander about on our own, but I was in for a treat. Just as Bobby in Boston had so generously shared his time and imparted his knowledge, Ronnie was equally passionate, knowledgeable, and generous.

Born and raised in Madera, he was proud of his home and of the cemetery he so diligently worked to maintain. This county burial site, not unlike the one in Hanford, was handled with care. Not only were the grounds of the large area maintained just as the rest of the cemetery, but each individual plot had a little plaque in the ground marking the burial spot, along with a full name and birth and death dates. One town/county over from Fresno, and yet so different. Ronnie called the plaques bronze, but when you touched them, you could feel that they were painted with a bronze-colored paint and were really a hard plastic. He was shocked to hear about Fresno County's mass burying of boxed cremations. Madera, too, had begun burying cremains to save space, and Ronnie pointed out where you could see the change happen—a few yards away from us, the plaques were spaced much closer together—but they still buried them individually. With a smaller population than Fresno, Madera could ultimately afford that extra bit of dignity.

There among the bronze-plated plaques were four temporary green plastic markers with a placard inside that noted the names of four of the recently buried, just earlier that week:

GUILBERT WALTER DULFET, AGE 90 (1928–2018)
SYLVIA YBARRA, AGE 62 (1955–2018)
ANTONIO SANCHEZ MARTINEZ, AGE 52 (1965–2018)
MICHAEL WALTER RASCH, AGE 47 (1971–2018).[1]

♦

I thought after the Madera visit that I wouldn't be going to any additional potter's fields for a while. But on a visit to my husband's family in Kentucky for the holidays at the end of 2018, my mother-in-law found links to indigent burial locations in the area, of which the closest ones were in Louisville. I got to Kentucky a few days before my husband, and knowing that he wouldn't have any interest in walking around cemeteries with me, I asked my brother-in-law, Lee, and his friend Courtney to join me. They were excited to come along, as it wasn't every day you went exploring cemeteries, particularly potter's fields. Courtney brought her five-year-old daughter, June, with us as well. The four of us piled into Lee's car and set off on a tombstone tour. It was just a few days before Christmas.

We were going to visit two cemeteries that contained potter's fields: River Valley and Meadow View. Both were on the outskirts of Lexington. We started with River Valley, the older of the two, which was nestled up against the Louisville Gas and Electric power plant, situated within a triangle-shaped lot right up against the reservoir walls. This was solely a potter's field; there were no paid-for plots in this cemetery. It was a gray day, and by the time we arrived, there was a drizzly mist about us. There was some initial confusion when we first arrived at where the GPS said the cemetery was located. The stacks of the power plant loomed above us, and buttressing the perimeter were large grassy berms that held a reservoir of water for the plant. There was a brief moment of head-scratching before I saw what looked like headstones just ahead of us. To the left of the road leading into the plant and situated against one of the berms was a small cemetery. When we drove in, we saw a little shelter that looked like a bus stop. We got out to inspect it and realized that it was a shelter for visitors. Along the back wall were a series of framed documents. Each was a list of names of those buried there, organized by burial year, last name, first name, date of birth, date of death, plot number, row number, and grave number. The burial years ranged from 2006 to 2010. I couldn't believe how organized it was, how out-in-the-open it all was, and how memorialized the occupants were. I noted only one Juan Doe. When I looked this up after our visit, I found an article that noted he had been a Mexican national who had been murdered here in Kentucky just shortly after his arrival. They didn't have any name or information to track down his family, so they gave him an indigent burial. After looking over the names, we pulled up our hoods and ventured out into the broader cemetery.

We began toward the back of the cemetery, where the car was parked, and started examining a hodgepodge of homemade and professional markers. Some were quite elaborate, with large slabs of stone, carved names, and dates, sometimes with sayings or pictures of the deceased. These expensive markers resided alongside the standard-issue "temporary" nameplates issued by the county, which were 3.5″ × 4.5″ metal frames, just a tad bigger than an index card, housed in a glass case and printed with the person's name and birth and death dates as well as the row and grave number.

But more numerous than either of these two grave marker options was a third: the homemade headstone. These captured our attention and imaginations; they were so imperfectly beautiful and so full of character that it was hard to not be drawn to them. There were several wooden crosses that dotted the cemetery, and sometimes the wood was old baseboards pulled from someone's home. Many had the names and dates carved into the wood, and others had the words painted on. One headstone was a metal handicap sign. Above the typical image of a stick-figure person in a wheelchair were letters that looked like the kind stuck onto mailboxes, which read: "RIP, You Are Missed, Ronnie K. Childs, JAN 9 1962–APR 29 2004."

Before this cemetery tour, I'd only ever gone by myself or with my dad. I didn't know what to expect. Would others be open to the experience and have the same interest we did? What would it be like bringing a child along? How would she react? When we had first pulled into River Valley, June began wiggling in her seat and said, "I'm a little scared."

Courtney had smiled at her and replied, "There's nothing to be afraid of, and besides, you like scary things, remember?"

June nodded in agreement, and before we knew it, she had immersed herself in the experience. She ran around in her pink polka-dotted rain boots and began calling us over to headstones, saying, "Look at this one." and "What does this one say?" She not only wasn't scared but also seemed to show sympathy. Even when we were in the infant section and Courtney explained that babies or children June's age were buried there, it didn't seem to faze her. Of course, it's hard to say how much she fully understood. I remember being five and just starting to grasp the idea of mortality. As we stood in front of a large monument dedicated to fifty people who had given their bodies to science, Courtney struggled to explain to June what that meant, finally acquiescing that trying to explain this more complex idea to a five-year-old was too tricky. I had to agree.

I had my own questions about the monument and those who had "given" their bodies to science. Was this something they had been able to opt into? What were the laws in Kentucky around the disposition of unclaimed bodies? In some parts of the country, the poor, homeless, or unclaimed sometimes ended up as cadavers upon whom mortuary students practiced embalming or were used for other scientific and medical endeavors, without any consent given. This practice has historical roots. In the article "The Poor, the Black, and the Marginalized as the Source of Cadavers in United States Anatomical Education," for example, Edward Halperin notes: "The physical and documentary evidence demonstrates the disproportionate use of the bodies of the poor, the Black, and the marginalized in furthering the medical education of white elites" (498). They would have had no idea that's what had become of them after death. Either way, I loved how most graves in this cemetery seemed to have a marker, including one for these people who had donated their bodies to science. According to a 2011 article in *Louisville Magazine*, the county always tried to provide headstones when they could.

We left after an hour or so and went to the newer Meadow View, which had been opened after River Valley filled up. There were about five rows of recent burials from earlier in the year that had become muddy grave-shaped holes due to the rain that had already fallen that winter. You could see where the graves were: sunken-down rectangles, each with temporary markers. Courtney and June stayed in the car while Lee and I walked around. Meadow View was smaller—or at least it didn't have as many people buried there yet—and unlike River Valley, it was void of any homemade, individualized headstones. Here, everything was very organized and uniform, each person having been buried sequentially by date, and each marker was printed with the person's name, their birth and death dates, and the internment date.

On our way home, I realized that I had seen Meadow View before in a 2016 documentary called *The Potter's Field*, which had highlighted indigent burials in Kentucky. The twist came in the form of a high school program that had students volunteer to come out to Meadow View whenever there was a burial for unclaimed people to help serve as pallbearers, choir members, and mourners. Courtney was proud of this place she called home, and she noted that in spite of the perceptions that those of us not from here might sometimes have of the area, the students who came out to unclaimed burials, as well as the county's efforts to give proper memorialization to those buried in the potter's field, showed how they took care of one another in the South, even in death.

◆

In *The Secret Cemetery*, Francis and her colleagues write, "Just as a person's literal home is a material symbol of the self and family, so, too, does the tomb, as home, embody the 'personhood' and meaning of the deceased. When a person dies, his or her social identity will not perish so long as it can be reconstructed through the memories and actions of the living" (21). Courtney's comments about how Southerners take care of their own through proper burial and memorialization made me reflect differently on the unclaimed burial I'd witnessed when I was at Fairview Cemetery earlier that year. It had been a sunny summer day in

Boston, and the place had no aura of solemnity leading up to the burial; it looked and felt like a worksite. I had stood under a tree, a lot across from where the burial was to happen. A backhoe trailed Bobby in his work truck, both of which were followed by a white hearse with two small American flags on the front hood. They parked and approached the pile of dirt, where four cemetery maintenance men stood nearby in their uniforms of gray T-shirts and blue trousers. Two people from the funeral home got out of the hearse and accompanied the maintenance men to the back of the car, from which they pulled out a pine box. They wrapped ropes around the box and lowered it down into the plot, dug deep enough to allow a second coffin to be placed on top. Ten minutes later the cemetery manager walked back to the office, the funeral home workers left, and one of Bobby's men got in the backhoe and began filling in the hole.

In *Wish You Were Here: Adventures in Cemetery Travel*, Loren Rhoads writes about cemeteries, "People take care of the things they love. If they have fond memories of a place, they'll watch out for it and donate time or money to keep it restored" (20). This seems to be the thing missing for many unclaimed dead, for those who are buried in county cemeteries, poor lots, pauper's graves, and potter's fields. Yet there are people within this complex machine who are still working to try to afford some dignity to the unclaimed dead, doing their jobs and doing the right thing. But the myriad of issues, including ever-expanding class disparities and a lack of governmental resources for dealing with the bodies of the poor, leaves many people in a forgotten limbo where bodies stack up with no one to pay for or claim them and where dignity in death is given only to those who can afford it.

Homeless Jesus—Manchester, England. Photo by author.

On Bodies and Embodiment

A T FIRST, I was ecstatic when my dad told me that he'd been able to get us a tour of the Fresno County morgue, but I then was disappointed when he added that we wouldn't be seeing any bodies. As I began delving further into the world of thanatology (the study of death and dying) I became heavily focused on the body and what happens to it in death, and so a trip to the morgue felt opportune. However, on the day of the tour, in the autumn of 2016, when the deputy coroner walked us into the cold storage room and we stood, surrounded by bodies, and witnessed an autopsy being performed on a gunshot victim, I felt a sense of excitement. It was as though I'd glimpsed what I was so desperately reaching for: a feeling of intimacy with death but without the mortal fear of it landing on my head.

Later that evening, I called my husband, furiously rambling on about all I had seen. All that adrenaline made me feel electric, alive. Why did I have such a strong reaction to being that close to the dead? Like Caitlin Doughty writes in *Smoke Gets in Your Eyes*, "I wanted the hard stuff: real bodies, real death" (6). She came to the deathcare industry for the same reason I'd come to it myself, a search for a "deeper understanding of death" and to reframe the grief she'd had from her own experiences. Seeing and being in the presence of real dead bodies made me feel alive, energized.

In the ethnographic study *Shelter Blues: Sanity and Selfhood Among the Homeless,* anthropologist Robert Desjarlais considers the experience of homelessness through various lenses, including culture, language, health care, and political agency. Desjarlais notes how journalists and the media tend to focus on the grotesqueness and the inability of unhoused people to contain their bodily needs and afflictions, displaying them as pitiful figures in an effort to draw attention to the issues of homelessness. But in doing so, they spectacularize and other the bodies of those who are homeless and, in effect, individual homeless people: "For [those in the media], homeless [people] are those who fail to restrain their bodies from an outpouring of scat, urine, words, or outstretched arms; they offend a spectator's sensory faculties" (3).

> Body (noun) | /ˈbä-dē/ | —the physical structure of a person or an animal, including the bones, flesh, and organs; the trunk apart from the head and the limbs; the physical and mortal aspect of a person as opposed to the soul or spirit; the main or central part of something, especially a building or text; a large or substantial amount of something; a mass or collection of something; a group of people with a common purpose or function acting as an organized unit; a mass of matter distinct from other masses. (*Oxford Languages*)

Our bodies, and the fact that they will all die and decay one day, is something we all have in common: We understand pain, shivering, fever, itch. I don't believe it's possible to talk about death or homelessness without talking about the body. Both things bring the physicality and temporality of our existence to the forefront in ways that we can ignore or deny in other aspects of our daily lives. Death leads to the decay and destruction of the body, and homelessness has immediate visceral effects on the body through exposure to the elements, lack of nutritious foods, injury, illness, restricted access to health care, and violence. Therefore, it felt unsurprising that my exploration of the body intersected with the research I was doing around dying while homeless. Yet I could still hear Desjarlais yelling from the pages of his book, "Shame, shame!"

Was I wrong to be focusing on the bodies of those who were homeless, spectacularizing them in an effort to induce empathy? Did my white, safe, housed, privileged body have any right to comment? On the other hand, it's not possible to talk about life and death and the inequalities and disparities that exist for the unhoused without talking about the physicality of such an experience. The body can be an entrance into seeing the person, the mind, and the humanity without reducing someone to only the physical.

It's a difficult proposition: wanting the housed to understand the unhoused by means of physicality, wanting to show both the horrible and the beautiful, the wretchedness and the survivorship. Yet such an approach risks ostracizing, othering, and marginalizing the experience of homelessness by parading it as a tourist attraction, something that unhoused people can dip into and out of, returning to relative comfort, rather than as a way for those unfamiliar with the homeless experience to develop a better understanding of and empathy toward it.

However, the body also provides the opportunity for us to become more intimately familiar with death and homelessness. Once a year, across cities in the United Kingdom, there are *sleep outs*, organized events that bring people together to sleep outside, usually in the late autumn, to raise awareness and money toward ending homelessness. A sanitized simulation of the real thing, sure, but a physically powerful one nonetheless. It's perhaps the closest way someone can physically embody one small facet of an experience that they might otherwise not know: Teeth falling out from years of alcohol abuse and lack of necessary dental care, staples in the head causing radiating nerve pain down the length of the body, trench foot from sleeping under bridges on rainy nights, blisters on feet from ill-fitting shoes and constant walking, eight toes down to the nubs—a result of frostbite after nights outside in a New England winter, sleeping in the backs of abandoned cars.

Those experiencing chronic homelessness will certainly suffer effects to their physical self, their lived bodies. But it's also evident how those physically visible effects can play out in a larger context as symbols and metaphors that relate to culture, society, and political control. Assumptions are often made about those who are homeless in relation to their levels of personal hygiene, looks, and other physical effects, and in some ways, when we see someone who is homeless exemplifying those assumptions (dirty, disheveled) this validates and confirms those assumptions. It could also be said that those physical stereotypes of someone who is homeless—including the negative connotations, moralistic judgments, and assumptions that people in that situation are lazy, have chosen to be unhoused, or are addicts or mentally unhealthy—all play into the body politic of maintaining class structures. Poor people are that way because of their own personal failings, the thinking goes, not because of systematic injustices that are near impossible to overcome.

Embody (verb) | *em·body* | /əm'bädē/ | embodied; embodying—give material form to something abstract; embodiment: the representation or expression of something in tangible or visible form. (*Oxford Languages*)

"Homelessness denotes a temporary lack of housing, but connotes a lasting moral career. Because this 'identity' is deemed sufficient and interchangeable, the 'homeless' usually go unnamed. The identification is typically achieved through spectral means: one knows the homeless not by talking with them but by seeing them" (Desjarlais 2). Homelessness is also often conflated with uselessness, criminality, or a lack of moral character or fortitude. Unhoused people are sometimes referred to as loitering, taking up space, dirty, or trash, thereby making it easier to justify moving them on or hiding them away, busing them out of one town and into a neighboring one, or fining them for sitting in public spaces. All this makes it easier to dispose of these humans like trash in death. You can't be forgotten if you're never remembered. You can't be seen if you're never visible.

The embodied homeless are sometimes seen as disruptive, potentially causing chaos in civilized places. They are blights on doorsteps and sidewalks, betrayed by their bodies, which transgress physically against social order. They fall out of chairs they're not meant to be sitting in, lie limp on floors from overdose as coffee and food orders are taken and filled.

In "Contemporary Hospice Care: The Sequestration of the Unbounded Body and 'Dirty Dying,'" Julia Lawton describes her study of the dirty, unbounded bodies of the dying sequestered within hospices when their symptoms of incontinence, vomiting, or bleeding become uncontrollable and spill forth from their bodies with impunity. Lawton suggests that one reason Westernized societies hide this away is because over time we have come to highly value independence and selfhood, the success of which can be judged by how able one is to control their bodily functions. Our identities have become inextricably bound to our bodies and our ability to control those bodies. Often the homeless are seen as lacking control over such things simply because they have no choice but to defecate, urinate, vomit, and bleed in public. The homeless body is regularly illustrated as the other—a defiance or opposition to the civilized, housed body—something that needs removing, exterminating, hiding, burying. This sometimes takes shape in the form of loitering and encampment laws to move along those without homes to places where they will not be seen.

Corpse (noun) | /kôrps/ —a dead body, especially of a human being rather than an animal; cadaver (noun) | ca·dav·er—a dead body; especially one intended for dissection. From Latin: from *cadere*, meaning "to fall." (*Oxford Languages*)

Found: Dead man in dumpster behind Amazon building. Frozen in a position on his hands and knees, as if trying to stand, blood-stained nose and dirt-caked hands, surrounded by ice cream, bananas, strawberries, frozen pizzas, cans, and packaging.

Vulnerable bodies, indigent bodies, unclaimed bodies, homeless bodies, Black bodies, female bodies, unwanted bodies, marginalized bodies, forgotten bodies. The streets can affect a social death, where a person is not fully accepted as human by the wider society. You die a social death the day the word *homeless* is attached to your person. Once labeled as homeless, this identification clings to the body, to the self. Nobody, no body, deserves to be thrown out, disposed of like trash.

Body a human being: PERSON. (*Merriam-Webster*)

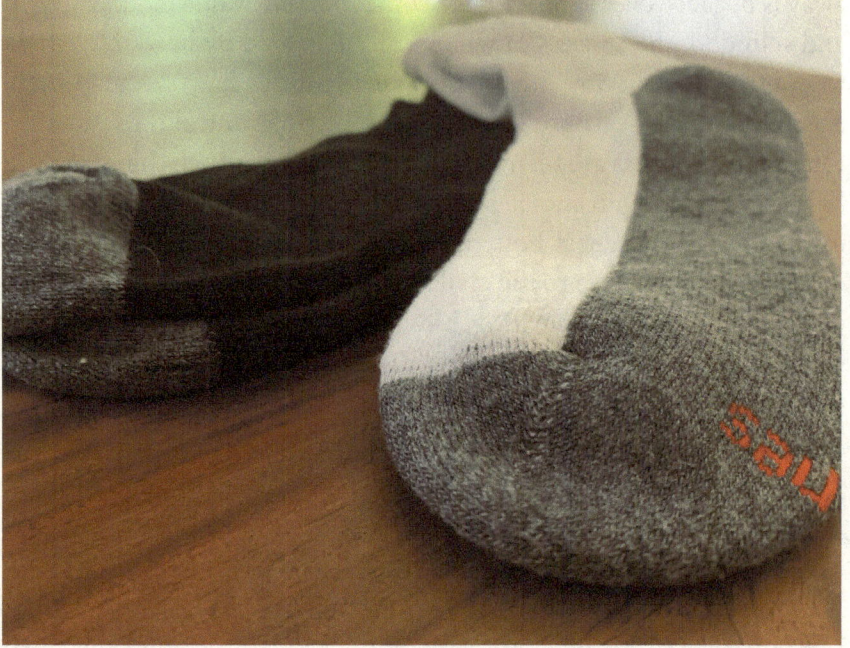

The Simple Comfort of Socks. Photo by author.

Sweet Feet

W HEN I FIRST met Rebecca, I was taken aback by her stature; she was thin, so thin, likely weighing no more than a hundred pounds. She was missing some teeth, and she kept her hair short, complaining of sometimes intense head pain. Her skin clung to her bones, and she walked with a cane. She was less than ten years older than me, in her late forties. Some days, she would come in spirited and energized, one time regaling us with a story of doing free sessions of goat yoga that had been offered near South Station in Boston. Other days, she'd come in more subdued and sit quietly, not making eye contact.

It was 2018, and for the summer, I was volunteering as a foot-care assistant at a day shelter for homeless people. Walking is a primary mode of transport for many who are homeless; therefore, foot health is a pressing issue. Problems can include athlete's foot, foot pain, improperly fitting shoes, immersion foot (a.k.a. trench foot), calluses, corns, blisters, and loss of toes due to untreated infection or frostbite. The most common ailments we saw in the clinic were blisters from ill-fitting shoes, as well as athlete's foot and immersion foot from wet and dirty socks and from using shared showers in the shelters.[1]

Dr. Jim O'Connell is the founder and president of Boston Health Care for the Homeless Program (BHCHP), which opened in 1985. In its thirty-plus years, it has grown into a behemoth of safe spaces for those in need, its jewel being the Barbara McInnis House, the 104-bed medical respite unit on the organization's main campus, plus additional sites around Greater Boston, including the foot-care clinic inside St. Francis House where I volunteered. The main campus, situated in downtown Boston across the street from Boston Medical Center, offers a plethora of services, including a dental clinic, a pharmacy, an eye clinic, an outpatient clinic for regular doctor visits for both adults and families, specialty care for those living with HIV, support for transgender people, a behavioral health unit, and a substance use disorder unit, as well as a street team who meets a subgroup of homeless people who can't or won't enter a shelter.

Dr. O'Connell wrote about his experience as a street doctor in the book *Stories from the Shadows: Reflections of a Street Doctor*. The first chapter, "The Footsoak," leads the reader through his introduction to street medicine by first tending to the feet (and other parts of the body) of homeless people in Boston's oldest and largest shelter, Pine Street Inn: "In keeping with the obvious biblical allusion, the footsoak inverts the usual power structure and places the caregiver at the feet of each patient and far from the head. . . . After wandering the city for hours, suffering exposure to the extremes of weather, and then standing in a series of queues awaiting entrance to the shelter, a bed ticket, and the evening meal, homeless persons relished the chance to sit and rest while someone cleansed and soothed their feet" (16). Having read about Dr. O'Connell's experience, I was compelled to apply as a foot-care assistant. Although I'd never been homeless, as a hiker and someone who didn't own a car, and therefore walked nearly everywhere, I understood the role that feet play in our health. Without healthy feet, so much of our autonomy can quickly be lost.

Leading up to my first day, I was given a foot-care assistant duties and responsibilities sheet that outlined the basics of what I'd be doing: setting up basins for foot soaks and working with nurses to assess the condition of patients' feet, distributing socks and towels, assisting patients with the application of creams and powder, engaging them in conversation (to establish rapport, which can result in the identification of further medical issues), disinfecting and washing basins, and assisting with restocking medical supplies and other administrative tasks. Yet I was still unsure of what the experience would actually be like. I was nervous about the unknown: not knowing how the place would look, feel, sound, and smell. I was concerned about whether I'd do a good job and be able to follow procedures and processes. I worried about trying to remember when you needed gloves on versus when you needed to take them off. What if I was bad at handling someone's feet? Or didn't know how to talk to the patients? Or got in the way of the medical staff?

Ultimately, I understood I couldn't know all and my fears wouldn't be assuaged until I got there and began putting my training materials into practice. But I hadn't expected to be schooled on the importance of something as small as the sock and its power to heal, to comfort, to offer a small moment of feeling human—of feeling normal.

How often do you think about socks? Socks get dirty and wet. Of course, you know that, and so did I. But working in the foot clinic helped place that knowledge in a new context. I had never thought about what might happen if you couldn't clean or easily replace your socks, and it hadn't occurred to me just how quickly they became unwearable.[2]

Before volunteering in the clinic, my sock buying had always happened passively. I'd be in Target and know that my husband had more holey socks than not, and so I'd throw a pack in for him and then wind my way through to the women's department, where I'd see some ankle socks and think, *Yeah, I could use some new ones too.* Those packs of socks would then get absorbed into the cost of all the other Target purchases. But when I started going to the store explicitly to buy socks for the shelter, I was taken aback. I'd think, *What do you mean it's fourteen dollars for a six-pack of men's crew socks? "Expect More. Pay Less" my ass.* Here's the thing: not all socks are created equal. I could have bought cheaper socks, but they wouldn't have the same padding, softness, or weight to them. A better-quality sock will go further in keeping blisters at bay, something that all too often plagues those who are homeless, because if you can't afford a home or food, you also probably can't afford a taxi or an Uber. Even a bus ride is likely beyond your means, which leaves you walking miles upon miles to pick up your social security check, meet your social workers, get to the doctor, go to the foot clinic, and then finally head to the shelter for the night, where you'll leave your socks on after that long day of walking and sleep with your shoes under your head. But as they say, Boston is a walkable city—thank god for small favors.

Most of the socks in the clinic came from donations. Some were individual one-off donations. Sometimes people would coordinate sock drives among their friends and family and bring in a larger haul. The biggest donations the clinic received came from the annually coordinated effort between BHCHP and the Red Sox baseball team: Sox for Socks. In 2017, they collected more than four thousand socks.

Of course, I should have expected to have more than just my ignorance of socks abated. One day when I came in for my volunteer shift, I wore a T-shirt from the local REI store that had an image of evergreen trees and "Take It Outside" written beneath. It was the first time I'd worn a shirt with writing on it to the clinic. I generally figured it was better to avoid this so as not to offend someone—no sports teams or sayings that could be otherwise contentious. But going outside, being out of doors, what was offensive about that? Oh. Shit. And I was totally called out for it. One man pointed at my shirt as he was bending down to scrub his feet with a small piece of pumice and said, "I'm outside all the time." What happens when you take something and place it in a new context? What might be considered virtuous or admirable can become mocking and distancing.[3]

Rebecca wouldn't be the only patient who would stand out and hold a space in my memory. On my first day at the clinic, I found myself tickling the feet of a grown man I'll call Daniel. He plopped down in the chair and boisterously answered the requisite questions for the intake form, including his name, date of birth, and other questions about his living situation, current health, and healthcare history. He was jovial, and as I examined his feet, he confirmed that he was in fact quite high. Due to his size, he was unable to bend over to take his shoes and socks off on his own and so needed help with the process. I crouched down and untied his shoes, placing them to one side, and took each sock off. Then we filled two buckets, one for each foot. It was hard to miss the large ankle monitor adorning his left foot. He, like so many others, seemed to be in a perpetual state of liminality. While his feet soaked in the warm, soapy water, he regaled the roomful of volunteers and other patients with soapbox banter about how certain local universities were known for their love of weed. After ten minutes or so, I took his feet out of the water, toweled them off, and began massaging cream into them. As I massaged, I heard giggling. I looked up at him, and he said, "Girl, that tickles!"

Then there was Mark, a man around my age who came into the clinic regularly. He was fit and muscular. He looked like a bodybuilder and was someone I would refer to as the "invisible homeless": If you saw him walking down the street, you'd never know that he stayed in a shelter. He was clean-shaven and had no other visual indicators that he might be experiencing homelessness. As Nick Flynn writes in his memoir, *Another Bullshit Night in Suck City*, "Eighty percent of the homeless are invisible, like the proverbial iceberg, [and] when I walk through the city now every other person I see is someone I know from the shelter, but if you didn't know you'd think they were on their lunch break, enjoying a little sun" (184).

One morning, Mark came in deflated and tired and told us about his previous day, which had begun with him needing to do laundry. He thought he had money on his card, but when he got there, he realized the card was empty, so he retraced the two miles he'd just walked with a forty-pound bag of laundry in tow to get money from someone he knew so that he could go back to the laundromat. First errand over; on to the next. He waited for the bus to take him to the Department of Transitional Assistance—the local social security offices—to pick up his check, but the bus never came (good old Massachusetts Bay Transportation Authority). So he walked there as well. A late summer afternoon spent walking from errands to chores and back. It was a day to treat himself: McDonald's. He'd saved enough money for a double cheeseburger—just enough for the burger. But thirst was getting the better of him on this hot and humid New England day. He asked for a free glass of ice water. The woman behind the counter looked at him like he was crazy and seemed to hesitate and mull over his request. He asked again, unable to understand why his question was such a difficult one to answer. Finally, after him asking multiple times, she gave him the water but no ice.

Daniel came in regularly, yet he still struggled to maintain good foot health. Some days, he was cheerfully belligerent, and other days, he was borderline abusive, depending on his level of sobriety. Whenever he was asked about allergies, his standard reply was, "Is alcohol an allergy?" This was accompanied by his toothless grin, which was not uncommon with homeless alcoholics. His immersion foot was so bad that the entire bottoms of his feet were covered in wet, ghostly white, pockmarked skin. They were always too bad to let him soak, as doing so would aggravate the condition, so we just had him apply a lot of powder to his skin and socks. We also gave him two pairs (against the one-pair policy, as stocks always ran low) that he could layer up in a feeble effort to stave off the damp. The first time I assisted with the care of his feet, they looked particularly bad, and when I made note of this to him, he shrugged. He'd spent the previous rainy night sleeping under a bridge and was soaked through by morning. What was to be expected? All the socks and foot powder in the world were no match for the streets.[4]

Walter, a veteran who lived upstairs, came in one day with an injury to two of his toes. After one look, one of the nurses insisted he go to the ER. Two of his toes were such a dark purple, they were nearly black, and the concern was that he had an infection that could lead to him losing them—or worse, the whole foot. He used a cane but could barely walk the block to the pharmacy. The nurse reassured him that she'd put him in a taxi to make sure he got to the hospital. I had seen lost toes previously that summer. They were usually the result of a neglected infection or hypothermia. When I asked one man, who was missing four toes, one of our routine questions about where he spent most nights, he replied, "Streets, sometimes the back of an abandoned car."

Once, toward the end of my time as a volunteer, a patient walked into the office, slowly and deliberately pushing a walker in front of him, which required all his effort and concentration to do so. Although we were technically past closing time, it wasn't hard to understand why they'd let him in: He had waited for so long to get into the clinic that day, and he was in a bad way. Thin and frail, he grimaced as he lowered himself into the plastic chair. His feet were in severe pain, sensitive to the gentlest of touch, and he winced as we helped him get them into the tubs.

After soaking, he needed help applying lotion and getting his fresh socks on. I pulled over the leg-support stand to rest his foot on so as to minimize his pain. I'd touched a lot of feet over my short time there, but as I rubbed the lotion into his legs, they felt scaly and gritty through my gloves, as though the skin would peel off just with my touch. I'd never felt anything like it before, and I had to swallow my shock, as I didn't want him to see it on my face. To put his socks on, I rolled them down to the toe and maneuvered over his toes (where his pain was the worst), with as little contact as possible. This was so difficult that he still had to brace himself to bear the pain.

One of the staff nurses explained that he likely had peripheral neuropathy, which is diabetic nerve damage leading to pain, numbness, and weakness, usually in the hands and feet. It's an all-too-common occurrence among homeless people and was something we often saw at the clinic. Without regular access to healthy foods, diabetes rates are high, and for those who are homeless, this can lead to severe complications that might otherwise be avoided through proper management. When you don't have a safe place to store your medications, your belongings are stolen all the time, and you can't afford to get to the doctor because the bus ride alone is too expensive, or you're in too poor health to walk the miles you need to, it's not surprising that something manageable for the housed becomes unmanageable when on the streets.

◆

Pain lived in the foot clinic. It came in all forms and intensities, and I dare think if you had the nerve to show the happy-face-to-sad-face pain scale to some in there, they'd happily shove it right up your backside and really illustrate for you what kind of pain they were in. For some, that pain was so limiting that they couldn't do basic things—removing their shoes and socks, placing their feet in a bucket of water, drying them off, then putting everything back on—on their own. I often wondered what they did when they weren't in the clinic if they needed to take their shoes or clothes off, use the restroom, or take a shower. Did they have friends who helped, or did they simply not remove their clothing or take showers?

Community also lived in the clinic. For staff and volunteers, we began each morning before opening the clinic with a team meeting, led by Cecilia, the director of nursing. We'd end the session by standing in a circle, each of us with a fist extended into the center. We'd pump our arms and chant, "One, two, three: SWEET FEET! WOO, WOO, WOO, WOO!" And our patients were no different. As with any group of people sharing a common experience, they created tight communities where they looked out for one another. They shared food, they shared clothing, they shared worries about their friend who heard voices, they shared jokes. We humans need one another.

On my final day at the clinic, I saw Rebecca once more, and she seemed worse than normal. She sat angled on the chair in evident pain. Every muscle in her face tensed as she winced. She had an abscess on her bottom. Sometimes it's hard to understand the kind of physical pain someone is experiencing. But I could feel her pain, if only a little. Years earlier, I'd had a yearlong battle with methicillin-resistant Staphylococcus aureus (MRSA)—the scary staph that no one wants—from a tattoo that had become infected. Boils would pop up randomly on my body, the worst being a large one on my lower back, right beneath the waistline of my pants. Even wearing soft yoga pants, I remember hunching over and crying in pain in the ten steps I had to take between the couch and the kitchen sink. But that's where my situation's similarity to Rebecca's ended. I had a kitchen sink and a couch. I had a place to shelter in. I had doctors throwing every antibiotic at me they could. I was able to keep my wounds clean so that they healed with no subsequent issues.

I took extra care with Rebecca that day, cupping her calf in one hand (so small it barely filled my palm) and her heel in the other to lower each foot softly into the warm water, then did the same to take them out. I wrapped a towel around her legs, as if I were swaddling a baby coming out of a bath, and massaged the cream into her skin, moving my thumbs in soft circles. It's such a small thing, but this contact creates a feeling of intimacy—to treat the body in a hands-on way creates a shared humanity between bodies.

Once her socks and shoes were back on, we helped her up, and the director of nursing herself took her into a room to look at the abscess. I wanted to give Rebecca a big bear hug, to show I cared, but I was afraid I would break her. I settled for tucking her feet into a warm pair of socks, tying her shoes, and helping her stand. Sometimes we need to feel useful, to help as much as, or more than, we need help. At the beginning of *Stories from the Shadows*, Dr. O'Connell writes, "Remember that people have lived through hell and listen carefully to their stories. . . . Each guest was invited into the clinic and addressed by name. Most homeless persons wander our urban landscapes for days without ever hearing someone call them by name, and the response was exuberant. Eyes opened, heads lifted, scowls became smiles" (15). The St. Francis shelter motto is "Homelessness is an experience, not an identity." The clinic embodied this in practice. I've never been homeless. I can't know what it's like, but in the foot clinic, the physical and mental effects of not having a home are loud and visible. Foot care may not be the ultimate solution, but it offers a brief sanctuary from that frenetic space, a sense of renewal, and improving health. Dirty and wet socks came in, pained faces and broken bodies came in. A bucket of warm water and soap would be offered up, along with a choice: gold-tipped, thick, thin, high, short, or specialty diabetic? People soaked their feet, sat quietly, conversed with others, or even dozed off, leaving with clean feet and the comfort of a new pair of socks.[5]

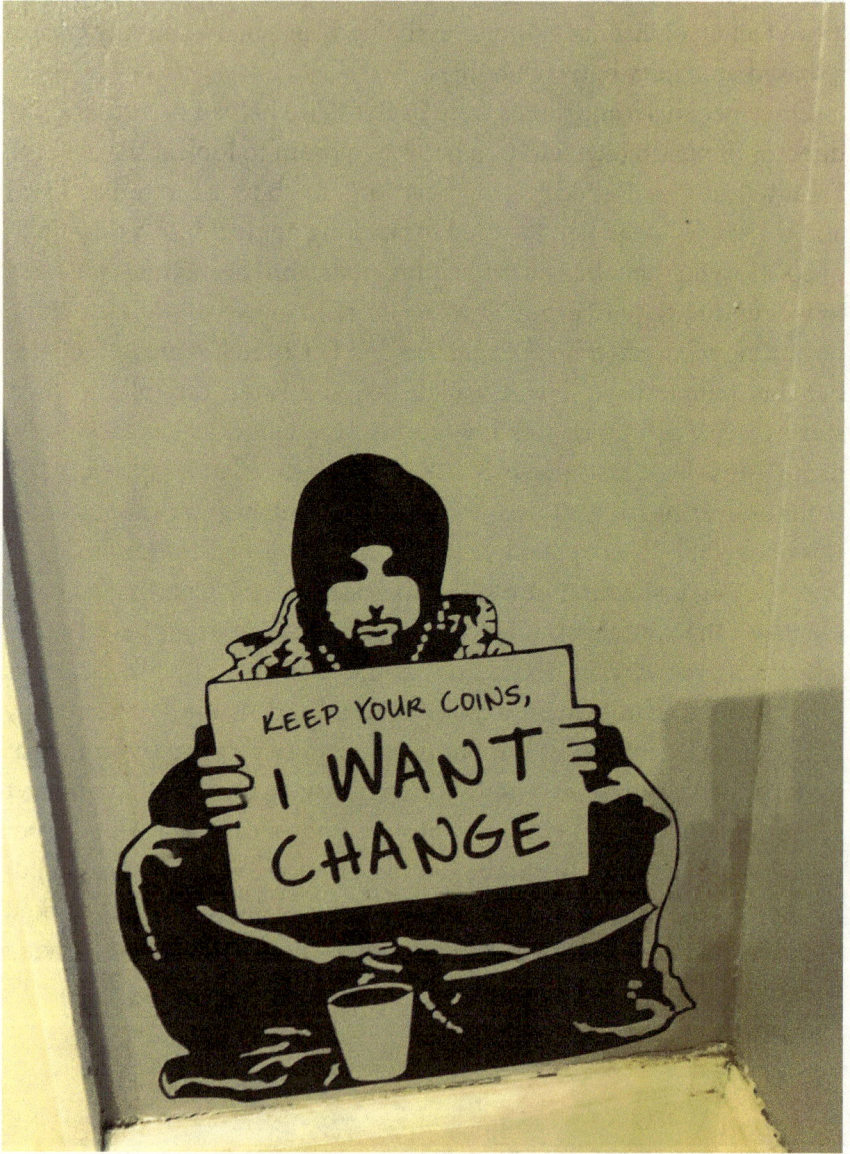

I Want Change. Photo by author.

Deaths of Disparity

Overdose on a Coffee Shop Floor

ONE MORNING, I was waiting in line for a coffee at a Dunkin' Donuts in downtown Boston. Two middle-aged homeless men were sitting at the bar-style seating along the window when one of them made a short, guttural sound and fell backward onto the floor, taking the chair with him. He lay flat on his back, not moving. I don't know how long I stood there watching the scene unfold; it could only have been seconds but felt like ages. No one else moved to help, so I scrambled out of line and asked the man's friend if he needed someone to call 911; he vigorously nodded his head in response. It was clear that the guy on the floor wasn't breathing.

When the operator answered, I told her that a man had collapsed on the floor of the Dunkin' Donuts on the corner of Tremont and Boylston Streets. But she needed an exact address, and I had no idea what that was. I looked around, but no one else seemed to notice there was a man lying flat out on the floor. People were still ordering their coffees and sausage-egg-and-cheese-on-a-bagel sandwiches. Employees were still making those coffees and sausage-egg-and-cheese-on-a-bagel sandwiches. I called out to someone behind the counter, "What's the address here?" Crickets. A man was dying on the dirty, cold floor of a Dunkin' Donuts. Why was nobody paying attention? Maybe people just didn't want to get involved—the workers themselves would have been used to seeing homeless people regularly and possibly had become inured to the drama that this reality brought—or maybe it was just plain old compassion fatigue.

Anger fueling me, I walked up to the counter and yelled at one of the guys making coffee, "Hey, what the fuck is the address? We need an ambulance." The man behind the counter shook his head, saying he didn't know, so I resorted to putting the operator on speakerphone while I looked up the address on Google Maps.

As I did, three construction workers came in and immediately surrounded the man on the floor. One of them happened to be a volunteer firefighter, and he began CPR as the emergency dispatcher reassured me that an ambulance was on its way. She wanted to know if the man was breathing, if anything was coming out of his mouth, what might have happened to him, did he have any conditions they needed to know about? I looked at the man's friend next to me and asked, "Do you know what's wrong with him? Do you know if he has any health issues?" They seemed like such stupid questions to ask. It was obvious that the man was overdosing. The guy looked at me incredulously and spit back, "Man, I don't fucking know. He's not breathing. Just get help."

I looked at him and responded, "I'm trying . . ." *I'm trying and I'm failing*, I thought.

The paramedics finally arrived, tables and chairs were moved out of the way to make room, a dose of Narcan was given to reverse the effects of the overdose, and the man was strapped to a gurney and wheeled out of the restaurant. I held the door open to let them through, and as they passed by, the man woke up screaming and kicking. He was pissed.

When someone is brought back from an overdose by Narcan, it can be a violent business: the body goes into immediate and intense withdrawal, and it can feel like you've had the shit kicked out of you. The person who has overdosed may be confused and terrified, and so it seems a reasonable response to be angry. A lot like what it must feel like to be born: ripped from nonexistence and unconsciousness into the bright, noisy, messy business of living.

The drama over, the space around us snapped back to normal: Tables were shoved together, chairs were picked up, and we all got back in line as though none of it had ever happened.

Lives of Disparity

Never before had I witnessed someone experiencing an overdose, and the scene got to me. But it was the nonreaction by others in that Dunkin' Donuts to a man dying on the floor that got *into* me. It was like watching a split-screen recording of the same location but in two separate moments, a dissonance I couldn't resolve. A chaplain from a nearby shelter had come into the restaurant just as the paramedics were leaving with the man and got in line behind me.

"It's so awful," I said, looking for some outlet to process what I'd just seen.

"Yes," he replied, before shrugging his shoulders and continuing, "Sadly, we see this all the time at the shelter."

The reality is that those who experience homelessness often lead lives more closely entwined with death than the housed. Although overdose may be one of the more visible and visceral afflictions suffered by someone on the streets, it doesn't stand alone as the primary cause of ill health or death. When someone experiencing chronic homelessness has an illness or injury, their journey through the health-care system can often be uncertain and complex. A combination of lack of access to housing and the discontinuity between systems creates barriers to care, particularly end-of-life care, for people experiencing homelessness (Hutt et al. 450). Trimorbidity, a common issue experienced by homeless people, problematizes this further through the intersection of mental health issues, poor physical health, and/or drug and alcohol misuse. The presentation of symptoms of an underlying disease can be missed and/or complicated by substance abuse or mental illness in addition to a lack of access to care. This is also true if patients are too busy trying to find shelter, work, or food, all of which can obstruct the ability or desire to address health concerns early on, allowing medical issues to grow into bigger, less treatable, and potentially more fatal conditions later.

"Deaths of despair" are defined by the U.S. Congressional Joint Economic Committee as, "deaths by suicide, alcohol abuse, and drug overdose or addiction." Many assume those who are homeless are so due to mental health and substance misuse issues, but this is inaccurate for a number of reasons; many may not be suffering from either condition, and many of those who do have such issues have them as a result of being homeless, not the other way around. These are also not the only, or even the primary medical concerns for people living on the streets.

Baggett and his colleagues studied homeless deaths between 2003 and 2008 in Boston and note that heart disease and lung cancer accompanied overdose as the top causes of death: In those five years, 219 people in the city died from overdose, 206 from cancer, and 203 from heart disease. While drug overdose was most common in people aged twenty-five to forty-four years, heart disease and cancer were most common in people aged forty-five to sixty-four years. It turns out that those who experience chronic homelessness and who end up dying while homeless suffer from "deaths of disparity" rather than "deaths of despair."

The Boston Health Care for the Homeless Program (BHCHP) manual, *The Health Care of Homeless Persons: A Manual of Communicable Diseases and Common Problems in Shelters and on the Streets*, details the most commonly seen ailments in unhoused people, and it's daunting:

bed bugs,
cellulitis,
conjunctivitis,
diarrhea,
hepatitis C,
HIV/AIDS,
influenza,
lice,
nosocomial infections (hospital-acquired infections),
scabies,
tuberculosis,
viral meningitis,
West Nile virus,
hyperthermia,

heat stroke,
heat exhaustion,
hypothermia,
frostbite,
traumatic brain injury,
hunger,
obesity,
diabetes,
nutritional deficiency disorders,
chronic pain,
depression.

Imagine being admitted to the hospital after falling and hitting your head on the sidewalk. Imagine you're treated; then, in the middle of the night, they deem you no longer sick enough to stay in the hospital. At up to $10,000 a night, hospitals can't keep you there for free. Imagine they hand you a bag with your clothes in it. Imagine they then drop you off at a bus stop in a hospital gown, far enough away from the hospital so that you won't easily make your way back. Imagine they do this in the dead of winter with freezing temps outside (Sweeney). This is one of the many hurdles homeless people potentially face when they get sick or injured and have nowhere to go. My dad once told me that a night in the hospital is the most expensive hotel stay we ever have, and he wasn't wrong.

Sometimes hospitals take this distasteful action, known as "patient dumping," which is defined as the "practice that occurs when a hospital prematurely discharges a patient, often to bus stops, homeless shelters or other hospitals. Victims typically fall into one or more of the following categories: those with a mental health condition, undocumented or under-documented immigrants, and the homeless" (Abraham). One hospital in Los Angeles agreed to pay a $550,000 legal settlement after being accused of leaving hundreds of homeless patients at bus and train stations or on the streets after discharging them (Sweeney).

In 1986, the U.S. Congress enacted the Emergency Medical Treatment and Labor Act to try to stem patient dumping. The law requires hospitals to take anyone who comes into the emergency room, regardless of their insurance or citizenship status or whether they are able to pay. But an analysis in 2019 showed that hospitals often got around these requirements by transferring patients to other hospitals. A majority of those patients were uninsured, pointing to a financial motive as the primary reason (Gavin). This isn't surprising, because as long as hospitals have to work within the reality of bad debt that regularly goes uncompensated, they have little incentive to care for patients who can't pay (American Hospital Association).

As Emily Maloney writes in her essay, "Cost of Living," "The hospital where I worked . . . was $54 million in debt. . . . We were to be careful when we distributed small stuffed animals to unhappy children in the ER, were told to dispense fewer scrub tops to adolescents with dislocated shoulders and bloodied shirts. . . . Everything cost money" (83). Anyone with means wouldn't stand for a hospital dumping their loved ones on the street like trash. But as David Wendell Moller writes in his book *Dancing with Broken Bones: Poverty, Race, and Spirit-Filled Dying in the Inner City*: "In [the United States], the tendency is to blame the poor for being poor. . . . They are responsible for the misery they suffer. Such a belief system leads to a conspiracy of denial that poverty is a real and harmful byproduct of the institutional arrangements of our society, and a refusal to believe that health [and] health care . . . are not equally available to all" (24–25).

The inequitable treatment of health care for those who are homeless extends beyond illness and injury—and beyond life. Mortality rates for the unhoused are three to four times higher than the general population (Ko et al. 423). Another study by Hutt and her colleagues determined the average age of death for those without homes is thirty-four to forty-seven years old. Some homeless people in their fifties and sixties have health problems—like cardiometabolic diseases, urinary incontinence, and cognitive, sensory, and mobility impairments—more commonly associated with someone in their seventies or eighties (448). I struggle to imagine how anyone recovers, let alone thrives, when trying to manage any of these issues while living unsheltered.

Housing (Not Death) Is the Great Equalizer

Even though I've spent only a small amount of time inside homeless shelters compared to those who have lived in them, I have been in them enough to empathize with homeless people who choose to avoid them completely. They aren't much better than the streets as a place to recover from a major illness or injury, and they certainly are no place to die.

Shelters are not known for being quiet places, nor for being safe. They're often crowded and full of spontaneous bursts of violence. Shelters are where your stuff gets stolen, where you're harassed, and where you're corralled and herded like cattle. When you walk through their doors, there is no doubt that you are in a land of chaos. A constant threat of crisis lies beneath the surface.

When I volunteered at the foot-care clinic, I witnessed a series of such incidents: a guest trying to get into the shelter but refusing to be seen or touched by a security guard, filling the lobby with arguing, chaos; a man gripped by the fits of a seizure because he couldn't get a refill on his medications; someone overdosing in the bathroom, the blue light wailing, and a security guard calmly calling out through the intercom system, "Code blue, lobby bathroom," then the staff responding with the crash cart and Narcan in hand. Around lunchtime, the food smells would become nauseating; the lounge rooms had the feeling of a nursing home but with none of the quiet calm, where almost none of the people were old. The room bulged, full of round tables with people sitting at them. The television would be on, with some watching but many not, and the staff would cram behind the safety of the counter, making periodic announcements into the microphone about food being served or calling for someone to come to the front desk.

Housing is health care.

I first heard this expression, this illuminating expression, from Jeff Olivet, former CEO of the Center for Social Innovation, when he spoke on the subject at a rally for housing rights: "Housing is healthcare. . . .

Housing is stability, housing is justice, housing is beautiful, housing is a basic human right not something that comes with strings attached, housing is for everyone not just those who are deemed worthy or deserving. Housing makes it easier to eat better, sleep better, and feel better" (Olivet and Dones). Being housed allows for certain things that the streets do not afford. For one, you have a safe, temperature-controlled place to store your medications, including those that may need to be refrigerated. You have the privacy to administer those medications, and they're not going to get stolen or lost. When you have a home, you're protected from the elements: wounds can be kept clean more readily, and clothes can be washed with regularity.

Not all roofs are created equal. Shelters, hotels, or someone's couch all may be examples of a roof over one's head, but they're not necessarily safe or sanitary. All these living situations are included in the definition of homelessness. In addition, if someone's been on the streets for a while and is used to some combination of chaos and institutionalization—or if someone has drug misuse, mental health, or serious physical health issues—all these things may make it difficult for that person to remain successfully housed. Giving someone a roof does not magically solve all their problems. That housing has to come with support, resources, and a sense of community.

Respite for the Dying

Circle the City, a medical respite unit (MRU) I visited in 2018, had these words etched into a frosted glass wall above the image of a nearby mountain range: *Everyone deserves a time and place to heal.*

Medical respite units are one example of how people working in homeless medicine try to fill the gaps in a health-care system that isn't designed to work for everyone, particularly not for those experiencing the instabilities and complexities of being homeless. When someone isn't sick or injured enough to remain in the hospital but is far too sick to be able to recover out on the streets or in a shelter, MRUs can provide short-term care and a place for the homeless to stay.

Medical respite units have become crucial stopgaps between the hospital and the street or shelter. They allow for bed rest, elevating limbs, dressing wounds cleanly and safely, storing medications at required temperatures, and administering medications and keeping them in a safe place where they won't be stolen or lost, and they offer a place of quiet, a place to rest and recover. The average stay is anywhere from a week to a month, and the staff also works with patients on other issues, including substance misuse, mental health issues, and moving them into housing. In 2018, almost 1.5 million people experienced homelessness, and at the time there were roughly ninety medical respite units (with additional ones in development) in the United States, varying in size and capabilities. Some MRUs are no more than a couple of beds set aside in a shelter. Others are separate, complex units housing a hundred beds or more with a repertoire of medical staff dedicated solely to respite care, such as the 104-bed unit of the Boston Health Care for the Homeless Program. According to the National Health Care for the Homeless Council, most MRUs are funded through various resources, including donations and fundraising as well as federal programs such as Medicaid and Medicare.

Circle the City is a fifty-bed medical respite unit in Phoenix, Arizona, that has also successfully incorporated hospice and palliative care (the difference between the two being that palliative care is care given to provide comfort and maintain a quality of life that may or may not include curative treatment, whereas hospice care is comfort care given, usually in the last six months of life, without curative treatment). In the summer of 2018, Melissa Sandoval, the chief medical officer of the unit, invited me to meet one of their patients. She took me into the men's dorms, where Richard was sitting on his bed. Richard (whose name has been changed for privacy) was there for hospice care. His wheelchair sat next to his bed, and on it was a seat cushion with a red cover in a Southwestern-style design. While I waited for Melissa to find a chair for me to sit on, Richard told me how he had made the cushion. At first, I was just grateful for a benign chat. I initially felt afraid of this slim, sixtysomething-year-old-man, who was hooked to an oxygen tank and had a passion for sewing. But the truth was, it wasn't Richard I was afraid of; it was myself. I knew that I was speaking to someone doubly vulnerable: homeless and in hospice. He had only two to three months to live, and here I was taking up precious moments. My inexperience in both realms, homelessness and death, felt evident. As he told me about sewing his cushion, in the back of my mind, I was telling myself, *Don't say anything stupid.*

Richard told the story of how, in the year leading up to his entering hospice, he'd let his youngest daughter move in with him. She'd called, saying that she was in an abusive relationship and she wanted to come home. He didn't hesitate to say yes, not realizing at the time that she was addicted to meth. Not long after she had moved in, he began experiencing bouts of illness, and finally, one of those sent him to the hospital for a short time. While he was away, he was robbed of everything, including his checkbook, and his bank account, with a meager savings of just over $2,000, was cleaned out. Unable to pay the rent, his landlord evicted him.

For a while, he couch surfed with friends; in the last of those homes, he found himself sleeping on a mattress on the floor. One morning when he went to get up, he rolled himself off the mattress and then tried to push himself to stand, but his arms wouldn't hold his weight, and he crashed to the ground, smashing his face up. His friends called 911, and then, following a smattering of tests, a week after being admitted to the hospital, the doctor delivered the news: He had a cold, pneumonia, emphysema, and lung cancer. To this, he replied, "Oh, is that it?" As he described this to me, he doubled over laughing.

I wasn't sure whether he was laughing over his response to the doctor's diagnosis, the irony of life, or the absurdity of it all, but it was hard not to laugh along with him. From the hospital, he was referred to the respite unit. Patients who end up in medical respite usually are referred from hospitals, clinics, or skilled nursing facilities. What Richard didn't say, but what the staff had pieced together, was that in all likelihood, it had been his daughter who had robbed him and left him homeless.

I thought our conversation might focus on his experience of homelessness in his final days, of spending this time in an MRU, and although we did talk about those things, our conversation quickly became a way for him to share memories and have something of a life review. He loved it at the medical respite unit, he said, and it wasn't hard to see why. The staff doted on him. The nurse manager helped him acquire a sewing machine. At first, she brought in an old one she had at home, but it needed a power cord and a foot pedal. After some searching, they determined that the best thing to do was buy a new one, and it arrived the next day: a small gray Singer.

Sewing had been a lifelong passion of Richard's, something he'd been doing since the age of ten. As a child, he'd wanted his mom to make him a country-western-style shirt, but as he put it, "She was always busy with other things." He pestered so much that, although she didn't have the time to make one, she got the pattern and materials for him and showed him how to use the sewing machine. It was the first thing he ever made, and he beamed with pride as he told Melissa and me how everyone at school had loved the shirt and wanted to know where he'd gotten it from. He continued sewing and made many of the clothes his two daughters wore. His oldest in particular loved the things he made for her. He lit up when he recalled a dress he'd made out of neckties, noting that it had been lost in the robbery.

He talked of his daughters, but his thoughts also led him to his mother, whom he believed to be in a nursing home. He couldn't remember the name of the place, though, or her exact birth date. His sister would know, but his phone had been stolen with his other belongings, so he had no way to contact any of them. He only had an old address for his sister. Melissa asked him if he had a good relationship with them, and whether he'd like to see or talk with his family if they could find them. He wanted that, so we scrambled together a pen and paper for him to note down any details he could remember. I didn't ask why his family didn't know what had become of him. I had been granted this privilege to speak with him and to have some of his time, and I was too fearful of squandering that gift by asking the wrong thing or offending. Yet I struggled to understand how he could have become so cut off from his family. And what about those friends he'd stayed with? I could only guess at how deeply the layers of complexity ran.

After speaking with Richard, Melissa took me on a tour of the respite unit, which included a brief chat with some nurses who worked on-site. Common ailments they treated there included diabetes, congestive heart failure, burns from lying on the hot summer sidewalk, heat exhaustion, and broken bones from being hit by cars.

Circle the City was able to offer hospice and palliative care through a partnership they had with a local hospice. Their staff acted as primary care physicians for patients, and the hospice nurses came in regularly to take care of all hospice-related issues. Yet even with all this, there were difficulties that sometimes prevented them from allowing patients to die comfortably there. For instance, they weren't always able to administer needed medications when someone became agitated or confused, and in those instances, they'd be forced to send those patients to the hospital to receive the medication needed to calm them down.

Melissa spoke of two hospice patients who both had followed such a trajectory. Jim had lung cancer and had been addicted to meth when he came to them. He had ignored early symptoms, but once he was diagnosed and settled in at Circle the City, he began to thrive. A 2019 paper found that a third of the patients they studied in Detroit, who were homeless, were diagnosed in the "distant tumor" stage, often meaning stage 4 or another late-stage cancer (Holowatyj et al.). Jim had a period where he "graduated" from hospice (i.e., he wasn't expected to die in the next six months), so he was released to supportive housing, but he failed to recover there and became sicker again, bringing him back to them for hospice care. Unfortunately, as he neared death during that time, he became confused, and they had to send him to the hospital for medication administration, but he died while there. It's not uncommon for patients to die during such hospital visits. When this happens, the staff takes it hard, having spent so much time caring for that patient. They'd much rather that person die surrounded by those who knew them, in a place they were comfortable and that had come to be home.

The other patient Melissa told me about was a young man in his early thirties with a heart defibrillator and congestive heart failure. As he grew sicker, he began experiencing heart erythema, and his internal defib began shocking him constantly. The staff asked him if they could take it out, but he was resistant. He was so young and assumed that this meant he would die sooner if they took it out. He said to them, "You're going to kill me faster!" Ultimately, they had to send him to another facility for an unrelated reason, and while there, his defibrillator was taken out. This patient served as a lesson to them, as they came to realize that they needed to ask these tough questions before patients got that sick. In response, the staff created a document, which wasn't a legal document, but gave patients an opportunity to put in writing things about themselves and their end-of-life care wishes (see appendix). The hope was that even in the worst cases, this document would help people take agency over their own dying.

Dying in Paradise

A few years after the day I witnessed the man overdosing in the Dunkin' Donuts, I found myself in Santa Monica, California, sitting across from Jeannie Meyer, a palliative care nurse, and Delia Cortez, a palliative social worker, both from UCLA, where they had started an organization called Hearing Their Voices. Jeannie told me the story of a man she had treated years ago while working in an intensive care unit. He'd been brought in by ambulance to the emergency room after having been found lying ill on the street. In the midst of admitting him, he went into respiratory distress, and after some tests, it was found that he had lung cancer. The good news was that it was a very treatable cancer. When the hospital staff went to speak with him, they assumed that they'd be having a conversation about his treatment: surgery, chemo, rehab. But he shut them down; he wanted no part of any of it. Clearly and bluntly, he explained to them that his idea of a quality life was getting the heck out of the hospital and back to one of the area parks, where he could be with his friends smoking and drinking until the cops ran him off. This was his community, and that's where he wanted to be. He understood that this decision meant that he would die sooner rather than later, but he was OK with that: What was the point of living longer if he lost his friends and the life and comfort he knew with them?

This experience stayed with Jeannie, as she could imagine his future pathway through the health-care system. He'd likely be found again at some point, having fallen down, and then transported to the hospital by the paramedics. He'd have his things rifled through as they tried to find someone to call who might know his wishes on being resuscitated. When they couldn't find anything, they'd place him on a ventilator and subject him to all the things he had explicitly expressed no desire to have happen to him.

This reminded me of a scene from the short Netflix documentary *Extremis*, where a man who is unhoused is seen in the intensive care unit, and the doctors are trying to work out how much he understands about his condition and what course of treatment he wants. The doctors painstakingly discuss among themselves their fears that he doesn't have the capacity to make decisions on his care for himself and that there's no one he knows who can advocate on his behalf. They try to confirm whether he'd prefer to make his own health-care decisions or if he'd be more comfortable with the doctors making them. To someone just off-screen, the doctor laments that if she can't get him to communicate his wishes, they'll be forced to do to him what they often do to patients in similar circumstances, "Plug them in and let them die on [the] machines."

Attitudes on death, dying, and end-of-life care among the homeless haven't been studied extensively, but there are a few studies that have tried to capture their voices, thoughts, beliefs, and feelings on death and dying. In a 2015 study, "What Constitutes a Good and Bad Death? Perspectives of Homeless Older Adults," the authors identify common themes around a good death, which included not suffering, experiencing a spiritual connection, and making amends. They also note that most participants consider the following "bad deaths": dying by accident or violence, being on life support, becoming physically dependent, and dying alone (Ko et al.). In another study, "Does End-of-Life Decision Making Matter?" end-of-life care is noted as not always being a priority among homeless people due to the prospects of trying to survive that many who are unhoused deal with day-to-day. As one of their participants states, "Some of them don't really care about their . . . end of life because many think that this is [the] 'end of life.' What end of life are you talking about? I'm on the street and nobody cares about me" (Ko and Nelson-Becker 186).

Yet Jeannie's experience with the man who refused treatment became an impetus for her to act. She knew that she needed to spread the word and educate those on the streets about their options. At a minimum, she wanted people to be armed with the knowledge of their rights to access or deny the care they needed. The best-case scenario would be for unsheltered people to complete advanced directives and either file them with local-area hospitals or have them carry the documents on their persons in the event that they ever found themselves unable to communicate their wishes.

She teamed up with Delia, who she had met through their work at the hospital and the two of them were able to secure a grant from the Coalition for Compassionate Care of California (CCCC) to create advanced directives and work with the Santa Monica homeless community to help them understand their rights. An advanced health-care directive is a legal document in which you can specify what you want and do not want for treatment and care if you are incapacitated or ill and cannot communicate or make such decisions for yourself. This can be anything from having a do not resuscitate (DNR) directive, so that if your heart stops beating, they won't perform cardiopulmonary resuscitation (CPR),[1] to not wanting to have life-sustaining measures at the end of life, such as being given food and water artificially or being put on a ventilator.

Jeannie and Delia created three documents. The first is a user-friendly advanced directive, written at a sixth-grade reading level, that includes pictures. The second is a "Go Wish Worksheet," which asks people to rank by importance thirty-five different potential elements of dying, such as dying alone, being free of pain, having their finances in order, and more. The third document they created is a "pocket" advanced directive, which is printed on a half sheet of paper and is meant to be kept on one's person, folded and carried in a wallet or pocket. This form includes basic information for medical staff, including name, date of birth, information on organ donation, whether they'd already completed an advanced directive, emergency contacts, and any medical centers at which they may have previously been treated (see appendix).

Once Jeannie and Delia had all their forms in place, they chose a local food bank that had a huge patio, picnic tables, and trees as the place to reach out to the local homeless community. Once a month, they'd set up a table with their advanced care planning materials, along with other resource information (on things such as medical, dental, and eye services; additional food banks; clothing donation centers; and even veterinary services for pet dogs and places for those living in their cars to get low-cost car maintenance). They couldn't just go in and blast people with information on death and dying.

Sometimes when people first approached Jeannie and Delia, they'd ask, "Are you going to harvest my organs?" or "Are you stealing my voice?" Building relationships and earning trust was a marathon, not a sprint. As Courtney Petruik notes in her article "Social Work Practices in Palliative and End-of-Life Care for Persons Experiencing Home-lessness: A Scoping Review," "Trust is required between patient/ client and social care providers. Many of their participants stated that they would not trust a doctor, nurse, family member, friend, or social worker, making it difficult to have highly personal and sensitive con-versations about EOL [end of life]. . . . [Yet], building trust occurs through repeated visits, which are not always possible with transient persons due to the unpredictability of their circumstances" (317).

As of September 2018, Jeannie and Delia had given out three hun-dred forms and had fifteen completed and returned to them. Of those fifteen people, there were two who stood out to Jeannie. Her first direc-tive was for a severe diabetic and had moderate kidney failure. This woman understood that she'd probably need to be on dialysis and in a nursing home soon, and Jeannie reported her as saying, "I know look-ing at me you probably think my life is terrible. But you know what, I love my life, and I try and find beauty in every single day, and I'll be able to do that until the time I die. I would want full aggressive treatment until everything is gone." The other was the young heroin addict she got to know, who knew full well the dangers of his drug use and so decided to fill out an advanced directive in case he was brought in from overdose. The work that Jeannie and Delia were doing reminded me of the man in the Dunkin' Donuts; if he had another overdose or some other serious incident and had a form like one of theirs in his pocket, he could have more agency in the care he received, and thereby more dignity.

Circle the City and the actions of Jeannie and Delia are small local operations, yet both suggest that if we collectively care enough, such efforts can be scaled up. And yet, although medical respite units do help, they don't replace the better alternative of stable housing.

As the world was steamrolled by the COVID-19 pandemic, like many other forms of social inequality, the disparities in health and end-of-life care for unhoused people were brought into even sharper focus. The real fallout from this disease won't be known for some time, but based on the full range of circumstances that create poor health outcomes for this group, including crowded shelters and no door to lock behind you at night, it stands to reason that the effects on the homeless may be devastating. Washing your hands, avoiding contact with others, and staying home are all ways to prevent the spread of such diseases. We were told to shelter in place, but that's difficult to do when you have no shelter. It's important to understand that despite the efforts of medical respite units, health-care staff for homeless people, and other services, this is a larger systemic problem that needs to be addressed for any real change to occur.

Medical respite units, after all, are meant to be for temporary stays, and most aren't set up for more than that; the percentage with hospice or palliative care capabilities is small. People eventually end up back on the streets or in shelters. Boston's biggest shelter, Pine Street Inn, sleeps 365 men in one large warehouse-like room and 120 women in a separate facility. Inside, "the air is thick, stale, dreamy, though barely masking the overpowering smell of stale sweat" (Flynn 30). Such conditions are a communicable disease's dream: bed bugs, lice, influenza, hepatitis, viral meningitis, staph infection (including MRSA), and COVID-19 all thrive with bodies in close proximity.

A Dignified Death

Death is inevitable, but deaths from disparity are not.

For those who are chronically homeless, institutionalization is both a life raft and an albatross. Many of the systems in place—shelters, soup kitchens, welfare programs, hospitals, and even prisons—keep people fed, clothed, temporarily sheltered, and alive. These systems also create an inertia that has the ability to suck people up into one institution and spit them out and on to the next until they reach their final destination: an unmarked grave in a potter's field.

The man who overdosed in Dunkin' Donuts was lucky that he didn't die that day on the floor of a coffee shop; in the years since, I have often wondered what became of him. I suspect his story was very different from that of Richard, who might be called one of the lucky ones. A few months after I met with him at Circle the City, Melissa emailed to confirm that he had passed away peacefully, surrounded by friends and caregivers from the respite unit, all of whom had come to love his gentle kindness and generosity.

Richard's experience reminds me of another story I was told by Julia Dobbins, a project manager at the National Health Care for the Homeless Council. They had a client who, like Richard, ended up at a medical respite unit. He had lived for twenty years on the street, yet the hardworking staff at the MRU where he was recuperating were able to get him housing. But after twenty years, all the damage done from living without a home couldn't be undone. Six months after he was housed, he was diagnosed with cancer and died shortly thereafter.

This man was found reclining in a La-Z-Boy chair, with a blanket pulled up over him and the television tuned to ESPN. Some might consider this a sad or lonely death. Although his previous caregivers at the medical respite unit were saddened, they also found some happiness and consolation in the way he died. It was a silver lining of sorts: his death had been on his terms. He died comfortably in a home of his own, not on the streets, not in a dumpster, not frozen to death on a park bench—and not hooked up to tubes in the intensive care unit.

When she finished telling me the story, Julia asked, "Isn't that what everyone deserves? To die with a blanket to cover you, in a place where you find comfort?"

139—The INN Between Butterfly Memorial Wall. Photo by author.

Rest in Place

Hospice for Unhoused Individuals

CRAIG RUSSELL DIED peacefully on May 12, 2022, surrounded by his friends at The INN Between. Craig had been suffering from dementia toward the end of his life, and as his condition deteriorated, he began asking more frequently for "cat." *Cat* was Roger, the female cat that belonged to Kimberly Peterson, the end-of-life doula at The INN Between. Roger would happily oblige, lying at the end of Craig's bed, keeping him company. When Craig began actively dying, meaning his body was finally shutting down and death was near, Roger went to his room and nestled up against his legs, where she remained until the mortuary arrived after he died.

I learned about Craig (and Roger) on a recent visit to The INN Between. It was a hot July day in 2024 when I flew into Salt Lake City, Utah, to spend the day with the residents and staff. The INN Between provides medical respite and end-of-life care for people experiencing homelessness.

After driving through a quiet, suburban neighborhood, the Uber driver slowed down and, just past a white picket fence, pulled into a long driveway where he dropped me off. I walked through a set of doors and the place was bustling: A staff member ran by, giving a quick wave, and a resident walked up with his big dog, named Bear, to find out more information about something going on later that afternoon. As I waited for Jillian Olmsted, the executive director, I sat in a cozy seating area with marigold walls just steps inside the main entrance. I was embraced by the immediate impression of a warm, vibrant place. It radiated a quiet energy with its murmurs of work being done and care being given.

The INN Between has an Assisted Living Facility Type II license, which enables them to provide residents with medical care and other assistance with the activities of daily living, including eating, bathing, toileting, dressing, and taking medication. In total, they can house around sixty adults, which includes thirty beds for hospice patients, those diagnosed with roughly six months or less to live, and others who need more extensive care. Additionally, they have twenty-five Congregate Care Facility beds, which are for adults who are capable of taking care of themselves but who could use added support as they recover and recuperate from illness or injury.

Shortly after arriving, I was greeted by Jillian, along with Kellie Mieremet, the community engagement manager, and the two of them proceeded to give me a full tour of the facility. I was struck by not only how welcoming the place was but how welcoming the people were as well. We began our tour at the butterfly memorial wall. On the wall was a house-shaped wood frame that held the number 139 written out using one hundred and thirty-nine blue paper butterflies.

When a resident on hospice begins actively dying, one of these blue butterflies is placed on the door of their room to notify people. Once that person dies, the butterfly is removed and used in a memorial service with staff, friends, family, and other residents, and someone is chosen to place the butterfly on the board where they keep track by arranging the butterflies in the number of people who have died to date at The INN. Dotted along the edges of the number were four gold butterflies. These symbolized people who had "graduated" from hospice. One of those gold butterflies represented a man who now lives in an apartment in Salt Lake City, has a job, and has a community to share his life with. Although rare, occasionally someone who previously was diagnosed with a life-limiting illness begins to recover and get better simply by having shelter and safety, receiving proper nutrition and medical care, and being surrounded by people who provide a space filled with calm, love, and respect.

From the butterfly wall, we meandered into the hospice wing, where each patient has a large room to themselves. The rooms are designed to house two patients, with a partial wall down the middle as a divider for privacy, but for the hospice patients, the front rooms have been turned into a sitting area. Each room is styled differently and has its own personality. Jillian and Kellie showed me one that was unoccupied. The sitting room was decorated with white leather high-back chairs, a mirrored console table, and a square chandelier encased in decorative glass beading. The window at the back part of the room, where the bed was, had been dressed with black-and-white paisley curtains.

From there, we continued down the hallways, past nursing staff giving residents their medication or taking their blood pressure, and past offices, including that of Kimberly, the end-of-life doula, where on the door hung a green paper skeleton with butterfly wings wearing a onesie that read, "I Play on Team USA" in celebration of the upcoming 2024 Olympics. We then ventured into the dining area, which felt like a casual restaurant. Here, I met two of the four kitchen staff, one of whom was Jillian's son. In one corner of the dining area were two couches, a small library, and an air hockey and a foosball table. There were also two outdoor spaces for residents to spend time in when it wasn't the height of summer.

As we moved through the building, and as Kellie and Jillian introduced me to both staff and residents that we passed, my head spun with the many plates they had to keep in the air to run such a large facility, easily the largest of its kind in the United States. This included Jesse Austin, who managed all their facilities and maintenance. He had saved them thousands of dollars by being handy enough to fix a multitude of the issues that regularly cropped up, avoiding the need to hire outside contractors. But in addition to maintenance, there were so many elements to keep track of: food preparation and running the kitchen; diet and nutrition training for residents; oversight of the nursing and hospice staff who manage treatments and medications; fundraising; planning and coordinating activities; volunteer recruitment; dealing with resident referrals, assessments, and intake; abiding by state regulations; and continually working to be a good neighbor.

Eventually, Jillian and Kellie left me at the jewelry-making room, a small space with a long table and workstations set up for residents to come in and make bracelets, necklaces, and more, some of which were sold to help raise funds. The jewelry making was overseen by two women who volunteered their time weekly, one of whom had been doing so for years. They invited me in and suggested that I try to make a bracelet (as someone who'd never made a piece of jewelry in her life), directing me to look through the stacks of supplies against the wall. After tentatively choosing some shells and silver pieces, I sat down to begin. One of the volunteers explained that this was a space where people often opened up about deeper issues and sometimes spent more time talking than crafting. The busying of hands allows anxiety to ease and barriers to fall. Before I was even able to put the first bead on the bracelet strand, one of the residents—JD, a man in his early sixties who sported a long beard and wore his hat backward over his wavy hair—introduced himself, and we fell into a deep conversation about the injury to his leg that led him to The INN Between to recuperate via their medical respite program.

We bonded over his experience having been incarcerated for ten years and the fact that my day job was working for a college for incarcerated people in San Quentin. His bright-blue, kind eyes sparkled as he told me about plans he had for helping homeless people in Salt Lake City, who like him, had been formerly incarcerated.

Later that afternoon I was scheduled to join JD along with other residents and the activities coordinator for an outing to Utah's statehouse. JD was a little apprehensive about going, as it had been just behind it that he'd injured himself after falling off his friend's bike. He'd been riding on the handlebars behind the statehouse. His friend didn't see the speed bump, and when they hit it, JD flew off and landed beneath a parked car. He worried that being back at the scene would bring up bad memories. His story drove home how easily injury and emotional trauma can pile up when someone is unhoused. Before I knew it, thirty minutes had flown by, and Kellie was back to collect me for lunch with some of the staff.

Lunch was in the community room with Kellie and Jillian along with Taelar Trujillo, director of nursing; Kim Pate, the assisted living administrator and a registered dietitian; and Adam Holm, a resident advocate. We sat in chairs already placed in a circle, munching on grilled cheese sandwiches and a creamy broccoli cheese soup from a local restaurant that was a staff favorite, as they explained to me some of the many services provided by The INN Between, including transportation to medical appointments, case management that helps residents sort out benefits or get onto housing lists (Salt Lake City has a two-to-six-year wait for affordable housing, but many residents qualify for long-term residential care, which can get them into housing much faster), substance use recovery support with daily transportation to methadone clinics, and activities to promote wellness (such as the jewelry room, the library, the games, and more) that can allow people to feel joy, to simply feel human.

As a registered dietitian, Kim spoke of the importance placed on providing nutritious meals and helping residents understand the importance of eating healthy and whole foods. This was something I saw in action when I met one resident, Larry.

Larry, like JD, was there on medical respite. I met the exuberant fiftysomething-year-old man as we piled into the back seat of a minivan to make the trip to the statehouse. In anticipation of the outing, he had styled his hair into a mohawk, using some gel to get it to stand straight up, and wore yellow-rimmed sunglasses and a tie-dyed tank top. As Larry and I sat crammed in the backseat along with another resident, Albert, Larry explained how he'd had two strokes in the span of a few months—the result of having uncontrolled diabetes. Albert and Larry had met in the hospital and knew they were both going to be discharged to The INN, and it seemed they had become fast friends. In his time at The INN Between, Larry had learned the importance of various vegetables and how they'd help him control his diabetes and hopefully prevent another stroke. We talked about the different ways to prepare our favorite foods. He'd decided cucumbers were a great addition to his diet, as they were a nutritious snack, low-calorie and hydrating.

Back in the community room over lunch, I also got to experience what I can only imagine is a tiny sliver of the huge repository of information and knowledge belonging to director of nursing Taelar Trujillo. Hers was such a large role, and she seemed so young yet so incredibly knowledgeable on all things nursing, as well as industry regulations and more. Not surprising, seeing as she'd started her career in mental and behavioral nursing, moved to the psychiatric intensive unit, then to the crisis team in an emergency room, then to home health hospice as an RN (registered nurse) case manager before landing at The INN. Our conversation eventually led to a discussion of some of the more difficult aspects of care, such as terminal agitation.

Terminal agitation is anxious, restless, or distressed behavior that may occur within the last few weeks of a person's life. For those who do experience terminal agitation, it can present differently depending on their diagnosis, what medications they're taking, their environment, and more. Examples of this agitated state include a persistent rubbing of legs together while in bed or crawling on the floor. One of The INN's patients, who was dying of liver failure and hepatitis C from alcohol/substance misuse and who experienced terminal agitation, became delusional, confused, and eventually aggressive, trying to eat his own feces and rip out his IVs. As I sat there listening to Taelar describe this patient's final days, I thought how horrible it must be to experience, and to witness as well. But I also thought how much more horrible the experience would be if you were alone, on the streets, without people skilled in hospice care there to intervene and provide support.

One of the core offerings of The INN Between is a program they have called No One Dies Alone (NODA). Volunteers who take part in NODA, go through a training that teaches them how to sit with hospice residents when they are actively dying. Depending on that person's wishes, they might play music, hold their hand, or sit silently. The most important thing is that the interaction is done with compassion and without judgment. And if a resident expresses the wish to not be alone, they are never left alone.

The INN had one resident, Paul Youngblood, who was written about in the article "A Place Where No One Dies Alone," by Lois M.

Collins. In the article, Collins speaks about how one of Paul's wishes at the end of life was for human touch. So in Paul's final hours, volunteers from the NODA program, along with staff from The INN Between, took turns holding his hand. As one volunteer would need a break, they would transition out by placing Paul's hand into that of a waiting volunteer, so that he never went a moment without being connected to someone. A simple wish honored through a community's commitment to provide dignity at the end of life, no matter the circumstances leading to that point.

◆

Unfortunately, the alternative for too many chronically unhoused individuals sits in stark contrast to Paul's passing. Dying on the streets is a very real possibility. A story of an elderly man named Ted, who died in a coffee shop in Vancouver, is one of the more visible examples of such a tragic death. Ted had been housed most of his life, but unexpected expenses related to a cancer diagnosis left him unable to pay rent. The shelter options were too scary for him, and so he made this coffee shop his home, where he spent his days, until one day he died there, slumped over at the table, potentially for hours, until it was discovered he was deceased. This is a horrifying tale of what might befall an elderly person who finds themselves homeless and without means at the end of life. Many others who die while homeless die in less visible ways: in tents, under bridges, in alleyways. Although there's an argument to be made that not everyone wants company in their final moments, I doubt there are many people who would opt for dying propped up against the back wall of a building down an alley, next to a dumpster, or publicly at a coffee shop table.

When chronic, life-limiting illness presents itself, hospice is a great option. Back in 2015, I signed up to volunteer with a hospice. When I initially joined, I'd had a vision that I'd be visiting a building, a place much like a nursing home but specifically dedicated to people who were on hospice—who were actively dying. But *hospice* is less a physical place one goes and more an existence, a way of being. Perhaps that's why we say *on* hospice instead of *in* hospice. Someone placed on hospice generally resides either in a care facility, such as a nursing home, or in their own home.

Homeless shelters may provide a roof over one's head, but they are not suitable places to be sick in or to age. Many shelters lack the services needed or have poor building structures for folks with reduced mobility. What if someone needs a bar on a wall or a seat for bathing? Or someone with vision loss has to share a dorm room full of beds, people, and belongings strewn on the floor? What if someone's legs hurt too much to carry themselves up three flights of stairs (Greenier)? Not great for aging, not great for dying, and certainly not great for being on hospice.

Where it's even harder to be on hospice is on the streets.

But with so few places like The INN Between, many are left trying to find alternatives. One option is street hospice. I was surprised to hear that such a thing existed. I recently reached out to Jeannie Meyer, who I had met with back in 2018 to learn more about the organization she'd started called Hearing Their Voices, where they work to get advanced care directives for unhoused people in Southern California. In addition to Hearing Their Voices, she had also started a think tank called Hospice Under the Bridge, which brings together people around the state working to find ways to provide hospice for unhoused people. She's the one who first introduced me to this idea of street hospice.

What fueled Jeannie's work with Hospice Under the Bridge was the memory of a homeless patient with whom she had worked. This woman had wanted to spend her final moments lying on the beach watching the sunset over the ocean. But Jeannie knew that much like the patient she'd encountered years earlier who had wanted to spend his final days drinking with his friends in the park, this woman wasn't likely to get that wish and would more likely be carted off to the hospital via an ambulance in the end. This story made me think of The INN Between resident Paul Youngblood, who had a volunteer play ocean sounds on their phone to remind him of his young day surfing on the beaches of California.

As Jeannie explained, when someone who is unhoused becomes terminally ill, nursing homes are not apt to take them in for a range of reasons: issues with insurance, concerns around security, and the inability, or unwillingness, to manage someone with substance misuse or mental health issues. John G. Cagle describes this issue in detail in his 2009 article, "Weathering the Storm: Palliative Care and Elderly Homeless Persons." He notes, as Jeannie did, that "homeless [people] are an often-stigmatized group. Individuals may be presumed to be criminals, crazy, violent, uneducated, or drug addled" (40). Cagle further elaborates, writing, "When trying to access hospice and palliative care services, homeless individuals in particular face several potential barriers, including limited social support, residential instability, and a lack of payment source. . . . In addition to numerous obstacles to care, these individuals are often struggling to meet their basic daily needs. . . . Moreover, palliative care providers may face complex challenges when providing comfort and support to homeless individuals who are dying. High rates of substance abuse, mental illness, and other co-morbidities may complicate care or pose ethical dilemmas" (29–30).

In 2024, not much had changed from Cagle's 2009 analysis, and so street hospice may be a last resort for some. Jeannie introduced me to Lena Beker, founder and CEO of Roze Room Hospice, located in the Greater Los Angeles area. Roze Room is a traditional hospice provider, but they do occasionally assist unhoused patients who remain living on the streets. Patients who receive street hospice are still mobile and self-sufficient enough to care for themselves, such as being able to use the bathroom or take a shower unassisted. These are people who have been referred to hospice but may not want to go into a recuperative care setting. Some of these patients are living under bridges or out of their cars. Nurses communicate with patients via cell phone and can often track them using the Find My Phone feature. Another piece of technology they adopted were fentanyl patches—these enable the nurses to help patients manage their pain while preventing them from being a target of robbery or selling their pain medications on the streets.

Hospice nurses from Roze Room go out in pairs or groups to assist an individual and are trained to meet people where they're at. One of their patients wasn't homeless but was living in a small rundown apartment and was a hoarder. They couldn't get inside to care for him, so when they needed to visit him, they would pitch a mobile shower and a privacy screen in his front yard where they'd bathe him, take his vitals, and administer any other care he needed.

Roze Room staff are trained not to judge someone by their own standards of what might be comfortable or desirable at the end of life and to respect someone's wishes and dignity when caring for them. In addition to providing hospice care, they've also been able to connect some folks with their family and help fulfill their final wishes through the Make-A-Wish and DreamCatchers Foundations. One patient was connected with a family member whom they'd lost touch with and before he died the two of them were able to catch a baseball game together.

◆

What originally drew my attention to the existence of hospice for homeless people was learning about Joshua's House, a planned hospice for homeless people in Sacramento. According to the Sacramento Regional Coalition to End Homelessness, between 2002 and 2022, one homeless person died every five days in Sacramento County. In the first half of 2022, that number had risen to one every three days. That's a lot of people dying on the streets. I'd been watching Joshua's House for years in anticipation of their opening. As far as I could find, there aren't any homeless hospices in the entire state of California, in spite of having 28 percent of the nation's homeless population (Senate Housing Committee).

In 2023, after years of their opening being delayed, I decided to do some online sleuthing to understand why Joshua's House struggled to open. I was unable to connect directly with the founders, yet from what I could gather, it was becoming clear that the reasons were partly due to a lack of funding and partly due to the fact that the community where they wanted to put Joshua's House was having none of it.

A Sacramento-area reporter pointed me in the direction of Rebecca Sandoval and she agreed to meet with me. I spent some time talking to Rebecca, a trustee of the Twin Rivers Unified School District board.

She has been the public face of the opposition to the opening of Joshua's House, which is slated to be built directly across the street from one of the district's elementary schools. It was an hour and a half drive, and I didn't know what to expect when I met with Rebecca. We ended up having a two-hour-long conversation that concluded with her driving me over to the proposed site of Joshua's House.

Being an outsider to this community, and without being able to connect with the folks at Joshua's House, I struggled to have a nuanced understanding of all the factors that were possibly at play with the impasse between the proposed hospice and the community, including some possible political wrangling with the city council. What I walked away with though, was equally important. I had expected a real Not In My Backyard attitude, one in which people don't want poor or unhoused people living, or shelters and other facilities that assist the poor operating, in their neighborhoods. And sure, some of that felt present, but it also wasn't so clear-cut. Rebecca was representing a community of first-generation and immigrant Mexican Americans, many of whom spoke Spanish as their first language. This neighborhood of Sacramento is a low-income community, and Rebecca pointed out that 1,800 students in their school district are homeless, many living with their parents in motel rooms just down the road from the potential site for Joshua's House, and walk by on their way to school each morning. The community already felt marginalized by the county and believed their neighborhood had been chosen for the hospice site because they were poor and under-resourced. The expectation was that they couldn't necessarily fight back with the same veracity as a wealthier community might.

In talking with Rebecca, it was clear that they also felt unheard. The school board had apparently offered a handful of other sites for Joshua's House to use that would have come with infrastructure already in place, but those locations were turned down, and they didn't know why. Rebecca clearly cared about the community she'd spent all but six months of her seventy-two years living in, and she said she would fight for them as long as she could. Eventually, our conversation led to what felt to be at the heart of their community's concerns—fear of the unknown. Rebecca raised several important questions about how Joshua's House would be managed. For instance, when someone died what would happen to the body and how would it be removed and transported? Would this happen during the day while kids were at school? What about the myriad of drugs that are often needed to manage pain, such as fentanyl? Who would be managing the drugs? Would they be on-site or brought in? What about visitors? Would there be specific visiting hours, or would people be milling about outside? There was mention of a curfew, did this mean that residents could hang out outside the facility until late at night? What about security? If there was a problem, how would the hospice handle that?

There are certainly answers to their questions, and some of that can be found in research articles or by visiting similar facilities' websites, including that of The INN Between. And other communities around the country have been able to embrace hospice centers for homeless people, including Plymouth Housing in Seattle, Washington; Rocky Mountain Refuge in Denver, Colorado; Solace Friends in Madison, Wisconsin; and Joseph's House in Washington, DC.

But it seemed to me that what Rebecca and her community wanted most was to hear those answers directly from Joshua's House. In my time with Rebecca, I'd learned more about the layers involved in creating these spaces for unhoused folks. It's never easy, and it's rarely simple, and this glimpse into that messiness revealed how deep those complexities run. I went home feeling sad—sad that there was so much unresolved in this particular situation. But I thought about The INN Between and knew that they too had experienced conflict with their potential neighbors but came out the other side of that with some new friends from the neighborhood who would come to eventually volunteer. There was hope for Joshua's House, a place desperately needed.

◆

My day in Salt Lake City spent at The INN was full-on. In addition to JD, Larry, and all the staff, I met a number of other memorable residents including Doug, who was on the resident board, and Kimberly, a fellow resident—the two had become an item after meeting in medical respite. Jillian noted that they'd already had two weddings on-site for residents who had met and fell in love.

Then there was Pops, who had another nickname: Papa Claus. He had a belly and a white beard, and when we went to the statehouse, he wore a T-shirt with a cartoon picture of Santa on the beach.

Albert, who sat in the back of the van with me and who pushed JD in the wheelchair through the statehouse, seemed a gentle soul who sometimes struggled to find words. He had previously been in construction. Albert's sisters lived in town, but when his mom had died the year before, he'd begun to lose touch with his siblings, as it seemed his mom was the glue that had kept the family together.

I sat with Michael over a dinner of baked chicken, rice, and corn. With his pink-and-white checkered button-down and khaki shorts, he told me how he'd gone to Cornell for his undergrad and had two master's degrees. He'd ended up on medical respite after being hit by a large truck while riding his bike. This had left him in a coma for months, and when he woke up he didn't remember who he was or what had happened. He too had prior strained relationships and loss in his life, including the death of his mother, which led him to drink excessively following her funeral and incur a DUI, and a bad relationship with an ex-wife who lived abroad with his daughters, with whom he no longer had contact.

And then there was Dennis, who was there on hospice: a soft-spoken, thin man with close-cropped hair and eyes, who'd lost a leg. I felt the positive vibes being in his proximity. We sat and talked next to his bed, and as we did so I took in his room: decorations made from rope and feathers hung on the wall, stacks of applesauce cups sitting on a table. His good friend Mark was there as well. Mark and Dennis had worked together sixteen years earlier for a security firm, and they'd become quite close over the years. So much so that Mark was his power of attorney and helped Dennis navigate the complicated business of dying.

Prior to coming to The INN Between, Dennis had lived alone in an apartment until he became sick and was hospitalized. He couldn't go back to his apartment, as he needed too much care, including assistance with bathing and using the toilet. This reminded me of Richard from Circle the City, who I'd met back in 2018 when he was on hospice. Like Richard, and like Ted from the coffee shop in Vancouver, Dennis too had not been homeless; it wasn't until circumstances at the end forced him from his home.

Mark was Dennis's de facto family, and it was clear he would drop everything to be there and help as needed. Dennis had been a long-time smoker and admitted he just couldn't give it up. Dennis chuckled when he told me how Mark joked that he might as well keep smoking, because he was going to die anyway. Like others I'd encountered over the course of the day, Dennis was estranged from his family. After he and his wife divorced, she took their two sons, and he'd lost touch with them. But since arriving at The INN, he had reconnected with both of his sons—one of them calling him almost every day, worried that he wouldn't get to visit before his dad died—and both had plans to come visit him in Salt Lake City. Knowing that his sons were coming to visit brought him immense joy, and he teared up as he spoke of their impending visit. As I stood up to leave, Dennis and I clasped hands, and I left him and Mark to continue their visit.

In death, there is room for beauty and joy. At the end of the day, before taking pictures with Kellie and Jillian, I sat alone in the community room with Kimberly, the end-of-life doula, and I asked her which patients had most stayed with her. Her eyes lit up as she exclaimed, "So many of them!" and she began to tell me about some of the individuals who had called The INN Between their final home.

Michael, who passed in January 2024, had been resistant at first but eventually opened up. He told Kimberly that his mom, who had died, had loved the U2 song "With or Without You." At the end, when he began struggling with terminal agitation, Kimberly convinced him to stay in bed. As he experienced a death rattle, Kimberly held his hand and said goodbye. Then playing U2's song on her phone, she told him to reach out for his mom's hand.

There was Do, originally from Vietnam; he was on hospice at The INN for six months. Do asked for help locating family, so Kimberly

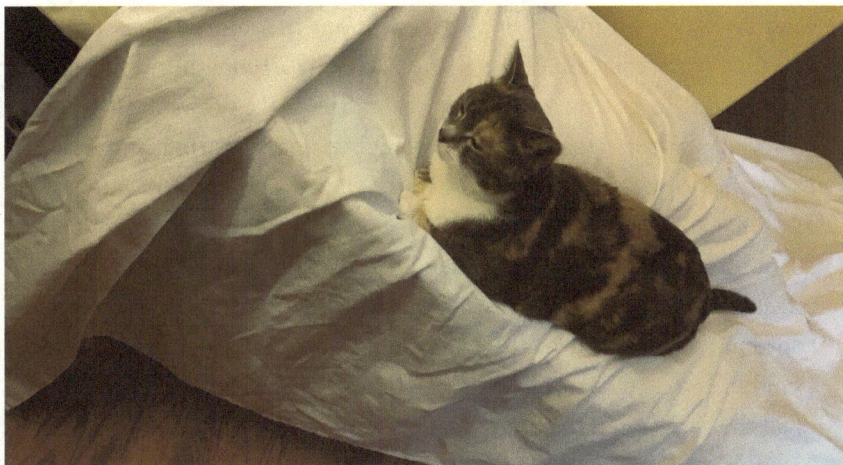

Unconditional Love from Roger. Courtesy Kimberly Peterson.

decided to look on Facebook. There were a lot of folks with the same last name as Do, and she was worried she wouldn't be able to narrow down her search. But she knew his favorite flower was the lotus, and when she found someone with his last name and an image of a lotus flower, she followed her instincts, and it turned out to be his daughter. Both Do's daughter and wife were able to Facetime with him the night before he died.

When another resident, Liz, began declining, Kimberly brought color chalk, and residents went outside and drew images and wrote notes to Liz. Then they all took pictures with her sitting in her wheelchair, saying goodbye while processing their emotions and grief through art.

And of course, Roger the cat stood out in some memories too, including one where Roger sat up against the head of a man who was actively dying and began purring. As Kimberly noted, Roger had taught her something incredibly important: It doesn't matter if you can't communicate via language; show up without judgment, show compassion, and show unconditional love.

The week after my trip, on my Instagram page, I posted a picture of the blue butterfly memorial and wrote,

Tuesday was a whirlwind of a day. I was out the door at 4am and in Salt Lake City by 10am. Then flying back and arriving home close to 2:30am. But in between flights, I was at The INN Between. It was a full-on day of conversations, smiles, laughter, tears, sharing, and more. I was able to spend time with residents, staff, and caregivers and have never felt so welcome so quickly somewhere before. Within minutes I felt at home, and within hours I felt like I had old friends. I even got to pile into a minivan in 99-degree temps with residents and the activities coordinator for a visit to the Utah state house. Walking out of there, I couldn't wait to share the joys of The INN Between, where in spite of all the challenges, they have managed to cultivate a place filled with community, home, and hope.

I then scrolled to The INN Between's Instagram and saw some posts memorializing residents who had died in 2024, including a message so simple and yet so profound: "130th individual to die in a bed, NOT on the street."

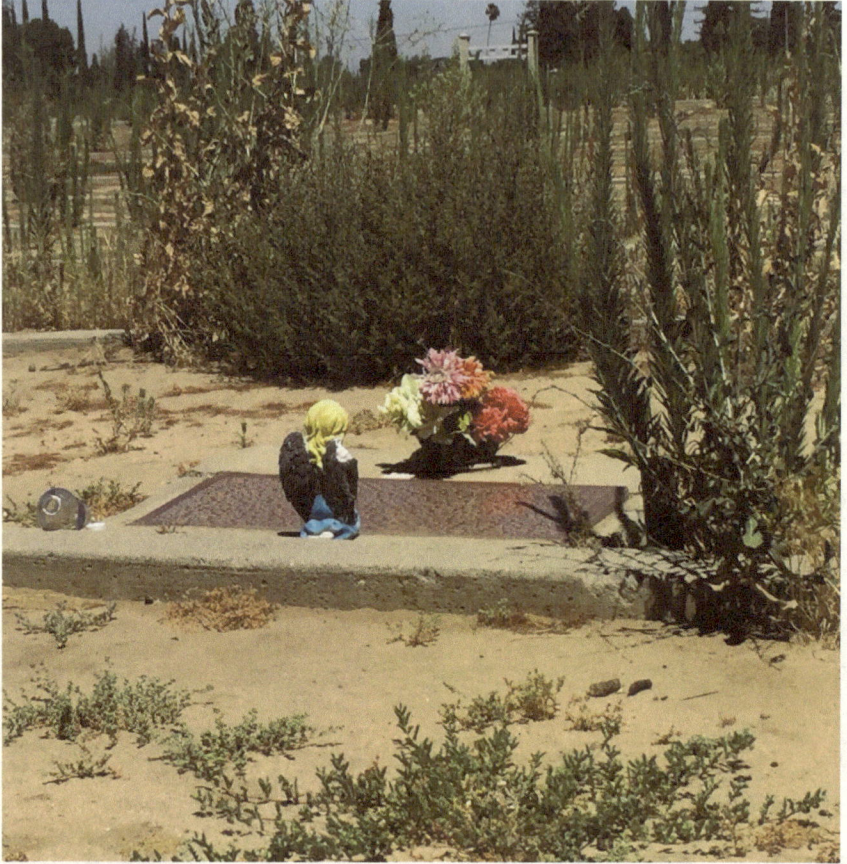

Fresno County Cemetery: Headstone for Deceased 1979 to 1989. Photo by author.

In Memoriam

Names from Fresno County Cemetery Memorial Headstone (1979–1989)

JOSE LUJAN + Eusebio Banuelus + Jose Torres + Juan Garcia + Frank Jernigan + John Doe, 9-8-79 + Victoriano Perea + Georgia Cooper + Maricel Stark + Robert Powell + A. D. Mike + Rose Ensada Bates + James Nichols + Baby Boy Doe, 10-5-80 + John Doe #2, 5-26-80 + Galvan Cruz Lopez + Verlie Garcia+ James Francis O'Rourke + Herbert Calander + Thomas Wood + Leroy Everett Morgan + John Doe, 12-1-80 + John Doe, 7-19-80 + Tony Medina + Robert Ford + Marcelino Mendujando + Hubert T. Rivers + John Ricks + Kei Fukuda + Charles Bradford + Comecindo Marta Gerardo + Carlos Rameriz + Everett Campbell + Arthur R. Camero + Baby Boy Luna #2 + Lois Mae Hallock + Ozell Welsh + Texas D. J. Darling + Jesus Mata +Thomas Jimenez + Margaret Ann Johnson + Guadalupe Valle + J. B. Cherry + Bufford Raymond Coffman + Jorge Villegas Gonzalez + Warren H. Young + John Doe, 9-5-81 + Wingston Church + Alejandro Luna + Virginia Fallis + Jessie Matson + Manuel Vasquez Munoz + Thomas King + Kamiel Coessens + John Doe, 5-12-81 + Louis Stone + Amos I. Thomas + John Doe, 8-18-82 + John Doe, 10-16-82 + Henry Johnson + Chun Cha Whitney + Raymond Stivers + Lloyd Edwards + John Doe, 6-8-82 + John Doe, 12-1-82 + Clarence Amway + John Doe, 3-6-82 + Lovell Lover + Ruben Serraro + Claud Ernest Collier + Theodore Byrd + Randolph Cochran + Jose Gonzales + Gregorio Vargas + Alex DeSoto + Arthur Morton + Stanley P. Bang + Felicano Vadlez Puente + Mario Carrero Ibarra + Winnie Maniscalco + Jesus Rojas + Milton Davis + Alfredo

Villareal + Ramon Mendoza + John Doe, 7-26-82 + Raymond Sebring + Emerry Dilks + Regino Hernandez + Ernest Fresquez + Edward Allman + Jose L. Valesquez + Harry Williams + Ignacio Aranda + Clinton Bismark Hendricks + Benjamin Hendry + Ernesto Castaneda + Bobby Neal Myatt + Levi Moore + John Shafer + Howard Ives + John Doe, 10-16-82 + Julia Chavez + Fermin Rodriquez Ramirez + Jose Morales + Patricia Hill + Roy Maurer + Manuel Mosqueda + Glendon Jones + Alonzo Pierson + Jan Mun Hee + Hattie B. Massie + Russell Bird + Frank Dunbar + Bounpan Phouangkco + William Tevis + Rosendo Fuentes + John Doe #2, 3-11-83 + Josephine Rios + Joe Mendoza + Infant Boy Ramirez + Baby Boy Vang + Jesus Vasquez Cansino + Willie Lee Mitchell + Herminio Torres + Anne L. McKay + Antonio Mota + Corine Joice + Esequeil Romero + John Doe, 1-5-83 + John Doe, 10-10-83 + Amezlua + Juan Marin + Edith Richardson + John Doe, 1-5-83 + Anisteo Cruz + Bruce L. Upton + Warren Wortman + Guadalupe Suarez + Francisco Gonzales + Edna Minyard + Mary + Gerthia Morgan + John Doe, 10-24-84 + Hazel Collins + Baby Girl Vang + John Doe, 6-21-84 + Alfred Delano Johnson + Carl Castle + Manuel Avila + John Doe, 12-23-84 + Howard Wilder + Frank Paul Martinez + Trinidad Rangel + Eula Mae Laws + James Mathews George Fish + Ramon Ruiz + Willard Johnnie Lee + John Doe, 5-18-84 + Juan Carrion + Oscard Hood + Tony Gonzales Martinez + Ruben Ayala Solis + Oral Maring + Angel Gutierrez Estrada + Joseph Gay + Marvin James Snider + Jose Santos + Viola Walker + Manuel Quintero Saldivar + Gus Allen + Colis Berry + Gene Ramos + Manuel Madrid Lopez + Jessica Adams + Juan Cisneros Ceballos + Robert Mitchell + Lloyd Hill + Bernice Tosko + Louise Victoria Heller + Kenneth Clifford Calvert + Florentino Acosta Soto + Samual Turnage + Robert Harold Fink + Trinidad Rodriguez Garcia + Jack Michelettii + Frank Briby + Salvador Felix + John Doe, 7-6-85 + John Doe, 6-15-85 + John Doe, 8-28-85 + John Doe, 10-16-85 + John Doe, 7-1-85 + John Doe, 6-29-85 + Eleanor W. Gentry + Torres + Daniel Gonzales + James Phillip Jackson + Merritt Lancaster + Evlin Scott + Jesus Guiterrez + Guadalupe Rodriquez + Edmund Vincent Douglas + Sarah Taylor Bennett + Joseph Marhala + Thomas E. Renfro + Miguel Andrade + Andrew

Binko + Pauline I. Kaht + Robert Vincent Portilla + Jay W. Strickland + John Doe, 9-3-87 + John Doe, 9-4-87 + Robert Simpson + Randell Cliff Watkins + Isaias Ramirez Cortez + Adania White + Harmilee Burrrough + Federico Gomez + Hilario Flores + Katrine Lynn Gibson + Baby Girl + Danny Jenkins + Quenton Ambus Dillard + Lee Brown + Charles Nelson + Denita Joan Singh + Robert Arthur Medina + Shiela Dale Adams + Max Stevenson Raines + Rudy Hernandez + Jenny Catalann + Ernest Peterson + Ronald Arieta + Marvin Walker + Preciliano Rodriguez + O. B. Patterson + Frank Ozuna + Edward Victor Cieselski + Margaret Mitcham Downey + Charles Edward Elliott + Marie Brass + Elizabeth Larson + Garret McCullock + Theodore Turner + Reynold Ace Williams + Baby Boy Xiong + Tococa Dayshaun Coleman + John Doe, 8-20-86 + John Doe, 7-1-86 + John Doe, 12-12-86 + John Doe, 4-23-86 + John Doe, 10-27-86 + Arturo Perez + Baby Boy Yang + Guillermo Herrera + Efrain Zuniga + Edward Bowers + Carlos Hernandez + Starrin Western Manson + Reyes Peres + Carlos Koeler + Jose Morales Robles + Julio Corona Salinas + Robert Boyd Shanch + Johnny Romain Sanchez + Frances Webb + Feuntin Guzman + John M. Blue + Joe Reyes + Vernie Thompson + Loraine Reed + James Strait + Miguel Garcia + Fernando Barreras + Liggins Lunnie + Taurino Moreno + Robert . . . + Juan . . . + John Unreadable + Susan Lamont + Overton Titto Spencer + Willie I. Gammon + Miguel Moran + Guadalupe Cruz + Miguel Perez + Rob McGlory + Paul Bautista Ramos + Raul Gaona Parra Jr. + Jorge Rodriguez

Destination: Unknown

TABLE 1. Fresno 2018 Mass Burial Spreadsheet. Courtesy of Gene Sibley.[1]

Name/ Gender	Age	Gender	Date of Death	Cemetery	Quadrant	Row	Plot #
Unknown Male	45		1945-08-07	County #2	North	22	46
Unknown Male			1911-06-18	County #1			
Unknown Male		M		County #1			
Unknown Male			1912-04-01	County #1			
Unknown Male		M		County #1			
Unknown Male Adult	Unk.		1945-04-18	County #2	North	22	28
Unknown Male Mexican	50		1939-07-12	County #2	North	20	08
Unknown Male Mexican	65		1940-06-20	County #2	North	27	42
Unknown Man	20	M		COUNTY		ROW 2	18
Unknown Man	About 4	M		COUNTY			01
Unknown Man	N/G	M		COUNTY		ROW 2A	28
Unknown Man			1913-05-05	County #1			
Unknown Man	30–35	M		County #1			
Unknown Man	About 60	M		County #1			
Unknown Man	65	M		County #1			

Name/ Gender	Age	Gender	Date of Death	Cemetery	Quadrant	Row	Plot #
Unknown Man	About 35	M		County #1			
Unknown Man	50	M		County #1			
Unknown Man	Unk.	M		County #1			
Unknown Man	Unk.	M		County #1			
Unknown Man	35	M		County #1			
Unknown Man	55	M		County #1			
Unknown Man	NR	M		County #1			
Unknown Man	About 55	M		County #1			
Unknown Man (white)	9	M		COUNTY		ROW 3A	30
Unknown Man (white)	80	M		COUNTY		3A	08
Unknown Man (white)	65	M		COUNTY		3A	11
Unknown Man (white)	35	M		COUNTY		3A	51
Unknown Mexican	40	N/G		County #1			
Unknown Mexican Male	55		1941-12-21	County #2	North	25	21
Unknown Negro	85	N/G		County #1			

(continued)

TABLE 1. Fresno 2018 Mass Burial Spreadsheet. Courtesy of Gene Sibley.[1] (*continued*)

Name/ Gender	Age	Gender	Date of Death	Cemetery	Quadrant	Row	Plot #
Unknown Skeleton	N/G	N/G		INDIGENT...			
Unknown White Man	50	M		COUNTY		ROW 1	15
Unknown White	45	N/G		COUNTY			
Unknown White Male	54		1938-01-11	County #2	North	30	06
Unknown White Man Bones	N/G	M		COUNTY		ROW 5	48 ½

Stevie W. + Sean D. + Gail T.+ Laura W.+ Michael J. + Robert M. + David S. + Bonnie + Frank B. + Billy G. + Nick + Juan L. + Danny N. + Precious + Tony L. + William B.+ Abdul A. + Francis C. + Rick H. + Mike G. + Tina G. + Walter W. + James B. + Mark O. + Timmy Copley Square + Jane Doe + Andrew R. + Michael C. + John T. + Don T. + Edward P. + Jack "Jackie" L. + John Doe + Anibel V. + Joseph S. + Raphael A. + John T. M. + Gary H. + Tomas Colliigan[2]

Fresno County Cemetery Mass Burial—September 13, 2018

Carl Abney + Donald Abney + John Abraugh + Joe Acevedo + Leonard Acosta + James Acquaviva + Albert Adams + Bobby Adams + Jesse Adney + Marcos Aguilar + Manuela Aguirre + David Alcaraz + Deandre Allen + Edward Allen + Ernest Allen + Steven Allen + Steven Allred + Al Almand + Juan Carlos Almanza + Steve Amador + Wallace Anderson + Larry Andrews + Victor Aparicio + Ronald A. Appling + Jose Aragon + Remigio Arellano + Gary Artrip + Sheila Arwood + Earl Atkinson + Robbie Atkinson + Ernesto Audelo + Raymond Austin +

Grave Markers in the City Poor Lot. Photo by author.

Ronald Autry + Jose Bacho + Jamie Bagwell + Richard Bailey + Robert Baker + William Baker + Carl Baldwin + Sean Baldwin + Donna Ballard + Donnie Banks + Pablo Barajas + Raymond Barilone + Jose Barrientos + Alex Barriga + Joseph Barriga + Rene Barton + Michael Barton + Gwendolyn Bates + Orville Bauch + Ricky Bautista + Charles Bayless + Lianthong Baysauvanh + Meing Baysouvant + Frank Beans + Pauline Beatty + Timothy Beatty + Armando Benitez + Jean Berkan + Gary Bertolatti Sr. + Franklin Bingham + Marion Birts III + Betty Bise + Carol Bitler + Shirley Black + Garrell Blackman + Burton Blair + Joseph Blancarte + George Blanchard + Thomas Blauvelt + Martin Boldt + Nancy Bonney + George Botich + Khamphat Bounmasanohn + Leslie Bovetti + Brenda Bowers + Donald Bowlin + Henry Box + Gregory Boyce + Donna Boyd + Wilma Boyd + Robert Bremer + Sandra Brent + Harold Bridges + Timothy Briggs + Ina Briney + James Brixey + Richard Brosnac + Robert Brouhard + Charles Brown + Donald Brown + Donald Brown + Eugene Brown

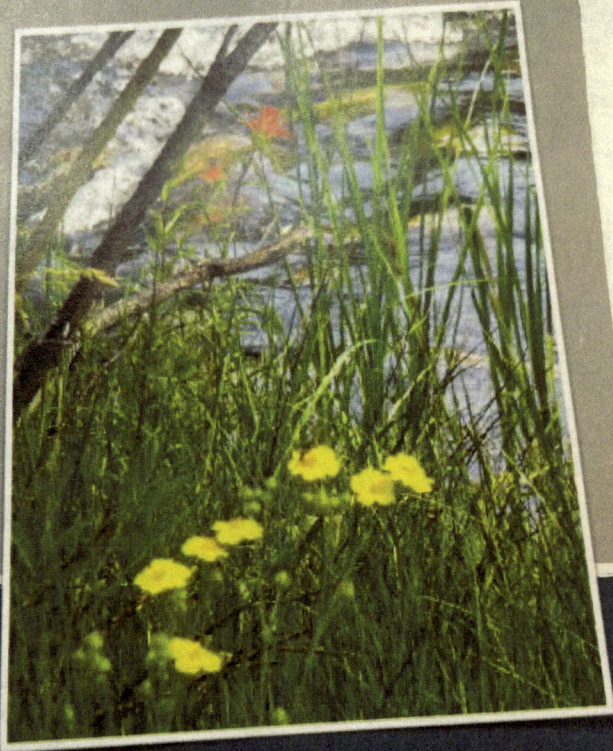

Fresno County Indigent Mass Burial Ceremony Program. Photo by author.

+ Legene Brown + Linda Brown + Rozell Brown + Martha Bruce + Paul Brugetti + Linden Brumley + Mary Brunton + David Bucio + Lester Budrow + Maxine Bunch + Thomas Burgess + Linda Burnett + Allen Burris + Barry Burton + Kenton Bustamante + Tommy Buswell + Robert Butler + Barbara Butz + Jesus Caballero + Trinidad Caballero Vega + Anna Caldwell + Robert Caldwell + Jose Camacho + Samuel Camacho + Donna Campbell + Jesus Campos + Joe Campos + Charles Cantwell + Jeanette Carbejal + Leonard Cardenas + John Carder + Ella Cardoza + Barbara L. Carmen + Lema Carpenter + Joanna Carrico + Kay Carson + Floyd Carter + Karen Carter + Irene Casey + Mark Cash + Hope Castanon + Linda Castellanos + Barbara Castello + Lynette Chambers + Vickie Chandler + Xieng Chanthaphanh + Juan Chavarria + Benigno Chavez + Florence Chavez + Juan Chavez Garcia + Nicolas Chavira + Joanne Chilberg + Darryl Childs + Paula Christian + Patricia Chumley + Brenda Clark + Laura Clayton + James Clinton Jr. + Kenneth Clyde + William Coleman + Joseph Conley + Annette Cook + James Copeland + Fidel Corona Perez + Daniel Cortese + Lashawn Cortese + Richard Coughlan + Cory Cousineau + Betty Cox + Edward Cox + Jon Cox + Dee Croft + James Crone + Burl Crouse + John Crown + Marilyn Cruikshank + Manuel Cruz + Rogelio Cruz + Beatrice Cummings + Clarence Cummings + Jack Cummings + James Cunningham + Lee Curtis + Manuel Dager + Kimberly Dale + Harry Daniels + Robert Darrell + Joseph Daugherty + Ralph Davidian + Allen Davis + Bobby Davis + Genevie Davis + Daniel Day + Soccorro De Fraijo + Paul De Herrera + Leslie + De St Aubin + Olga Dean + Charles Deentremont + Jamie Dehnert + Arlen Deitsch + Daniel Delgadillo + Ramon Delgado + Steven Depue + Kathleen Desalvo + Andres Diaz Cisneros + Robert Dixon + Velma Dodd + Jerome Donofrio + Michael Dowell + Eugene Dowling + Effie Drake + Danny Droullard + Frank Duffy + William Dungam + Ronald Dunkel + Lawrence Dupont + Leonard Edwards + Thurman Edwards + Phillip Edwards + Debra Elerick + Janette Elliott + Garcia Ernest + Juanita Eroles + Anthony Escamilla + Carlos Espaniol + Jennie Espinoza + Manuel Espinoza + Sharon Espinoza + Santillan Estanislao + Douglas Eurich + Michael Evett + Stephen Ewell + William

Fahy + Donna Falls + Mark Farens + Daniel Farias + Annette Farkas + Charles Farray + Victoria Fees + Jack Fennell + Frank Finley + Harold Fischer + Keith Fisher + Bernard Fleming + Charles Fleming + Alfredo Flores + Jose Flores + Luis Flores + Miguel Flores Lozano + Jimmy Flowers + Jeanie Ford + Floyd Foster Sr + John Fowler +Catherine Fox + Efrain Franco + Honest Franco + William French + Richard Frescholtz + Danny Fruitt + Rogelio Fuentes + George Fulp + Karen Fye + Paul Galabis + Linda Gallardo + Francisco Gallegos + Joe Galvez + Antonio Garcia + Aurelio Garcia + Cruz Garcia + Ernest Garcia + Juan Garcia + Johnnie Garcia + Darin Gardner + Jose Garibay + Janet Garner + Willard Wayne Garrison + Richard Garza + Nick George + Russell Giacalone + Reginald Gilliam + Howard Gilliand + Alice Gilliland + David Gipson + Andres Gomez + Erica Gonzales + Mary Gonzales + Olga Gonzales + Victor Gonzales + Joe Gonzales + Alvaro Gonzalez + Jose Gonzalez + Lazaro Gonzalez + Michael Goodman + Glen Gordon + Lawrence Gove + Leslie Graham + Carmen Granados + Darryl Grant + Aron Gray + Edward Greathouse + Judy Greek + Claymon Gren + William Grey + Kenneth Gridley + Perry Griffin + David Grimes + Darlene Groves + Connie Grubbs + Manuel Gutierrez + Napoleon Gutierrez + Vincent Gutierrez Sr. + Lee Guy + Diego Guzman + Edythe Hall + Elmer Hallford + Cheryl Hamilton + Donald Hamilton + James Hamilton Jr. + Janice Handley + Loretta Haney + Erma Harley + Jamie Harper + Patricia Harper + Payton Harrelson + Duane Harris + William Harris + Sherry Harrison + Rebba Hart + Frances Hauch + Jeffery Hawkins + Thomas Hayhurst + Vicky Hays + Kenneth Helmer + Woodrow Henderson + Jack Hendricks + Deborah Hendrickson + Terry Henry + Floyd Herbert + Jose Hernandez + Jose Hernandez + Maria Hernandez + Mark Herndon + Edward Hicks + Henry Hickson + David Higgins + Lydia Hinojos + Mary Hitti + Bryan Hobbs + Raymond Hodges + Patricia Hoffman + Robert Hoffman + Janet Hogue + Daniel Holcomb + Kimberli Holden + Gary Holland Sr. + Debra Hood + Bobby Hopkins + Leonettia Hopkins + Esther Horg + Jeff Horn + Leona Hornberger + Jo Ann Howard + Calvin Howell + Kendra Huffman + Virene Hughes + Edward Hulbert + Isaac Hundley + Franklin Hysell + John Hysell +

Bonnie Ibarra + Theodore Illenberg + Joann Imperatrice + Samuel Imperatrice + Anthony Imperial + Larry Ingle + Gene Ingledue + James Ivie + Jose Izaguirre + Mark Jackson + Patricia Jackson + Larry Jaquay + Raymond Jaquay + Sally Jarrett + Edward Jeanes + Bill Jefferson + Mark Jennings + Gerald Jewell + Alejandro Jimenez + Alejandro Jimenez + Leonard Jimenez + Clifton Johnson + Steven Johnson + Janet Johnson + Robert Johnson Sr. + Leslie Johnston + Joe Jones + Joyce Jones + Ronald Jones + Rosia Jones + Shirley Jones + Stephen Jones + Jimmie Jones + Amadeo Juarez + Galen Judd + John Justice + Wolf Kasten + William Kavet + Robert Keller + Jacqulyn Keltner + Chester Kemp + Opal Kent + Kevin Kenworth + Ruth Kessell + Helen Kessinger + Donald Kester + Kimberly Ketcher + Savaeng Khamkheuang + Judith Kilman + Larry Kimberlin + Jarvis King Sr. + Ralph Kinman + David Kluesner + Steve Knowles + David Knutson + Kathleen Koch + Tyrone Kopp + Jeannie Krause + Ron Kruser + Victor Kuykendall + Ada Lackey + Jose Laguna + Edward Lajoie + Rosie Lamb + Debra Lamonica + Dixie Lamorie + David Landrith + Conrad Landry + Herman Landsem + Stephen Larson + Ronnie Leckel + Jimmie Ledbetter + Roger Lee + Darlene Leggett + Roman Leon-Limias + Mary Licon + Alviezola Limbrick + Michael Lindsey + Charles Lipka + Shelly Lollis + Judy Long + Catarino Lopez + Edward Lopez + Elicia Lopez + Felipe Lopez + Jaime Lopez + Raymond Lopez + Raymond Lopez + Rogelio Lopez + Isaac Lozano + Ismael Lozano + Jose Luis + Diana Luttrell + Demetrice Lyday + Thomas Macarthur + Billye Maiberger + Gutrude Maltese + Barbara Maltsberger + Fanny + Mann + Richard Maria + Mark Marloe + James Marshall + Frederick Martin + Rodney Martin + Sherilyn Martin + Wayne Martin + Peter Martinella + George Martinez + Inocencio Martinez + John Martinez + Jose Martinez + Hermene Martinez Saucedo + Cary Massey + Raymond Mata + Michael Mathews + Saundra Matthews + Jennifer Maulding + William Maulding + Sandra McClendon + Linda McCracken + Stuart McDonald + Jack McGaughey + Belinda McGill + Ruth McGill + William Mcknown + Arthur Mckown + Stephen Mckown + Tamara McPhail + Evarista Medrano + Juan Medrano + Duane Meekma + Joshua Mehr + Carrol

Meinz + Santos Mejia Gonzales + Julius Melan + Ruben Mellin + Jessie Melton + Concepsion Mendez + Santiago Mendoza + Heike Meron + Thaddeus Meron + Dianne Merrel + Jose Meza + Lauren Michael + Daryl Miears + Dolores Milano + James Mills + Loretta Mitchell + William Mitchell + Russell Mitchum Jr. + Mary Mitilinos + Roberto Molina + Antonio Montano + Emilio Montenegro + Gary Moore + Terrill Moore + Jesus Mora + Andres Morales + Jose Morales + Ramon Morales + Ramon Morales + Yolanda Moran + Reina Moran Ramirez + Jose Moreno + Patricia Morgan + Bonnie Morris + Charles Morrison + Edward Mosely + Joseph Moser + William Mouradick + Clyde Murphy Jr. + Norma Myers + Raul Narbaiz + Francisco Narras + Todd Natho + Dan Neely + Mary Neff + Kirk Joesph Nefroney + Lymas Nelson + Daniel Nichols + Rebecca Nichols + William Nicoson + Deborah Nielsen + Sherry Noisey + Dora Noriega + Peggy North + Jerry Nykerk + Abel Ochoa + Domingo Odiaga + Gary Ogle + Joan Ohiggins + Patrick Ohler + Donny Oneal + Patrick Oneal + Deborah Orlosky + Robert Ornellas + Alberto Ortega + Victor Ortega + Juan Ortiz + Juan Lopez Ortiz + Juan Manuel Osegueracampos + Sam Oudomrak + Evalyn Oust + Randolph Overstreet + Johnny Owens + Karen Owens + Rhiannon Owens + Steve Pace + Robert Page + Bernard Para + Jan Pardew + Precious Parker + Leona Parks + Billy Parson + Donna Patterson + Teddy Pearce + Daryl Peebler + Vernon Pennington + Herman Perez + Jose Luis Perez + Marisela Perez + Richard Perez + Barbara Perez-Fugate + Carol Perrier + Gale Persons + Donna Peters + Zelma Peters + Cheryl Peterson + Wanda Pettitt + Vincent Pharris + Jimmy Phea Jr. + Sylvester Phillips + Hobert Phipps + Khampane Phongsavath + Maylene Poe + Allen Pool Sr. + James Potter + Charles Powell + Anthony Powers + Jeffrey Pratt + Miguel Preboste + Alton Preslie + Gary Price + Ralph Prieto-Garcia + Jeffery Pullem + Ginger Putnam + Joe Rafay + Ruth Rambo + Alfredo Ramirez + Daniel Ramirez + Juan Ramirez + Rosie Ramirez + Jose Ramirez Jr. + Albert Ramonoff + Manuel Ramos + Grady Ramsey + Gabriel Rances + Mariana Rances + Gina Redwine + Phillip Reed + Ronald Reed + Douglas Reedy + William Reeve + Patrick Reich + Lynn Reyes + Billy Rice + Paul Rice + Cornelius Richardson + Dick

Richardson + Franklin D Richardson + Lester L. Richardson + Marjorie Riley + Martha Ring + Louisa Rios + Dean Ristan + Consuelo Rivera + Lydia Rivera + Tarsha Rivers + Marilyn Robbins + Angela Robinson + Michael Rocha + Christina Rodriguez + Enrique Rodriguez + Guillermo Rodriguez + Peter Rodriguez + Ronald Rodriguez + Susan Rodriguez + Diane Roland + Edward Romanoff + Michele Ronzone + Beatrice Roque + Neary Rorth + Delores Rouse + Curtis Rowe + Anna Rubio + Luis Ruiz + David Rush + Nanette Russell + Naomi Russell + Sy Russell + Ronald Sabernaik + John Safina + William Safko + Julian Salazar + Donald Salter + Rodolfo Sanches + Daniel Sanchez + George Sanchez + Brian Sander s+ Larry Sanders + Jorge Sandoval + Barbara Santiago + Manuel Santiz + Edward Sargoto Jr. + Leola Saunders + Leroy Savage + Carmyn Scharffenburg + Ronald Schendel + Pedro Sebastian + Raymond Sepeda + Stephen Sharp + Marsha Shaw + James Shepard + Susan Shirk + Dani Shope + Billie Shrauger + Leanard Siderman + Linda Sides + Rodrigo Sifuentes + Louis Silva Jr. + Melissa Silverman + Daniel Simmons + Kathy Simmons + Joshua Simpson + Joy Sims + Bart Singleton + Joe Sinohui + Carol Skipper + Mary Slaughter + Karen Smallwood + Basil Smith + Brian Smith + Carl Smith + Dennis Smith + Jerry Smith + Jerry Smith + Lawrence Smith + Scott Smith + Thomas Smith + Thomas Smith + Cnell Smithe Liscano + James Snedeger + Larry Snyder + Gina Sosa + Bounpheng Sounthala + William Spear + Albert Spearman + Donald Spears + Paul St. Arnaud + Arthur Stallings + Zella Stevens + Robert Stevenson + Bobby Stimson + Betty Stone + Mary Storvold + Margaret Stout + Saundra Stress + Jimmy Strickland + Beatrice Strombeck + Mikel Stubblefield + Audrey Stuckman + Kathlyn Sullivan + Wayne Summers + Patsy Sumpter + Joanne Sutton + Ralph Svara Sr. + Craig Swanson + Janice Sweatt + Mildred Swimmer + Marjorie Sykes + Rodney Taylor + Tommy Taylor + Hadaline Thiesen + Hans Thiesen + Hane Thiphanet + George Thomas + William Thomas + George Thomas + Mary Thomas + Terrance Thomas + Kenneth Thurman + Luis Tinajero + Katherine Toca + Leo Torreblanca + Carlos Torres + Kathryn Torres + Maria Torres + Juan Torrez + Rosendo Toscano + Larry Towe + Mari Tsuboi + Albert Turner + Arthur Tyler Jr. + Linda

Uhl + Gay Urbina + Everardo Valencia + Franciso Valencia + Abraham Valencia Jr. + Raul Valle + James Vanderford + Lynn Vanness + Jorge Vargas + Frank Vargas + Mary Vaughan + Simplicio Vazquez + Domingo Vega + Macario Velazquez + Clarence Veney III + Marie Villane + Peter Villarreal + Silvino Villegas + Marylou Vogel + Breann Voigt + Herman Volke + Christopher Vulich + Donna Wade + Andrew Waldhauser + Essie Waldhauser + Dianne Waldron + Ruth Walker + Terri Walker + Danny Wallace + Lee Walls + Richard Walthall + Adan Ward + Michael Ward + Ronald Ward + Curtis Washington + Robert Watson Jr. + Deborah Wegener + Cornelious Welch + Linda Welch + Lise Wellingsworth + AY Wells + Linda Wells + Robert Whalen + Joel Wheeler + Latisha Whitaker + Marshall White + Therman Whitney + Ronald Wiggins + Abron Wilkerson + Troy Wilkins + James Williams + Otis Williams + Sherri Williams + Sylvia Williams + Thomas Williams + Eddie Willoughby + Sidney Wilmoth + Michael Wilson + Arnett Woods + Lowbell Woods + Gregory Wright + Ralph Wright + Eleanor Yanoff + Ignacio Zavala + Abel Zavaleta + Anna Zimmerman + Christopher Zuniga

The Fresno County Burial program provides funding for cremation of indigent, unclaimed, or abandoned decedents in Fresno County. This program serves to remember those who died in Fresno County that were homeless, poor, could not afford burial, were left abandoned or unclaimed or where we were unable to locate relatives.

—Fresno County Sheriff's Department

Indexing the Life & Death Experience of Homelessness

A Poem

.

.

.

beggar, 5
    begging, 5, 113, 213, 214, 271
    stemming, 271
    See also bum, hobo, homeless, tramp, transient, vagrant, and vagabond

bum, 66, 272
    See also beggar, hobo, homeless, tramp, transient, vagrant and vagabond

burial, 5, 16–22, 72–77, 85–86, 90–98, 103–107, 110–120, 230, 260, 269, 274
    mass, 21, 112, 230, 246–247, 257, 261, 274
    See also county disposition and potter's fields

choice, 12, 38, 57–58, 60, 62, 69, 76, 81–82, 90, 97, 120, 127, 139, 148, 150, 153, 163, 187, 219, 247
    See also lacking

conditions
    frostbite, 131, 133, 161, 175
    heatstroke, 175
    hypothermia, 133, 175
    hyperthermia, 175

county disposition, 65, 68, 75, 83
    See also burial and potter's field

On the day he dies, a lot will happen around him but will not necessarily be
about him.

Maybe someone will notice, maybe not.

Maybe someone will claim her, maybe not.

Maybe she will be given a proper burial with family and mourners and her name
will be felt on people's tongues and heard in people's hearts, but maybe not.

Perhaps his body will languish on the streets for a few hours or days, or he'll get
lucky and be picked up right away by the coroner.

He might walk into an emergency room and never walk back out.

She might walk into an emergency room and be sent back out.

Maybe they'll die on a park bench.

Maybe they'll die on the edge of a heating grate on the street, having warmed up
briefly in winter, only to roll off in his sleep and freeze to death.

Maybe he'll develop a cancer he doesn't know he has and doesn't treat because
he's too busy standing in line at the social security office, waiting in the shelter for food, begging on the streets for money, until the symptoms can finally
be ignored no longer and they scream terminal.

He may have the fortune of being sent to a medical respite unit and provided
hospice care, compassion, and dignity.

She may end up hooked to machines in an ICU with no voice, no agency in how
she dies.

After death, his body may be collected and paid for by someone who knew him
and loved him, still loves him, even if they don't know him anymore.

Or he might languish in cold storage at the county morgue until the requisite
bureaucratic time is up and he's buried unceremoniously in a two-body-deep
grave with only a number as a marker.

Or she'll be cremated, boxed and stored for a future mass indigent burial.

Labeled: outcast, a beggar, indigent, destitute, poor, needy, broke, and broken.

Maybe those around him don't see him, have forgotten him.

But death has not.

APPENDIX

IMPORTANT NOTICE TO EMERGENCY MEDICAL PERSONNEL

My name is _____

My date of birth _____

- ○ I have completed an Advanced Health Care Directive.
- ○ I wish to be an organ donor.
- ○ I have a prehospital DO NOT RESUSITATE (DNR) form.

In the event of an emergency please contact

1. Name: _____
   Phone # _____
2. Name: _____
   Phone # _____
3. Name: _____
   Phone # _____

I have received services in the past at (check off all that apply):

☐ Venice Family Clinic
☐ OPCC
☐ St. Joseph's Homeless Center
☐ VA
☐ Southern California Hospital at Culver City (previously Brotman Medical Center)
☐ St. John's Medical Center
☐ Marina del Rey Hospital

UCLA "Pocket" Advanced Directive, Courtesy of Jeannette Meyer, APRN-CNS, MSN, CCRN, CCNS, PCCN, ACHPN

Wishes for End of Life

Survey for patients to find out what's most important for them done in service of research and drafting of an advanced directive.

This is not a legal document but gives you an opportunity to write down important things about yourself and your wishes for end of life. You can say what you would like to happen if you are seriously ill and how you want things to be handled before and after you die. A copy of this paper should be kept with your other important papers. You may want to give a copy to a trusted friend, family member, or doctor and also discuss it with them.

- What I am most proud of in my life.
- How I want to be remembered.
- What is most important to me about how I am cared for at or near the end of my life.
- Fears I have about being seriously ill or dying.
- Spiritual or religious beliefs and traditions that are important to me.

- Religious rites or ceremonies that I would want performed when I am dying or have died.
- List anyone you would want to have contacted to assist with your spiritual needs if you are seriously ill.
- Wishes about what happens to your body (burial or cremation) and where you would want to be buried or have your ashes stored, if possible.
- Would you want to have a memorial service? If so, please describe anything that you would like to include such as music, readings, or other specific requests.
- People you want to be contacted in case of serious illness or death:
- People you do not want to be contacted in case of serious illness or death:
- Do you have a will or any specific directions about what you want to happen to your personal belongings? If you have a will, where is it located?
- Other comments:

End-of-Life Wishes Worksheet, Courtesy of Melissa Sandoval, MD; Diane Elmore, MD; and Circle the City

ACKNOWLEDGMENTS

THERE ARE SO many people to whom I owe my undying gratitude. First, I am beyond grateful for my parents, who instilled a deep love of learning, reading, and creating. They also instilled the belief in me that all people deserve to be treated with respect, dignity, and as equals and to not be complacent in the face of witnessing injustice. My dad has gone above and beyond to help me in my research, by sharing his own research with his cemetery work, connecting me to people to speak with, and letting me discuss my work. Thank you to my high school English teacher, Andrea Crisp, and to my grandmother, Carmella Rago—both showed an unwavering support in my education and development as a writer.

I am equally thankful for my amazing partner and husband, Eric, who has provided unwavering support for all my crazy ideas over the last twenty years, including quitting my stable job to pursue advanced education. He has been there for me in innumerable ways, encouraging me and moving to Scotland with me when I pursued my MFA in creative writing; reading my work honestly; and supporting nearly three years of me moving back and forth between the United States and the United Kingdom while working on the doctorate.

Of course, none of this would ever have happened without my two amazing doctoral supervisors, and friends, Dr. Elizabeth K. Reeder and Dr. Naomi Richards. I am thankful that they both saw potential in this project and were willing to take it on and work with me. This has been one of the most rewarding and fulfilling professional collaborations I've ever experienced. Their brutal honesty and their steady guiding mentorship helped me move through the most challenging project I've ever worked on.

I also am full of gratitude for Chrissy Davies, who has been my best friend for nearly twenty years. She generously donated her time to read my final draft and gave invaluable feedback on early drafts and assistance with promoting the book. She's not the sister I never had, she *is* my sister, and I owe her more bottles of wine than I can count for the work she did. I deeply appreciate her love and generosity.

I couldn't have written this without all the medical and nursing staff, CEOs, funeral industry professionals, and others who were willing to speak with me and give me hours (sometimes full days) of their time to provide insight into aspects of homeless health care and the world of professionals in death and dying. Some of those I'd like to thank include: Sheri Manning-Cartwright, Bobby Watts, Melissa Sandoval, Jeannette Meyer, Delia Cortez, Dr. Jim O'Connell, Jeff Olivet, Julia Dobbins, Laura Helme, Bobby, Ronnie, Rev. Alex T. McAspurren, Kelly A. Matlock, Mary Paulson-Ellis, Jack Sarafian, James Copner, Kate Carter, and Alison Colclough. Thank you to the lovely residents and the staff at The INN Between, including Jillian Olmstead, Kellie Mieremet, Kim Pate, Taelar Trujillo, Jesse Austin, and Jaimee Davis. Thank you as well to the staff at Brydon Court and Boston Health Care for the Homeless.

The first day of the doctorate program, when our creative writing cohort all met, I walked into the classroom and there was Sally Gales. I knew almost immediately we were going to be great friends; I had no idea how great. I couldn't have gotten through this without her. Same goes for Gillian Shirreffs, another fellow doctoral student and dear friend. Having you ladies to go through this with made all the difference. Thank you to the rest of the creative writing PhD cohort, including Gilly McDougall, Tawnya Selene Renelle, and Oliver K. Langmeade. And thank you to the Death Writes network—having a like-minded community means the world.

Thank you to GrubStreet: Center for Creative Writing in Boston, whose classes I've taken for more than a decade and where some of the first inklings of this book were developed. Thank you to the Writer's Room of Boston and the Somerville Library, where I spent many hours writing in beautiful spaces filled with books and good writing vibes. Thank you to Laura Pagluica, Caroyln Pershouse, and Carolyn Allard for making sure I had a clean, copyedited manuscript. Thank you to Mike Jauchen at The Artful Editor who provided the most amazing developmental edit that helped get the manuscript query-ready! Thank you to new writing friends who helped review and edit the final stages of this manuscript, including Andrea Firth and the women from the Equitable Disposition Alliance. I must also thank all the other friends and family who supported me during this endeavor, who encouraged and cheered me on.

Lastly, I cannot forget to acknowledge the amazing and strong individuals experiencing homelessness who I had the privilege of meeting throughout this journey. It was their stories that kept me motivated during challenging times when writing. This is for them.

The following essays were previously published:

"Deaths of Disparity." *Massachusetts Review*, vol. 58, no. 3, Fall 2021.

"Indexing the Life & Death Experience of Homelessness." *Portland Review*, Spring 2021.

"Remembering the Forgotten: The Space That Remains." *NEXT: Visions Toward a Less-Divided America*, edited by Artress Bethany White, Pangyrus, 2022, pp. 37–72.

"Sweet Feet." *Missouri Review*, 1 Jul. 2022, https://missourireview.com/sweet-feet-by-amy-shea/.

NOTES

Remembering the Forgotten

1. An annual weed, mare's tail, also known as horseweed (*Conyza canadensis*), is named as such because each plant has a single unbranched, roughly five-foot-tall stem covered in willow-like leaves. Horseweed prefers coarse, well-drained, and fertile loam soils. It can grow in organic soils and tolerates drought.

The Department of Transitional Assistance

1. Mount Auburn Cemetery was the first rural cemetery in the United States. This cemetery is more than just a burial ground. It also is used as a park, a wildlife habitat, a garden, and a conference center. It's lush, luxe, and peaceful. To be interred here will cost you a minimum of $25,000 to $30,000.

Field Notes of a Tombstone Tourist

1. County burials for Madera County are $498.70 (which includes the urn vault, handling charge, opening/closing the plot, county marker, and tax).

Sweet Feet

1. **Registration:** To get to the foot clinic, go through security downstairs at the main entrance of the shelter, take the stairs or elevator up to the second floor, and then pass by the clothing dispensary (with its quaint, country-like wooden

sign hung on the wall behind the ticket counter) and the folding chairs, set up ten wide and four rows deep, that serve as the waiting area for the medical and foot clinic—you have arrived.

2. **The Intake Form:** There are two towels on each of the three chairs. Lay one out on the floor underneath the feet, and set the other one aside to dry off after the soak. Take the patient's shoes and socks off. Complete the intake form with the patient and repeat the following script: "Please tell us the following: name; date of birth; whether you have diabetes (if so, this will trigger a blood sugar test); whether you have any allergies; whether you've had all your vaccinations (the flu shot is vital during the winter, and this summer we've had a hepatitis A outbreak in the shelters); whether you smoke (cigarettes specifically); whether you have a primary care doctor and, if so, where are they located (here, BHCHP, or elsewhere), and if you don't, whether you want to sign up with one; and finally, where you sleep most nights."

3. **The Visual Examination:** Put gloves on for visual examination of the feet. Things to look for include the following: immersion foot (if present, skip the foot soak or do only a very short one), athlete's foot (any noticeable odor can indicate this; use plenty of powder and lotion and scrub with the pumice, plus a shot of foot spray into the shoes), blisters (A+D ointment and Band-Aids), and signs of frostbite during winter. Ask the patient if they have any pain or itching. I always crouched down to do this and often would lift their foot up onto my thigh (many days, I'd get on the subway to go home and smell a faint odor of feet, and sometimes my black workout leggings would be covered in powder and lotion). Remove gloves to record the patient's foot condition on the flip side of the intake form.

4. **The Foot Soak:** Place a hard-plastic shell inside a square basin and fill with water and a few pumps of soap. The faucet temperatures are finicky, so keep feeling the water with your hands. Once full enough, place at the patient's feet and have them dip their toes in to check the temperature (adjust as needed by adding warm or cold water with the plastic cup by the sink). During those ten minutes of soaking, patients will have their blood pressure and temperature taken, be given small cups of powder and lotion to apply after the soak, be offered a fresh pair of socks, and be given nail clippers and pumice, if requested, as well as time to chat, nap, or sit quietly.

5. **Wrap Up with Clean Feet:** Put on a new pair of gloves, dump the water (athlete's foot can be transmitted very easily), and place the plastic shell in the trash. Clean out the plastic basin and set it to dry on the counter. Have the patient dry their feet, apply lotion and/or powder, and put fresh socks and shoes on. Send them on their way with clean feet, wipe the chair down, add two fresh towels, and get ready for the next person.

Deaths of Disparity

1. Many don't realize how violent CPR is—that ribs often get broken; even fewer realize that less than 8 percent of people who have CPR performed survive a month later, that 3 percent have a good outcome, that another 3 percent end up in a chronic vegetative state, and that the last 2 percent are generally comatose: Everyone else dies (Radiolab).

In Memoriam

1. "After I've passed, my biggest fear would be not making it back home . . . they'll throw you in a pauper's grave someplace and nobody's going to mourn you" (homeless man qtd. in Song et al.).

2. From the 2017 Homeless Memorial Service at Church on the Hill in Boston, Massachusetts—sixty-two names they were unable to obtain from the coroner's office, so those are not listed here.

Indexing the Life & Death Experience of Homelessness

1. Kusmer 37.

WORKS CITED AND CONSULTED

@A_Finucane. "Investigating the need for palliative care among people who are homeless in Scotland." *Twitter*, 28 Nov. 2018, 11:53 a.m., https://www.twitter.com/A_Finucane/status/1067823798148321280.

Abbey, Edward. *Desert Solitaire: A Season in the Wilderness*. Random House, 1968.

Abel, David. "Year Since Long Island's Close Finds Safety Net Tattered." *Boston Globe*, 8 Oct. 2015, https://www.bostonglobe.com/metro/2015/10/07/year-after-long-island-closed-big-holes-remain-city-safety-net/cbcOVyA2ZWGkGcisj2fUNP/story.html.

Abraham, Tony. "Patient Dumping a Symptom of Health System Woes." *Healthcare Dive*, 5 Feb. 2018, https://www.healthcaredive.com/news/patient-dumping-symptom-of-health-system-woes/516018/.

Abruzzini, Marissa. "Film Review: 'A Certain Kind of Death' by Grover Babcock and Blue Hadaegh." *SevenPonds*, 23 Sep. 2016, https://blog.sevenponds.com/lending-insight/film-review-a-certain-kind-of-death-by-grover-babcock-and-blue-hadaegh.

Academy of Medical Royal Colleges and Faculty for Homeless and Inclusion Health. *Academy of Medical Royal Colleges and Faculty for Homeless Inclusion Health Joint Position Statement*. Academy of Medical Royal Colleges and Faculty for Homeless and Inclusion Health, 2017.

"Aging Matters, Episode 2: End of Life." *NPT Reports*. Nashville Public Television and PBS, 2017, https://www.pbs.org/video/npt-reports-aging-matters-aging-matters-end-life/.

Aguilera, Diana. "Residents at Fresno Apartment Remain Without Heat, Hot Water." *KVPR*, 24 Nov. 2015, https://www.kvpr.org/post/residents-fresno-apartment-remain-without-heat-hot-water.

Alcoff, Linda M. "The Problem of Speaking for Others." *Cultural Critique*, no. 20, Winter 1991–1992, pp. 5–32.

Allen, Arthur, and Lorraine Woellert. "VA Kills Plan to Cut Homeless-Vet Program After Outcry." *Politico*, 6 Dec. 2017, https://www.politico.com/story/2017/12/06/homeless-veterans-benefits-trump-207781.

American Hospital Association. "Fact Sheet: Uncompensated Hospital Care Cost." https://www.aha.org/fact-sheets/2020-01-06-fact-sheet-uncompensated-hospital-care-cost. Accessed 12 May 2025.

Andrzejewski, Adam. "Mapping San Francisco's Human Waste Challenge—132,562 Cases Reported in the Public Way Since 2008." *Forbes*, 5 Apr. 2019, https://www.forbes.com/sites/adamandrzejewski/2019/04/15/mapping-san-franciscos-human-waste-challenge-132562-case-reports-since-2008/#762a2c6a5ea5.

Anthony, Caryn. "Bring Soup, Not Salad." *Modern Loss*, 22 Aug. 2017, https://www.modernloss.com/bring-soup-not-salad/.

Anwar, Liyna, and Emma Bowman. "They Comfort Strangers, So No One Dies Alone." *NPR*, 24 Nov. 2017, https://www.npr.org/2017/11/24/565948727/they-comfort-strangers-so-no-one-dies-alone.

Appleton, Rory. "Aggressive Panhandler Cited for 11th Time in 2016, Found with $1,800 in His Pocket." *Fresno Bee*, 18 Jan. 2016, https://www.fresnobee.com/news/local/crime/article55370835.html.

"Arbor Vitae Cemetery: Basic Pricing." *Madera Cemetery District*, https://www.maderacemetery.org/basic-pricing/. Accessed 24 Jul. 2019.

Aries, Philippe. *The Hour of Our Death: The Classic History of Western Attitudes Toward Death over the Last One Thousand Years.* 2nd ed., Vintage, 2008.

Association for the Study of Death and Society. https://www.deathandsociety.org/index.php. Accessed 25 Jul. 2020.

Baggett, Travis P., et al. "Mortality Among Homeless Adults in Boston: Shifts in Causes of Death over a 15-Year Period." *Journal of American Medical Association*, vol. 173, no. 3, 2013, pp. 189–195.

Baily, Isaac J. "Why Didn't My Drug-Affected Family Get Any Sympathy?" *Politico*, 10 Jun. 2018, https://www.politico.com/magazine/story/2018/06/10/opioid-crisis-crack-crisis-race-donald-trump-218602.

Barry-Jester, Anna Maria. "Sweeps of Homeless Camps in California Aggravate Key Health Issues." *NPR*, 10 Jan. 2020, https://www.npr.org/sections/health-shots/2020/01/10/794616155/sweeps-of-homeless-camps-in-california-aggravate-key-health-issues.

Bätschmann, Oskar, and Pascal Griener. *Hans Holbein: Revised and Expanded Second Edition.* Reaktion, 2014.

Bauer, Douglass. *What Happens Next? Matters of Life and Death.* U of Iowa P, 2005.

Bebinger, Martha. "Tent Medicine to Treat Those with the Coronavirus in Boston's Homeless Community." *WBUR Boston*, 23 Mar. 2020, https://www.wbur.org/commonhealth/2020/03/23/tent-medicine-to-treat-those-with-the-coronavirus-in-bostons-homeless-community.

Becker, Ernest. *The Denial of Death*. Simon and Schuster, 1973.

Behar, Ruth. "Death and Memory: From Santa Maria del Monte to Miami Beach." *Cultural Anthropology*, vol. 6, no. 3, 1991, pp. 346–384.

"Being Mortal." *Frontline*. PBS, 10 Feb. 2015, https://www.pbs.org/wgbh/frontline/film/being-mortal/.

Beker, Lena. Personal interview. 26 Jul. 2024.

Bell, Chris. "Design Crimes: How a Bench Launched a Homelessness Debate." *BBC UGC and Social News*, 14 May 2018, https://www.bbc.com/news/blogs-trending-44107320.

Bellafante, Gina. "Are We Fighting a War on Homelessness? Or a War on the Homeless?" *New York Times*, 31 May 2019, https://www.nytimes.com/2019/05/31/nyregion/homelessness-shelters.html.

Benson, Joseph, et al. *Protecting the Unprotected: A Survey of Violence Experienced While Homeless*. National Consumer Advisory Board and National Health Care for the Homeless Council, 2010.

Bernstein, Nina. "How to Avoid the Fate of a Common Grave." *New York Times*, 15 May 2016, https://www.nytimes.com/2016/05/15/nyregion/how-to-avoid-the-fate-of-a-common-grave.html.

———. "Unearthing the Secrets of New York's Mass Graves." *New York Times*, 15 May 2016, https://www.nytimes.com/interactive/2016/05/15/nyregion/new-york-mass-graves-hart-island.html?mtrref=www.bing.com&gwh=C2F2A461077A1246C5B721A857129434&gwt=pay&assetType=REGIWALL.

Bird, Walter, Jr. "Person of the Year: Peter Stefan." *Worcester Magazine*, 26 Dec. 2013, https://www.worcestermag.com/2013/12/26/person-year-peter-stefan.

———. "Unclaimed: Dead and Buried Alone in Massachusetts." *Worcester Magazine*, 20 Mar. 2014, https://www.worcestermag.com/2014/03/20/unclaimed-dead-buried-alone-massachusetts/21843.

Biss, Eula. *Notes from No Man's Land: American Essays*. Graywolf Press, 2011.

———. *On Immunity: An Inoculation*. Graywolf Press, 2015.

"The Bitter End." *Radiolab*. NPR, 15 Jan. 2013, https://www.wnycstudios.org/podcasts/radiolab/articles/262588-bitter-end.

Blumberg, Antonia. "A Growing Movement of 'Death Dulas' Is Rethinking How We Die." *Huffington Post*, 5 Jun. 2017, https://www.huffingtonpost.com/entry/end-of-life-doulas_us_591cbce2e4b03b485cae51c2.

Bobby. Personal interview. 7 May 2018.

Borba, Jeanie. "Gathering to Remember Burying the Grief of So Many Years." *Fresno Bee*, 22 Sep. 1995.

"Boston Common." *Freedom Trail Foundation*, https://www.thefreedomtrail.org/trail-sites/boston-common. Accessed 22 Mar. 2019.

Boston Health Care for the Homeless Program. https://www.bhchp.org/about-us. Accessed 28 Jan. 2018.

Boston Parks and Recreation Department. "Part 4: Open Space Management Mission—Cemeteries." *Open Space Plan 2002–2006*, Boston Parks and Recreation Department, 2002–2006, https://www.cityofboston.gov/parks/pdfs/os4a.pdf. Accessed 24 Jul. 2019.

Boydell, Katherine M. "Narratives of Identity: Re-Presentation of Self in People Who Are Homeless." *Qualitative Health Research*, vol. 10, no. 1, Jan. 2020, pp. 26–38.

Brash, Jimmy. Personal interview. 18 Oct. 2018.

Brennan, Dave. "Dying Destitute in the United States." *Funeral and Cemetery Law Blog*, 2 Apr. 2014, https://www.deathcarestudies.com/2014/04/dying-destitute-in-the-united-states/.

Brenoff, Ann. "When Loved Ones Die at Home, Family Caregivers Pay the Price." *Huffington Post*, 1 Jun. 2017, https://www.huffingtonpost.co.uk/entry/dying-at-home-family-caregivers_us_592738e6e4b0df34c35ab57f.

Briere, Tiffany. "Vision." *The Best American Essays 2015*, edited by Ariel Levy, Houghton Mifflin Harcourt, 2015, pp. 45–55.

Brody, Jane E. "The Surprising Effects of Loneliness on Health." *New York Times*, 11 Dec. 2017, https://www.nytimes.com/2017/12/11/well/mind/how-loneliness-affects-our-health.html?_r=0.

Brooks Olsen, Hanna. "Homelessness and the Impossibility of a Good Night's Sleep." *Atlantic*, 14 Aug. 2014, https://www.theatlantic.com/health/archive/2014/08/homelessness-and-the-impossibility-of-a-good-nights-sleep/375671/.

Brothers Grimm. *The Complete First Edition: The Original Fairy Tales of the Brothers Grimm*. Translated and edited by Jack Zipes, Princeton UP, 2014.

Brown, Rebecca T., et al. "Geriatric Syndromes in Older Homeless Adults." *J Gen Internal Medicine*, vol. 27, no. 1, 31 Aug. 2011, pp. 16–22, https://doi.org/10.1007/s11606-011-1848-9.

Brydon Court. Personal interview. 13 Feb. 2019.

Buchan, Lizzy. "Homeless People with Terminal Illnesses Could Be Offered Automatic Right to Housing." *Independent*, 5 Feb. 2018, https://www.independent.co.uk/news/uk/politics/homeless-illness-terminal-housing-right-parliament-ed-davey-liberal-democrats-a8191391.html.

Buhl, Larry. "In California, Helping the Homeless to Make Their Medical Preferences Clear." *Undark Magazine,* 19 Mar. 2018, https://www.undark.org/article/homeless-advance-care-directives/.

Buscaglia, Leo. *The Fall of Freddie the Leaf.* Slack, 1982.

Butler, Judith. "Precariousness and Grievability—When Is Life Grievable?" *Verso Books,* 16 Nov. 2015, https://www.versobooks.com/blogs/2339-judith-butler-precariousness-and-grievability-when-is-life-grievable.

"CA Health & Safety Code § 7054.7." *Justia,* https://www.law.justia.com/codes/california/2011/hsc/division-7/7050.5-7055/7054.7/. Accessed 25 Jul. 2020.

Cagle, John G. "Weathering the Storm: Palliative Care and Elderly Homeless Persons." *Journal of Housing for the Elderly,* vol. 23, 2009, pp. 29–46, https://doi.org/10.1080/02763890802664588.

Calix, Brianna. "How Many People Are Homeless in Fresno and Madera? A Tally Happens This Week." *Fresno Bee,* 23 Jan. 2018, https://www.fresnobee.com/news/local/article196063594.html.

———. "'We Have to Do Better.' Will Fresno Finally Get a New Homeless Shelter?" *Fresno Bee,* 21 Sep. 2018, https://www.fresnobee.com/latest-news/article218794730.html.

"Callahan v. Carey, No. 79-42582 (Sup. Ct. N.Y. County, Cot. 18, 1979)." *ESRC-Net,* https://www.escr-net.org/caselaw/2006/callahan-v-carey-no-79-42582-sup-ct-ny-county-cot-18-1979. Accessed 25 Jul. 2020.

Cameron, Ailsa, et al. "From Pillar to Post: Homeless Women's Experiences of Social Care." *Health and Social Care in the Community,* vol. 23, no. 3, 2016, pp. 345–352, https://doi.org/10.1111/hsc.12211.

Care Quality Commission. *A Different Ending: Addressing Inequalities in End of Life Care.* Care Quality Commission, 2016.

Care Quality Commission. *A Second Class Ending: Exploring the Barriers and Championing Outstanding End of Life Care for People Who Are Homeless.* Care Quality Commission, 2017.

Carino, Jerry. "Forgotten Marlboro Graveyard Recalls Psychiatric Hospital's Grim Past." *app.com,* 16 Apr. 2018, https://www.app.com/story/news/history/2018/04/16/marlboro-psychiatric-hospital-cemetery/505785002/.

Carlson, Lisa. *I Died Laughing: Funeral Education with a Light Touch.* Upper Access, 2010.

Carlson, Lisa, and Joshua Slocum. *Final Rights: Reclaiming the American Way of Death.* Upper Access, 2011.

Carter, Kate. Personal interview. 15 May 2017.

Castle, Lauren. "Who Cares for the Homeless When They Die on Phoenix Streets?" *Arizona Republic,* 18 Sep. 2018, https://www.azcentral.com/story/news/local/

phoenix/2018/09/18/arizona-homeless-die-phoenix-streets-heat-white-tanks
-cemetery-buried/830454002/.

Caswell, Glenys, and Morna O'Connor. "Agency in the Context of Social Death:
Dying Alone at Home." *Contemporary Social Science*, vol. 10, no. 3, 2015,
pp. 249–261.

———. "'I've No Fear of Dying Alone': Exploring Perspectives on Living and Dying
Alone." *Mortality*, vol. 24, no. 1, 2019, pp. 17–31.

Cemetery and Funeral Bureau. https://www.cfb.ca.gov/about_us/index.shtml.
Accessed 25 Jul. 2020.

A Certain Kind of Death. Directed by Grover Babcock and Blue Hadaegh, New Box
Media, 2003.

Cervantes, Racquel. "Blighted, Vacant Homes 'Magnets' for Fires." *Your Central Valley*, Jul. 2017, https://www.yourcentralvalley.com/news/local-news/blighted
-vacant-homes-magnets-for-fires/128978033.

Charlesworth, Lorraine. Personal interview. 18 Oct. 2018.

Chasan, Paula. "Embalming: In History and Today." *Funeral Consumers Alliance of
Eastern Massachusetts Annual Newsletter*, Mar. 2018.

Choi, Chris. "ITV News Investigation Finds 70% Rise in 'Paupers' Funerals'—with
Some Councils Preventing Relatives from Attending." *ITV News*, 15 Jun. 2018,
https://www.itv.com/news/2018-06-15/itv-news-investigation-finds-70-rise-in
-paupers-funerals/.

"City of Angels." *Dateline*. NBC, 19 Aug. 2018.

Clark, David, et al. "Interventions at the End of Life—a Taxonomy for 'Overlap-
ping Consensus.'" *Wellcome Open Research*, vol. 2, no. 7, 2017, https://doi.org/10
.12688/wellcomeopenres.10722.1.

Clayton, Alex, and Andrew Klevan, editors. *The Language and Style of Film Critics.*
Routledge, 2011.

Clemson, Sue. Personal interview. 18 Oct. 2018.

Coalition for the Homeless. *The Callahan Consent Decree: Establishing a Legal
Right to Shelter for Homeless Individuals in New York City*, 2014, https://
www.coalitionforthehomeless.org/wp-content/uploads/2014/06/Callahan
ConsentDecree.pdf.

Coalition on Homelessness. *Punishing the Poorest: How the Criminalization of Homelessness Perpetuates Poverty in San Francisco.* Coalition on Homelessness, 18 Jun.
2015, https://www.cohsf.org/Punishing.pdf.

Cochrane, Kira. "Bucket Lists: Are They a Good Idea?" *Guardian*, 26 Sep. 2012,
https://www.theguardian.com/lifeandstyle/2012/sep/26/bucket-lists-are-they
-good-idea.

Colclough, Alison. Personal interview. 15 Feb. 2019.

Cole, Elaine. "Ensuring Dignity in Death." *Nursing Standard,* vol. 32, no. 1, 30 Aug. 2017, https://doi.org/10.7748/ns.32.1.18.s22.

Collier, Roger. "Bringing Palliative Care to the Homeless." *Canadian Medical Association Journal,* vol. 183, no. 6, 5 Apr. 2011, pp. E317–E318.

Collins, Lois. "The Place Where No One Dies Alone." *Deseret News,* 19 Sep. 2023, https://www.deseret.com/2023/9/19/23217478/homeless-streets-dying-hospice-not-alone-inn-between-utah/.

Combs, Scott C. *Deathwatch: American Film Technology and the End of Life.* Columbia UP, 2014.

Conan, Neil. "Bedside Manner: Conversations with Patients About Death." *NPR,* 6 May 2013, https://www.npr.org/2013/05/06/181636287/bedside-manner-conversations-with-patients-about-death.

Conniff, Richard. "This Is How I Want to Be Dead." *New York Times,* 1 Jul. 2017.

"Consider It." *Vox Media,* https://studios.voxmedia.com/show/consider-it.html.

Cook, Aimee. "Exhibition: Dancing with Death." *Special Collections, University of Glasgow Library,* 2009, https://www.gla.ac.uk/myglasgow/library/files/special/exhibns/death/deathhome.html.

Cooper, Jason, and Jay Armitage. *The Unclaimed: How to Die on the Streets of LA.* Directed by Jason Cooper & Jay Armitage, King Toledo Entertainment, 2023. *YouTube,* uploaded by King Toledo Entertainment, 14 Dec. 2023. https://www.youtube.com/watch?v=zyfLieekOSo.

Copner, James. Personal interview. 15 Jul. 2016.

Coroner/Public Administrator. *Fresno County Sheriff's Office.* https://www.fresnosheriff.org/coroner.html.

Cortez, Delia. Personal interview. 11 Sep. 2018.

"Costs of Care." *US Department of Health and Human Services,* https://acl.gov/ltc/costs-and-who-pays/costs-of-care. Accessed 25 Apr. 2018.

"County of Los Angeles Register of Cremations 2012." *County of Los Angeles,* https://file.lacounty.gov/SDSInter/dhs/239924_CremationLog.pdf. Accessed 18 Nov. 2019.

Courtenay, Tamsen. "Dead Dogs Are Treated Better Than Dead Homeless People. It's a Disgrace." *Guardian,* 11 Oct. 2018, https://www.theguardian.com/commentisfree/2018/oct/11/dead-dogs-treated-dead-homeless-people-government-count?CMP=Share_iOSApp_Other.

———. *Four Feet Under: Thirty Untold Stories of Homelessness in London.* Unbound, 2018.

Cousins, Mark. *The Story of Film.* Pavilion, 2004.

Crawford, Sybil F. *AGS Field Guide No. 3: Guide to Forming a "Cemetery Friends" Organization.* Association of Gravestone Studies, 2003.

"Cremation Services Los Angeles, CA." *Tulip*, https://www.tulipcremation.com/service-areas/service-area/california/los-angeles-ca.html. Accessed 18 Nov. 2019.

"Criminalization." *National Coalition for the Homeless*, https://www.national homeless.org/issues/civil-rights/. Accessed 27 Feb. 2020.

Culhane, Dennis, and Randall Kuhn. "Patterns and Determinants of Public Shelter Utilization Among Homeless Adults in New York City and Philadelphia." *Journal of Policy Analysis and Management*, vol. 17, no. 1, 1998, pp. 23–43.

Cullen, Kevin. "Giving a Veteran a Much-Deserved Sendoff." *Boston Globe*, 6 Feb. 2016, https://www.bostonglobe.com/news/nation/2016/02/06/making-sure -their-service-their-country-not-forgotten/ucoEBWSiFpGEVRtMTygy6N/ story.html.

Cummins, Eleanor. "Why Millennials Are the 'Death Positive' Generation." *Vox*, 22 Jan. 2020, https://www.vox.com/the-highlight/2020/1/15/21059189/ death-millennials-funeral-planning-cremation-green-positive?fbclid=IwAR 2Ip2MrTVRHqB-niEci2CQ_pAsnWwGu5hnoTRMPx3pAmOXbwUK IrtbdQrQ.

Currid-Halkett, Elizabeth. *The Sum of Small Things: A Theory of the Aspirational Classes*. Princeton UP, 2017.

Dale, Mariana. "End-of-Life Care Is a New Beginning for Some Homeless Patients." *KJZZ*, 24 Jan. 2018, https://www.kjzz.org/content/597185/end-life-care-new -beginning-some-homeless-patients.

Daniel, Seth. "South End Burial Ground: Thousands of Unknown, Untold Stories." *Boston Sun*, 10 Aug. 2017, https://www.thebostonsun.com/2017/08/10/south -end-burial-groundthousands-of-unknown-untold-stories/.

Dart, Herman. *Gods of Death: An Encyclopedia of Death Deities*. CreateSpace, 2016.

"Dave." Personal interview. Mar. 2019.

Davey, Edward. *Early Day Motion 353: Homelessness and End of Life Care*. Session: 2017–2019, 10 Oct. 2017.

Davis, Jason R. Personal interview. 23 Jul. 2024.

Davis-Berman, Jennifer. "Contributing Cause of Death: Poverty." *Journal of Social Work in End-of-Life and Palliative Care*, vol. 9, no. 2, 2013, pp. 244–46.

Dawes, Glen S. Personal interview. 23 Jul. 2024.

de Chesnay, Mary, et al. *Caring for the Vulnerable: Perspectives in Nursing Theory, Practice and Research*. Jones and Bartlett Learning, 2016.

"Death Cafe—Map of Obit Words." *Pallimed*, 18 Sep. 2017, https://www.pallimed .org/.

Death Rookie. "The Politics of Death and Dying: A Challenge to the Death Posi-tive Movement." *Death Rookie*, 26 Sep. 2016, https://www.deathrookie.com/ 2016/09/26/the-politics-of-death-and-dying-a-challenge-to-the-death-positive -movement/. Accessed 8 Oct. 2016.

"Deaths and Death Rates: Los Angeles County." *Los Angeles Almanac*, https://www
.laalmanac.com/vitals/vi11.php#years. Accessed 18 Nov. 2019.

Deith, Jane. "Dying on the Streets." *File on 4*. BBC Radio 4, 18 Feb. 2018, https://
www.bbc.co.uk/programmes/b09r4qdr.

Demers, Phil. "Abandoned Bodies: Massachusetts' Poor and Unwanted Are Spending Months Waiting for Burial." *MassLive*, 1 Feb. 2018, https://www.masslive.com/
news/index.ssf/2018/02/when_poor_people_die_who_buries_them.html.

"Department of Transitional Assistance." *Commonwealth of Massachusetts*, https://
www.mass.gov/eohhs/gov/departments/dta/. Accessed 5 Dec. 2019.

Desjarlais, Robert. *Shelter Blues: Sanity and Selfhood Among the Homeless*. U of Penn-
sylvania P, 1997.

DiAngelo, Robin. *White Fragility: Why It's So Hard for White People to Talk About
Racism*. Beacon Press, 26 Jun. 2018.

"Dining with the Dead." *The Food Chain*. BBC World Service, 31 Oct. 2016, https://
www.bbc.co.uk/programmes/p04cscdc.

Diski, Jenny. *In Gratitude*. Bloomsbury, 2016.

Dlouhy, Jennifer A. "Trump Administration Proposes Restrictions to Protests in
D.C. Public Spaces." *Boston Globe*, 12 Oct. 2018, https://www.bostonglobe.com/
news/nation/2018/10/12/trump-administration-proposes-restrictions-protests
-public-spaces/X2pYpMBy9cMgXbXk7bTaoH/story.html.

Dobbins, Julia. Personal interview. 15 Apr. 2018.

Doughty, Caitlin. *Ask a Mortician* [channel]. *YouTube*, https://www.youtube.com/
channel/UCi5iiEyLwSLvlqnMio2u5gQ. Accessed 17 Jan. 2018.

———. *From Here to Eternity: Traveling the World to Find the Good Death*. W. W.
Norton, 2017.

———. *Smoke Gets in Your Eyes: And Other Lessons from the Crematory*. W. W. Norton, 2015.

———. *Will My Cat Eat My Eyeballs? Big Questions from Tiny Mortals About Death*.
W. W. Norton, 2019.

Dreams of a Life. Directed by Carol Morley, Channel Four Television / The British
Film Institute, 2011.

Edge of Life. Performance by Louis Theroux, Documentary Heaven, 2014, https://
www.documentaryheaven.com/edge-life/.

Ehrenreich, Barbara. *Natural Causes: An Epidemic of Wellness, the Certainty of Dying,
and Killing Ourselves to Live Longer*. Twelve, 2019.

———. *Smile or Die: How Positive Thinking Fooled America and the World*. Granta,
2010.

"Eighth Amendment: Excessive Fines, Cruel and Unusual Punishment." *National
Constitution Center*, https://www.constitutioncenter.org/interactive-constitution/
amendment/amendment-viii. Accessed 15 Jan. 2020.

End Game. Directed by Rob Epstein and Jeffrey Friedman, Netflix, 2018.

Entzel, Lila. Personal interview. 23 Jul. 2024.

Epstein, Eve. "Potter's Fields Still Serve Nameless Poor." *Los Angeles Times*, 17 Jan. 1993, https://www.latimes.com/archives/la-xpm-1993-01-17-mn-2075-story.html.

Extremis. Directed by Dan Krauss, performance by Jessica Zitter, Netflix, 2016.

"Faces of Death." *National Geographic Explorer Documentary*. National Geographic, 3 Apr. 2016, https://www.documentarytube.com/videos/national-geographic-explorer-documentary-faces-of-death-bbc-documentary.

Farragher, Thomas. "In Death, Roxbury Latin Students Get a Lesson in Life." *Boston Globe*, 5 Jan. 2016, https://www.bostonglobe.com/metro/2016/01/05/lesson-life-for-roxbury-latin-students-comes-cemetery-for-indigent/2cTeyl3cTYpGVMZi6iKEaL/story.html.

Fazey-Koven, Gian. *A Model to Support End of Life Care for the Homeless—Year 2 Evaluation Report*. St. Luke's Hospice, 2018.

Featherly, Jessica. *I Will Die: A Creative Journal for Mortals*. Deep Down Press, 2016.

Federici, Silvia. *Caliban and the Witch: Women, the Body, and Primitive Accumulation*. Autonomedia, 2017.

Feldman, Ilana. "Humanitarian Care and the Ends of Life: The Politics of Aging and Dying in a Palestinian Refugee Camp." *Cultural Anthropology*, vol. 32, no. 1, 2 Feb. 2017, pp. 42–67, https://doi.org/10.14506/ca32.1.06.

Fenwick, Peter, and Elizabeth Fenwick. *The Art of Dying: A Journey of Elsewhere*. Continuum, 2008.

Flynn, Nick. *Another Bullshit Night in Suck City*. W. W. Norton, 2004.

"Foot." *Bible Study Tools*, https://www.biblestudytools.com/dictionary/foot/. Accessed 25 Feb. 2019.

Ford, Matt. "America's Largest Mental Hospital Is a Jail." *Atlantic*, 8 Jun. 2015, https://www.theatlantic.com/politics/archive/2015/06/americas-largest-mental-hospital-is-a-jail/395012/.

Foucault, Michel. *The Birth of the Clinic*. Vintage, 1974.

Francis, Doris, et al. *The Secret Cemetery*. Berg, 2005.

Funeral Consumers Alliance. https://www.funerals.org/about/. Accessed 25 Jan. 2020.

Funeral Ethics Organization. https://www.funeralethics.org. Accessed 25 Feb. 2019.

Gaeta, Jessie, et al. "Providing a Safe Space and Medical Monitoring to Prevent Overdose Deaths." *Health Affairs*, 31 Aug. 2016, https://www.healthaffairs.org/content/forefront/providing-safe-space-and-medical-monitoring-prevent-overdose-deaths.

Galvin, Gaby. "'Patient Dumping' Still a Problem Despite Law." *U.S. News and World Report*, 1 Apr. 2019, https://www.usnews.com/news/health-news/articles/2019-04-01/patient-dumping-still-a-problem-despite-federal-law.

Gammon, Katharine. "The Future of Death Is Greener—and a Bit Creepy." *NBC News*, 27 Dec. 2016, https://www.nbcnews.com/mach/environment/future -death-will-be-lot-greener-bit-creepy-n699261.

Gavin, Christopher. "Homeless People Slept Under This Route 2 Bridge. Then Spikes Were Installed Where They Once Rested." *Boston.com*, 3 Jan. 2019, https://www.boston.com/news/local-news/2019/01/03/arlington-cambridge -homeless-camp-route-2-bridge-spikes.

Gee, Alistair. "At Night on Skid Row, Nearly 2,000 Homeless People Share Just Nine Toilets." *Guardian*, 30 Jun. 2017, https://www.theguardian.com/us-news/2017/ jun/30/la-skid-row-homeless-toilet-access-report.

———. "Death in an Amazon Dumpster." *Guardian*, 28 Dec. 2017, https://www .theguardian.com/us-news/2017/dec/28/amazon-dumpster-death-homeless -man-frank-ryan.

George, Carmen. "Her Ashes Were Almost Buried in a Mass Grave. Hundreds Will Be Unless Claimed Soon." *Fresno Bee*, 6 Sep. 2018, https://www.fresnobee.com/ news/local/article217489065.html.

"Getting Medicine to Homeless People on the Streets of Edinburgh." *BBC Scotland*, 14 Dec. 2018, https://www.bbc.com/news/av/uk-scotland-46573082/getting -medicine-to-homeless-people-on-the-streets-of-edinburgh.

Gilbert, Sandra M. *Death's Door: Modern Dying and the Ways We Grieve*. W. W. Norton, 2006.

Gladstone, William. *AZ Quotes*, https://www.azquotes.com/quote/934227. Accessed 23 Apr. 2025.

Gladwell, Malcolm. "Million-Dollar Murray." *New Yorker*, vol. 81, no. 46, 2006, p. 96.

Gonzales, Vicki. "Dying with Respect: Sacramento Doctor Starts Homeless Hospice." *KCRA*, 21 Dec. 2017, https://www.kcra.com/article/dying-with-respect -sacramento-doctor-starts-homeless-hospice/14430038.

Goodwin, Karen. "The Glasgow Effect: 'We Die Young Here—but You Just Get on with It.'" *Guardian*, 10 Jun. 2016, https://www.theguardian.com/cities/2016/ jun/10/glasgow-effect-die-young-high-risk-premature-death.

———. "Revealed: 'Glasgow Effect' Mortality Rate Blamed on Westminster Social Engineering." *The Herald*, 15 May 2016, https://www.heraldscotland.com/ news/14493634.Revealed___Glasgow_effect__mortality_rate_blamed_on _Westminster_social_engineering/?ref=fbshr.

Gorer, Geoffrey. "The Pornography of Death." *Encounter*, Oct. 1955, pp. 49–52. *Unz Review*, 2003, https://www.unz.com/print/Encounter-1955oct-00049/.

Goulding, Tom. "What Happens When You Die Alone?" *Vice UK*, 8 Dec. 2016, https://www.vice.com/en_uk/article/4xw4jd/chto-proishodit-kogda-vy-umir aete-v-odinochestve.

Grabar, Henry. "The Alarming Rise in Homelessness Doesn't Tell the Whole Story."
   Slate, 8 Dec. 2017, https://www.slate.com/business/2017/12/a-dramatic-increase
   -in-homelessness-in-los-angeles-accounts-for-the-first-national-increase-in
   -nearly-a-decadeif-you-believe-the-numbers.html.

"Green Burial in Massachusetts: Frequently Asked Questions." *Green Burial Massachusetts*, https://greenburialma.org/resources/faq/#:~:text=Is%20Green%20Burial
   %20an%20Option,your%20local%20board%20of%20health. Accessed 25 Jul.
   2020.

Greenfield, Patrick, et al. "At Least 440 Homeless People Died in UK in Past Year,
   Study Shows." *Guardian*, 8 Oct. 2018, https://amp.theguardian.com/society/
   2018/oct/08/homeless-people-die-uk-2017.

Greenhalgh, Stephen. Personal interview. 18 Oct. 2018.

Greenier, Amanda. *Late-Life Homelessness: Experiences of Disadvantage and Unequal
   Aging*. McGill-Queen's UP, 2021.

Griffin, Gabriele, editor. *Research Methods for English Studies*, 2nd ed. Edinburgh UP,
   2013.

Gutkind, Lee, et al. *Twelve Breaths a Minute: End of Life Essays*. Southern Methodist
   UP, 2005.

Guwande, Atul. *Being Mortal: Medicine and What Matters in the End*. Metropolitan,
   2014.

Habegger, Becca. "Homeless Hospice Planned near South Natomas School." *ABC
   10*, 27 Jun. 2023, https://www.abc10.com/article/news/local/homeless-hospice
   -planned-south-natomas/103-bac1e3f3-d44c-4cd0-aecf-251b498e49d4.

Halperin, Edward C. "The Poor, the Black, and the Marginalized as the Source of
   Cadavers in United States Anatomical Education." *Clinical Anatomy*, vol. 20,
   no. 5, 2007, pp. 489–495.

Hanley, Ryan. "How Much Does a Night in the Hospital Cost?" *Trusted Choice*,
   17 Dec. 2013, https://www.trustedchoice.com/insurance-articles/life-health/
   cost-night-hospital/.

Hanson, Melissa. "Who Buries Massachusetts' Poor? State Pays So Little Only a
   Couple of Funeral Homes Will Take Them." *MassLive*, 2 Feb. 2018, https://www
   .masslive.com/news/index.ssf/2018/02/can_you_have_a_funeral_for_jus
   .html.

Hatry, Heide. *Icons in Ash*. Station Hill Press, 2017.

He, Sophie. "What Wong Kar-Wai's Films Meant to Young Asians in America." *Cat-
   apult*, 7 Nov. 2018, https://www.catapult.co/stories/wong-kar-wai-film-asians
   -america-sophie-he.

"A Healing and Meditative Landscape." *Sweet Auburn: Magazine of the Friends of
   Mount Auburn*, vol. 1, 2018.

Health Care for the Homeless Clinicians' Network. *Adapting Your Practice: Recommendations for End-of-Life Care for People Experiencing Homelessness.* Health Care for the Homeless Clinicians' Network, 2018.

Helme, Laura. Personal interview. 20 Feb. 2019.

Hemley, Robin. "Field Notes for the Graveyard Enthusiast." *The Inevitable: Contemporary Writers Confront Death,* edited by Bradford Morrow and David Shields, W. W. Norton, 2011, pp. 195–207.

Herring, Chris. "Complaint-Oriented Policing: Regulating Homelessness in Public Space." *American Sociological Review,* vol. 84, no. 5, 2019, pp. 769–800.

Hewett, Nigel, et al. "A General Practitioner and Nurse Led Approach to Improving Hospital Care for Homeless People." *British Medical Journal,* vol. 28, 2012, https://doi.org/10.1136/bmj.e5999.

Hirst, Victoria. "An Exploration of Homeless Patients' Experience of General Practice in an Outreach Setting." *Homelessness and Inclusion Health,* 29 Mar. 2018, https://www.homelessnessandhealth.co.uk/events/2018/dr-victoria-hirst/.

"The History." *The Hart Island Project,* https://www.hartisland.net/history. Accessed 5 Dec. 2019.

Ho, Vivian. "Blocked Sidewalks: How Boulders Became a Flashpoint in San Francisco's Homeless Crisis." *Guardian,* 3 Oct. 2019, https://www.theguardian.com/us-news/2019/oct/02/san-francisco-boulder-homeless-crisis.

Hodge, James G., et al. "Homelessness and the Public's Health: Legal Responses." *Journal of Law, Medicine and Ethics,* vol. 45, no. 1, 2017, pp. 28–32.

Hollars, B. J. "The Girl in the Surf: Exploitation vs. Documentation." *Creative Nonfiction,* vol. 44, 2012, https://www.creativenonfiction.org/online-reading/girl-surf.

Holm, Adam. Personal interview. 23 Jul. 2024.

Holowatyj, Andreana N., et al. "The Epidemiology of Cancer Among Homeless Adults in Metropolitan Detroit." *JNCI Cancer Spectrum,* Mar. 2019, https://doi.org/10.1093/jncics/pkz006.

Home Less Home. Produced by Bill Brand, edited by Joanna Kiernan, BB Optics, 1990.

"Horsetail." *RHS Gardening,* https://www.rhs.org.uk/advice/profile?PID=257. Accessed 25 Jul. 2020.

Horvath, Mark. "Let's Talk About Homeless People, a.k.a. 'People Experiencing Homelessness.'" *Invisible People,* 15 Feb. 2019, https://invisiblepeople.tv/saying-people-experiencing-homelessness-will-not-influence-change/.

"Housing Solutions for People Experiencing Homelessness." *Healing Hands,* vol. 22, no. 2. National Health Care for the Homeless Council, 2018, https://www.nhchc.org/wp-content/uploads/2019/08/healing-hands-housing-solutions-for-people-experiencing-homelessness.pdf.

Hoy, William G. *Do Funerals Matter? The Purposes and Practices of Death Rituals in Global Perspective.* Routledge, 2013.

Hudson, Briony F., et al. "Challenges to Access and Provision of Palliative Care for People Who Are Homeless: A Systematic Review of Qualitative Research." *BMC Palliative Care*, vol. 15, no. 1, 2016, pp. 1–18.

Hulkower, Raphael. "From Sacrilege to Privilege: The Tale of Body Procurement for Anatomical Dissection in the United States." *Einstein Journal of Biology and Medicine*, vol. 27, no. 1, 2011, pp. 23–26.

Hunt, Chris. "Life Lessons." *Real Simple*, Sep. 2016, https://www.realsimple.com.

Hutt, Evelyn, et al. "Addressing the Challenges of Palliative Care for Homeless Veterans." *American Journal of Hospice and Palliative Medicine*, vol. 35, no. 3, 2018, pp. 448–455.

"Information and Resources About Cancer: Breast, Colon, Lung, Prostate, Skin." *American Cancer Society*, https://www.cancer.org/. Accessed 25 Jul. 2020.

"The INN Between Provides Dignity in End-of-Life for Utah's Unhoused Community." *Sarah Lawrence College*, https://www.sarahlawrence.edu/health-advocacy/blog/the-inn-between-provides-dignity-in-end-of-life-for-utahs-unhoused-community.html. Accessed 10 Apr. 2024.

Innis, Michelle. "Affordable Underground Furniture: D.I.Y. Coffin Clubs Catch on in New Zealand." *New York Times*, 25 Feb. 2017, https://www.nyti.ms/2lH6SV4.

Irons, Meghan E. "Inmates Push Fund to Cover Funerals." *Boston Globe*, 17 Mar. 2012, https://www.bostonglobe.com/metro/2012/03/16/mci-norfolk-inmates-press-create-fund-help-families-pay-for-headstones/HsvYHopwDC5PjaMrwYvPDJ/story.html.

James, Stephanie. Personal interview. 19 Feb. 2019.

Jamison, Leslie. Introduction to *The Best American Essays 2017*, edited by Leslie Jamison, Houghton Mifflin Harcourt, 2017, pp. xvi–xxvi.

———. "Lost Boys." *The Empathy Exams: Essays*. Graywolf Press, 2014, pp. 161–184.

Janus, Andrea. "Woman Who Died Trapped in Toronto Donation Bin Lived Tough Life, Friends Say." *CBC News*, 8 Jan. 2019, https://www.cbc.ca/news/canada/toronto/woman-who-died-trapped-in-toronto-donation-bin-lived-tough-life-friends-say-1.4969545?fbclid=IwAR3QvkRnMggyM8lgrDVzbQZ5Dy9z1gWb6aPMB1L_uGDhX8_gjLh_FGiSqZY.

Jean, Melissa, et al. "Patient-Centered Care: Case Studies on End of Life." *Healing Hands*, National Health Care for the Homeless Council, vol. 22, no. 1, Winter 2018, https://nhchc.org/wp-content/uploads/2019/08/hh-end-of-life-care-final-2.pdf.

Jolicoeur, Lynn. "'I Finally Did It': Homeless for Years, Lenny Gets a Home." *WBUR Boston*, 16 Nov. 2017, https://www.wbur.org/news/2017/11/16/lenny-housed-boston.

Jong, Jonathan. "How Scared of Death Are We Really—and How Does That Affect Us?" *The Conversation,* 8 Feb. 2016, https://www.theconversation.com/how-scared -of-death-are-we-really-and-how-does-that-affect-us-54258.

Kalanithi, Paul. *When Breath Becomes Air.* Random House, 2016.

Kaplan-Weismann, Laura, et al. "Feasibility of Advance Care Planning in Primary Care for Homeless Adults." *Journal of Aging and Health,* pp. 1–23, https://doi .org/10.1177/0898264319862420.

Kassam, Ashifa. "Death of Canadian Man Living in 24-Hour Coffee Shop Sparks Housing Outcry." *Guardian,* 7 Jun. 2018, https://www.theguardian.com/world/ 2018/jun/07/canada-death-homeless-man-tim-hortons-vancouver.

Kellehear, Allan. "Dying Old—and Preferably Alone? Agency, Resistance and Dissent at the End of Life." *International Journal of Ageing and Later Life,* vol. 4, no. 1, 2009, pp. 5–21.

Kelly, Lynn. Personal interview. 18 Oct. 2018.

Kinkade, Lynda. "America's Poor Becoming More Destitute Under Trump, UN Report Says." *CNN,* 22 Jun. 2018, https://www.cnn.com/2018/06/22/us/ america-poverty-un-report/index.html.

Kleinfeld, N. R. "The Lonely Death of George Bell." *New York Times,* 18 Oct. 2015, https://www.nyti.ms/1jKA89f.

Klinenberg, Eric. "A Review of: 'A Certain Kind of Death.'" *Political Communication,* vol. 22, no. 3, 2006, pp. 417–418.

KMPH. "Resting in Weeds: Problems in Keeping Up Fresno Chinese Cemetery." *KMPH,* 10 Jul. 2012, https://www.kmph.com/archive/resting-in-weeds -problems-in-keeping-up-fresno-chinese-cemetery.

Ko, Eunjeong, and Holly Nelson-Becker. "Does End-of-Life Decision Making Matter? Perspectives of the Older Homeless Adults." *American Journal of Hospice and Palliative Medicine,* vol. 31, no. 2, 2013, pp. 183–188.

Ko, Eunjeong, et al. "What Constitutes a Good and Bad Death? Perspectives of Homeless Older Adults." *Death Studies,* vol. 39, no. 7, 2015, 422–432.

Kowalczyk, Liz. "A Double Diagnosis—Cancer While Poor." *Boston Globe,* 30 Dec. 2018, https://www.bostonglobe.com/metro/2018/12/29/double-diagnosis/6dl K3khlR6jrOBXpNIMiiI/story.html.

Kramer, Mark, and Wendy Call. *Telling True Stories: A Nonfiction Writer's Guide.* Plume, 2007.

Kubler-Ross, Elisabeth. *On Death and Dying: What the Dying Have to Teach Doctors, Nurses, Clergy, and Their Own Families.* Scribner, 2014.

Kushel, Margot. "How the Homeless Population Is Changing: It's Older and Sicker." *The Conversation,* 8 Jan. 2016, https://www.theconversation.com/how-the-home less-population-is-changing-its-older-and-sicker-50632.

Kusmer, Kenneth L. *Down and Out, on the Road: The Homeless in American History.* Oxford UP, 2002.

Labriola, Albert C. *The Mirror of Salvation [Speculum Humane Salvationis]: An Edition of British Library Blockbook G. 11784.* Translated by John W. Smeltz, Duquesne UP, 2002.

Larsen, Michael. Personal interview. 23 Jul. 2024.

Lawton, Julia. "Contemporary Hospice Care: The Sequestration of the Unbounded Body and 'Dirty Dying.'" *Sociology of Health and Illness,* vol. 20, no. 2, 1998, pp. 121–143.

Lea, Rachel. "'The Shitful Body': Excretion and control." *Medische Antropologie,* vol. 11, no. 1, 1999, pp. 7–18.

Lebrun-Harris, Lydie A., et al. "Health Status and Health Care Experiences Among Homeless Patients in Federally Supported Health Centers: Findings from the 2009 Patient Survey." *Health Research and Education Trust,* vol. 48, no. 3, 2013, pp. 992–1017.

LeDuff, Charlie. "What Killed Aiyana Stanley-Jones?" *The Best American Essays 2011,* edited by Edwidge Danticat, Houghton Mifflin Harcourt, 2011, pp. 107–125.

Lee, Barrett A., and Christopher J. Schreck. "Danger on the Streets: Marginality and Victimization Among Homeless People." *American Behavioral Scientist,* vol. 48, no. 8, Apr. 2015, https://doi.org/10.1177/0002764204274200.

Lee, Phuong. "Seattle Repeals Homeless-Aid Tax After Amazon Objects." *PBS Newshour,* 12 Jun. 2018, https://www.pbs.org/newshour/nation/seattle-backs-down-from-homeless-aid-tax-after-amazon-objects.

Legal Information Institute. "U.S. Constitution." *Cornell Law School,* https://www.law.cornell.edu/constitution. Accessed 5 Mar. 2020.

Leland, John. "The Positive Death Movement Comes to Life." *New York Times,* 22 Jun. 2018, https://www.nytimes.com/2018/06/22/nyregion/the-positive-death-movement-comes-to-life.html.

Levy, Jay S., and Robin Johnson, editors. *Cross-Cultural Dialogues on Homelessness: From Pretreatment Strategies to Psychologically Informed Environments.* Love Healing Press, 2017.

Lewer, Dan, et al. "Health-Related Quality of Life and Prevalence of Six Chronic Diseases in Homeless and Housed People: A Cross-Sectional Study in London and Birmingham, England." *British Medical Journal,* vol. 9, 2019.

Lichterman, Paul. "Interpretive Reflexivity in Ethnography." *Ethnography,* vol. 18, no. 1, 2017, pp. 35–45.

Lloyd, Larry. Personal interview. 23 Jul. 2024.

Lofland, Lyn H. *The Craft of Dying: The Modern Face of Death.* MIT Press, 2019.

The Long Goodbye. Commissioned by Good Life, Good Death, Good Grief. *YouTube,* uploaded by Rosetta Life, 19 Oct. 2012, https://www.youtube.com/watch?v=4x6_CBpJtPM.

Lopate, Phillip. *The Art of the Personal Essay*. Anchor, 1995.

Lopez, Steve. "He Handed Water to Homeless People When Temps Topped 100. Some Silver Lake Neighbors Jeered, Others Cheered." *Los Angeles Times*, 11 Jul. 2018, https://www.latimes.com/local/california/la-me-lopez-water-homeless -20180711-story.html.

Lynch, Michael. "Against Reflexivity as an Academic Virtue and Source of Privileged Knowledge." *Theory, Culture and Society*, vol. 17, no. 3, 2002, pp. 26–45.

Magnatta, Marisa. "Someone Made an Interactive San Francisco Poop Map." *WMMR*, 17 Apr. 2019, https://www.wmmr.com/2019/04/17/someone-made-an -interactive-san-francisco-poop-map/.

Mahdawi, Arwa. "So, Do You Come Here Often? An Evening at New York's Death Cafe." *Guardian*, 21 May 2016, https://www.theguardian.com/lifeandstyle/2016/ may/21/evening-at-new-york-death-cafe.

Malone, Scott. "Cold Comfort: U.S. Homeless Shelters Overwhelmed in Brutal Weather." *Reuters*, 5 Jan. 2018, https://www.reuters.com/article/us-usa-weather -homelessness-feature/cold-comfort-u-s-homeless-shelters-overwhelmed-in -brutal-weather-idUSKBN1EU1ZE.

Maloney, Emily. "Cost of Living." *The Best American Essays 2017*, edited by Leslie Jamison, Houghton Mifflin Harcourt, 2017, pp. 82–90.

Manning Peskin, Sara. "The Symptoms of Dying." *New York Times*, 20 Jun. 2017, https://www.nytimes.com/2017/06/20/well/live/the-symptoms-of-dying .html.

Manning-Cartwright, Sherri. Personal interview. 15 Jul. 2016.

Mannix, Kathryn. *With the End in Mind: How to Live and Die Well*. William Collins, 2017.

Marin Health and Human Services. "Fact Sheet: Deaths Uncounted: Using Local Data to Act on Unnecessary Tragedy." *NHCHC*, Oct. 2022.

Marsh, Sarah. "Death in Westminster: A 'Wake-Up Call' on Homelessness." *Guardian*, 20 Dec. 2018, https://www.theguardian.com/society/2018/dec/20/death-in -westminster-a-wake-up-call-on-homelessness.

Massey, Heather. "Direct Cremation Costs." *Funeral Consumers Alliance of Eastern Massachusetts Annual Newsletter*, Mar. 2018.

Masters, Alexander. *Stuart: A Life Backwards*. Harper Perennial, 2005.

Matlock, Kelly Anne. Personal interview. Jan. 2015.

McAspurren, Alex T. Personal interview. 27 Nov. 2018.

McCarthy, Todd. "A Certain Kind of Death." *Variety*, 18 Feb. 2003, https://www .variety.com/2003/film/reviews/a-certain-kind-of-death-1200543357/.

McClenaghan, Maeve, and Charles Boutaud. "Dying Homeless: Counting the Deaths of Homeless People Across the UK." *Bureau of Investigative Journalism*, 23 Apr. 2018, https://www.thebureauinvestigates.com/stories/2018-04-23/dying -homeless.

McCormick, Erin. "Big Brother on Wheels? Fired Security Robot Divides Local Homeless People." *Guardian*, 17 Dec. 2017, https://www.theguardian.com/us-news/2017/dec/16/san-francisco-homeless-robot.

McCormick-Cavanagh, Conor. "Rocky Mountain Refuge Providing Hospice Care for Homeless in Denver." *Westword*, 3 Mar. 2022, https://www.westword.com/news/rocky-mountain-refuge-providing-hospice-care-for-homeless-in-denver-13565955.

McManus, John. "The World Is Running Out of Burial Space." *BBC News*, 13 Mar. 2015, https://www.bbc.com/news/uk-31837964.

Meltzer, Marisa. "How Death Got Cool." *Guardian*, 12 Jan. 2018, https://www.theguardian.com/news/2018/jan/12/how-death-got-cool-swedish-death-cleaning?CMP=Share_iOSApp_Other.

Merriam-Webster. "Body, n. (2)." https://www.merriam-webster.com/dictionary/body. Accessed 12 May 2025.

Mettler, Suzanne. *The Submerged State: How Invisible Government Policies Undermine American Democracy*. U of Chicago P, 2011.

Meyer, Jeannette. Personal interview. 11 Sep. 2018; 16 Jul. 2024.

Mieremet, Kellie. Personal interview. 23 Jul. 2024.

Miles, Lizzy. "Do Hospice Patients Reveal the Secrets to the Universe?" *Pallimed*, 5 Sep. 2016, https://www.pallimed.org/2016/09/do-hospice-patients-reveal-secrets-to.html.

———. "FAQ for New Hospice Volunteers: 15 Simple Questions You're Afraid to Ask." *Pallimed*, 16 Nov. 2016, https://www.pallimed.org/2016/11/faq-for-new-hospice-volunteers-15.html?m=1.

Miller, Thaddeus. "Fresno Agrees to Pilot Plan That Employs Homeless People. Here's What It Looks Like." *Fresno Bee*, 30 Jan. 2020, https://www.fresnobee.com/news/local/article239815873.html.

Mills, Stu. "Smiths Falls, Ont., Funeral Business Dissolves the Dead, Pours Them into Town Sewers." *CBC News*, 20 Jun. 2016, https://www.cbc.ca/news/canada/ottawa/bodies-dissolved-sewers-smiths-falls-funeral-1.3635063.

Mitchel, Susan. "Notes Toward a History of Scaffolding." *The Next American Essay*, edited by John D'Agata, Graywolf Press, 2003, pp. 231–250.

Mitchell, Don. "The Annihilation of Space by Law: The Roots and Implications of Anti-Homelessness Laws in the United States." *Antipode*, vol. 29, no. 3, 1997, pp. 303–335.

Mitford, Jessica. *The American Way of Death*. Simon and Schuster, 1963.

Mohdin, Aamna. "'I'm Exhausted': Life in England's Homelessness Hotspot." *Guardian*, 26 Nov. 2018, https://www.theguardian.com/society/2018/nov/26/homeless-hotspot-newham-east-london-rough-sleeping.

Moller, David W. *Dancing with Broken Bones: Poverty, Race, and Spirit-Filled Dying in the Inner City*. Oxford UP, 2012.

Morales, Mark, et al. "New York May Bury Unclaimed Coronavirus Victims on Hart Island, but Mayor Says 'No Mass Burials.'" *CNN*, 10 Apr. 2020, https://www.cnn .com/2020/04/10/us/new-york-hart-island-burials/index.html.

Morrison, Blake. "Natural Causes by Barbara Ehrenreich Review—Against Health Sages and Fitness Gurus." *Guardian*, 12 Apr. 2018, https://www.theguardian .com/books/2018/apr/12/natural-causes-by-barbara-ehrenreich-review.

Moss, Josh. "Remembering the Forgotten." *Louisville Magazine*, 24 May 2011, https://archive.louisville.com/content/remembering-forgotten-louisville -magazine.

Mossburg, Cheri. "Deaths Among Homeless People in Los Angeles Have Doubled Since 2013, Report Says." *CNN*, 29 Oct. 2019, https://www.cnn.com/2019/10/ 29/us/los-angeles-county-homeless-deaths/index.html.

Mount Auburn Cemetery. https://www.mountauburn.org/about/. Accessed 25 Jul. 2020.

Murray, Sarah. "Remains of the Day: Here Are the New Ways to Dispose of Your Body." *Observer*, 7 Jun. 2016, https://www.observer.com/2016/06/remains-of -the-day-the-burial-industry-breaks-new-ground/.

Musumeci, Natalie, and Reuven Fenton. "Vault Full of Skeletons Found Under Washington Square Park." *New York Post*, 5 Nov. 2015, https://www.nypost.com/ 2015/11/05/vault-full-of-skeletons-found-under-washington-square-park/.

Nathonson, Rick. "Endings and Renewals: Former Inmates Build Kosher Caskets." *AP News*, 9 Aug. 2017, https://apnews.com/general-news-231de182eco8 4228a4ba99cdeb8a076d.

National Alliance to End Homelessness. "Rapid Re-Housing Performance Benchmarks and Program Standards." *NAEH*, Mar. 2016, https://www.endhomeless ness.org/wp-content/uploads/2016/02/Performance-Benchmarks-and -Program-Standards.pdf.

National Coalition for the Homeless. *Tent Cities in America: A Pacific Coast Report.* National Coalition for the Homeless, 2010.

National Health Care for the Homeless Council. *The Hard, Cold Facts About the Deaths of Homeless People.* National Health Care for the Homeless Council, 2006.

National Law Center on Homelessness and Poverty. *Housing Not Handcuffs 2019: Ending the Criminalization of Homelessness in U.S. Cities.* National Law Center on Homelessness and Poverty, 2019.

Newsbeat. "Hungary Enforces 'Cruel' Ban on Rough Sleeping." *BBC News*, 15 Oct. 2018, https://www.bbc.com/news/newsbeat-45860488.

"Newsletter Archive." *Boston Health Care for the Homeless Program*, https://www .bhchp.org/news-events/news/newsletter-archive/. Accessed 28 Jan. 2018.

Nichols, Bill. *Introduction to Documentary*, 3rd ed. Indiana UP, 2017.

"Nosedive." *Black Mirror*, season 3, episode 1, Netflix, 21 Oct. 2016.

Notarnicola, Christopher. "Indigent Disposition." *The Best American Essays 2017*, edited by Leslie Jamison, Houghton Mifflin Harcourt, 2017, pp. 176–179.

Nuwer, Rachel. "What If We Knew When and How We Would Die?" *BBC Future*, 18 Jun. 2018, https://www.bbc.com/future/story/20180618-what-if-we-knew-when-we-were-going-to-die.

O'Connell, James J., editor. *The Health Care of Homeless Persons: A Manual of Communicable Diseases and Common Problems in Shelters and on the Streets*. BHCHP Press, 2004.

———. *Stories from the Shadows: Reflections of a Street Doctor*. BHCHP Press, 2015.

———. Personal interview. 18 Jun. 2018.

O'Connell, James J., et al. "The Boston Health Care for the Homeless Program: A Public Health Framework." *American Journal of Public Health*, vol. 100, no. 8, 2010, pp. 1400–1408.

O'Flaherty, Brendan. "Homelessness Research: A Guide for Economists (and Friends)." *Journal of Housing Economics*, vol. 44, 2019, 1–25.

Olivet, Jeff. Personal interview. 16 Feb. 2018.

Olivet, Jeff, and Marc Dones. "Homelessness Is a Symptom of Racism: Interview with Jeff Olivet and Marc Dones." *YouTube*, uploaded by Invisible People, 26 Sep. 2016, https://www.youtube.com/watch?v=GXHkFFeHP-0.

Oliviere, David, et al. *Death, Dying, and Social Differences*. Oxford UP, 2011.

Olmsted, Jillian. Personal interview. 23 Jul. 2024.

Omundson, Joe. "Stop Confusing Homeless and Houseless." *Medium*, 2 Sep. 2019, https://medium.com/ecofrugality/stop-confusing-homeless-and-houseless-39b055d29ea3.

"The Open Museum." *Glasgow Life*. https://www.glasgowlife.org.uk/museums/the-open-museum. Accessed 8 May 2025.

Order of the Good Death. https://www.orderofthegooddeath.com/about. Accessed 25 Jan. 2020.

Orenstein, Natalie. "Homeless? Unhoused? Unsheltered? Word Choice Matters When Reporting on Oaklanders Who Don't Have Permanent Housing." *Oaklandside*, 10 Nov. 2020, https://oaklandside.org/2020/11/10/homeless-unhoused-unsheltered-word-choice-matters-when-reporting-on-oaklanders-who-dont-have-permanent-housing/.

Orwell, George. "How the Poor Die." First published November 1946. *George Orwell's Library*, 29 Dec. 2019, https://www.orwell.ru/library/articles/Poor_Die/english/e_pdie.

Oxford Languages. "Body, n." https://languages.oup.com/google-dictionary-en/. Accessed 10 May 2025.

Padgett, Deborah K., et al. *Housing First: Ending Homelessness, Transforming Systems, and Changing Lives*. Oxford UP, 2015.

Page, Stacy A., et al. "Causes of Death Among an Urban Homeless Population Considered by the Medical Examiner." *Journal of Social Work in End-of-Life and Palliative Care*, vol. 8, no. 3, 2012, pp. 265–271, https://doi.org/10.1080/15524256.2012.708111.

Pate, Kim. Personal interview. 23 Jul. 2024.

Paulson-Ellis, Mary. *The Other Mrs. Walker*. Mantle, 2016.

———. Personal interview. 4 Jun. 2018.

———. "'Who Were His Pals, Where Did He Go'? Solving the Mysteries of Those Who Die Alone." *Guardian*, 27 Aug. 2016, https://www.theguardian.com/global/2016/aug/27/solving-mysteries-those-who-die-alone-mr-lobban.

Payne, Keith. "How Inequality Shortens Lifespan." *Literary Hub*, 5 May 2017, https://www.lithub.com/how-inequality-shortens-lifespans/.

Pegues, Jeff. "Man Captures Video of 'Patient Dumping' Outside Baltimore Hospital." *CBS Evening News*, 10 Jan. 2018, https://www.cbsnews.com/news/man-captures-video-of-patient-dumping-outside-baltimore-hospital/.

"Peripheral Neuropathy." *National Health Service*, https://www.nhs.uk/conditions/peripheral-neuropathy/. Accessed 25 Feb. 2019.

Peschek, Joseph G. "The Submerged State: How Invisible Government Policies Undermine American Democracy." *New Political Science*, vol. 35, no. 1, 2013, pp. 153–155.

Peterson, Kimberly. Personal interview. 23 Jul. 2024.

Petruik, Courtney R. "Social Work Practices in Palliative and End-of-Life Care for Persons Experiencing Homelessness: A Scoping Review." *Families in Society*, vol. 99, no. 4, 2018, pp. 317–328.

Phelps, Dennis. Personal interview. 23 Jul. 2024.

Pidd, Helen. "Council Proposes £1,000 Fines for Homeless People Sleeping in Tents." *Guardian*, 24 Nov. 2017, https://www.theguardian.com/society/2017/nov/24/council-proposes-1000-fines-for-homeless-sleeping-in-tents.

———. "'It's Not a Lifestyle Choice': Homelessness on the Streets of Manchester." *Guardian*, 10 Mar. 2016, https://www.theguardian.com/uk-news/2016/mar/10/homelessness-streets-manchester-outreach-rough-sleepers-housing.

Piehler, Jeffrey M. "Ashes to Ashes, but First a Nice Pine Box." *New York Times*, 1 Feb. 2014, https://www.nytimes.com/2014/02/02/opinion/sunday/ashes-to-ashes-but-first-a-nice-pine-box.html.

Pine Street Inn. https://www.pinestreetinn.org/about-us. Accessed 25 Feb. 2019.

Podymow, Tiina, et al. "Shelter-Based Palliative Care for the Homeless Terminally Ill." *Palliative Medicine*, vol. 20, no. 3, 2006, pp. 81–86.

Pogash, Carol. "Colma, Calif., Is a Town of 2.2 Square Miles, Most of It 6 Feet Deep." *New York Times*, 9 Dec. 2006, https://www.nytimes.com/2006/12/09/us/09cemetery.html.

Pogrund, Gabriel. "Nameless Babies in Pile 'Em High, Sell 'Em Cheap Grave." *Sunday Times*, 11 Mar. 2018, https://www.thetimes.co.uk/article/nameless-babies-in-pile-em-high-sell-em-cheap-grave-3mqpmoxs8.

Policy Advocacy Clinic. "California's New Vagrancy Laws: The Growing Enactment and Enforcement of Anti-Homeless Laws in the Golden State." Berkeley Law, University of California, Jun. 2016, https://considerthehomeless.org/pdf/CA_New_Vagrancy_Laws.pdf.

Pollefeys, Patrick. *La Mort Sans l'Art*, https://www.lamortdanslart.com/main.htm. Accessed 25 Jul. 2020.

Porter, Catherine. "At His Own Wake: Celebrating Life and the Gift of Death." *New York Times*, 25 May 2017, https://www.nytimes.com/2017/05/25/world/canada/euthanasia-bill-john-shields-death.html.

Porter, Max. *Grief Is the Thing with Feathers*. Graywolf Press, 2016.

Powell, John A., and Eloy Toppin Jr. "Health Equity and the Circle of Human Concern." *AMA Journal of Ethics*, vol. 23, no. 2, Feb. 2021, pp. 166–174.

The Potter's Field. Directed by: Edward Heavrin, produced by Gill Holland and Alex Koch. *YouTube*, uploaded by Edward Hearvin, 15 Feb. 2016, https://www.youtube.com/watch?v=pwN_rfOoIuA&t=27s.

"Principles of Harm Reduction." *Harm Reduction Coalition*, harmreduction.org/about-us/principles-of-harm-reduction/. Accessed 14 Nov. 2018.

"Public Health Funerals." *North Ayrshire Council*, https://www.maps-north-ayrshire.opendata.arcgis.com/datasets/public-health-funerals/data. Accessed 12 Nov. 2018.

"Quality. Access, Justice. Community." *National Health Care for the Homeless Council*, https://www.nhchc.org/. Accessed 24 Jul. 2020.

QualityWatch. "Hospital Bed Occupancy." *Nuffield Trust*, 22 Aug. 2020, https://www.nuffieldtrust.org.uk/resource/hospital-bed-occupancy.

"Racial Disparities in Homelessness in the United States." *National Alliance to End Homelessness*, 6 Jun. 2018, https://www.endhomelessness.org/resource/racial-disparities-homelessness-united-states/.

RainCity Housing. "Housing First: Principles into Practice—Animated Overview." *YouTube*, uploaded by Gwen Haworth, 15 Oct. 2014, https://www.youtube.com/watch?time_continue=6&v=pwdq2VWavtc&feature=emb_title.

Rankine, Claudia. *Citizen: An American Lyric*. Graywolf, 2014.

"Rescue. Restore. Empower." *Fresno Rescue Mission*, https://www.fresnomission.org/. Accessed 25 Jul. 2020.

Reslock, Debbie. "Coping with the Death of Old Friends and Siblings." *Next Avenue*, 21 Mar. 2017, https://www.lithub.com/how-inequality-shortens-lifespans/.

Rhoads, Loren. "Cemetery Travel: Your Take-Along Guide to Graves and Grave-yards Around the World." *Cemetery Travel*, https://www.cemeterytravel.com. Accessed 25 Feb. 2018.

———, editor. *Death's Garden*. Automatism Press, 1995.

———. *Wish You Were Here: Adventures in Cemetery Travel*. Western Legends Press, 2013.

Rhodes, Mike. "Fresno Homeless Moved into Toolsheds." *Central Valley*, 22 Nov. 2004, https://www.indybay.org/newsitems/2004/11/22/17067361.php.

"Richard." Personal interview. 10 Sep. 2018.

Richards, Naomi. "Old Age Rational Suicide." *Sociology Compass*, vol. 11, no. 3, 2017, doi.org/10.1111/soc4.12456.

Roach, Mary. *Stiff: The Curious Lives of Human Cadavers*. W. W. Norton, 2005.

Robert, Martin, and Laura Tradii. "Do We Deny Death? I. A Genealogy of Death Denial." *Mortality*, vol. 24, no. 5, 2017, pp. 247–260.

Robertson, Jennifer. "Reflexivity Redux: A Pithy Polemic on 'Positionality.'" *Anthropological Quarterly*, vol. 75, no. 4, 2002, pp. 785–792.

Rocha, Veronica. "Baby's Body Found in Bag of Concrete in Fresno Canal." *Los Angeles Times*, 16 May 2014, https://www.lithub.com/how-inequality-shortens-lifespans/.

Ronnie. Personal interview. 15 Aug. 2018.

Rosenbloom, Megan, and Caitlin Doughty. *Death Salon*, https://www.deathsalon.org/. Accessed 25 Jul. 2020.

Rylands, Harry W., and George Bullen. *The Ars Moriendi (Editio Princeps, Circa 1450): A Reproduction of the Copy in the British Museum*. Trieste, 2017.

Sacramento Regional Coalition to End Homelessness. *Sacramento County 2016 Homeless Deaths Report*. Sacramento Regional Coalition to End Homelessness, 2016.

———. *Sacramento County 2022 Mid-Year Homeless Deaths Report*. Sacramento Regional Coalition to End Homelessness, 2022, https://www.srceh.org/_files/ugd/ee52bb_bd3a0b861eb94511942020fc1f421543.pdf.

Sadler, Catharine. "Working with the Homeless." *Nursing Standard*, vol. 30, no. 21, 2016, pp. 64–65.

Sandoval, Melissa. Personal interview. 10 Sep. 2018.

Sandoval, Rebecca. Personal interview. 15 Aug. 2024.

Sarafian, Jack. Personal interview. 15 Jul. 2016.

Saunders, George. "Tent City, U.S.A." *GQ*, 15 Sep. 2009, https://www.gq.com/story/homeless-tent-city-george-saunders-fresno.

Scheper-Hughes, Nancy, and Margaret M. Lock. "The Mindful Body: A Prolegomenon to Future Work in Medical Anthropology." *Medical Anthropology Quarterly*, vol. 1, no. 1, Mar. 1987, pp. 6–41.

Schmalz, Timothy. *Homeless Jesus*. Sculpture. https://www.sculpturebytps.com/large-bronze-statues-and-sculptures/homeless-jesus/.

Schulman, Caroline, et al. "End-of-Life Care for Homeless People: A Qualitative Analysis Exploring the Challenges to Access and Provision of Palliative Care." *Palliative Medicine*, vol. 32, no. 1, 2018, pp. 36–45.

Seale, Clive. "Media Constructions of Dying Alone: A Form of 'Bad Death.'" *Social Science and Medicine*, vol. 58, no. 5, 2004, pp. 967–974.

Seale, Clive, and Sjaak van der Geest. "Good and Bad Death: Introduction." *Social Science and Medicine*, vol. 58, no. 5, 2004, pp. 883–885.

Seftel, Joshua. "The Many Sad Fates of Mr. Toledano." *New York Times*, 20 Sep. 2016, https://www.nytimes.com/video/opinion/100000004653100/the-many-sad-fates-of-mr-toledano.html?mcubz=0.

Selbin, Jeffrey, et al. "California's New Vagrancy Laws: The Growing Enactment and Enforcement of Anti-Homeless Laws in the Golden State." *UC Berkley School of Law*, 12 Feb. 2015, https://www.homelesshub.ca/resource/californias-new-vagrancy-laws-growing-enactment-and-enforcement-anti-homeless-laws-golden.

Semuels, Alana. "Living, and Dying, at Home." *Atlantic*, 1 May 2015, https://www.theatlantic.com/business/archive/2015/05/living-and-dying-at-home/391871/.

Senate Housing Committee. "Fact Sheet: Homelessness in California." *California State Senate*, https://shou.senate.ca.gov/sites/shou.senate.ca.gov/files/Homelessness%20in%20CA%202023%20Numbers%20-%201.2024.pdf. Accessed 22 Aug. 2024.

Serving Life. Directed by Lisa R. Cohen, narrated by Forest Whitaker, Oprah Winfrey Network, 28 Jul. 2011.

Shea, Amy. *Greetings from Fresno*. U of Glasgow, 2014.

Sheehan, Tim. "Ban on Homeless Camping Wins Fresno City Council Approval." *Fresno Bee*, 17 Aug. 2017, https://www.fresnobee.com/news/local/article167906722.html.

Sherwood, Harriet. "Windsor Council Leader Calls for Removal of Homeless Before Royal Wedding." *Guardian*, 3 Jan. 2018, https://www.theguardian.com/society/2018/jan/03/windsor-council-calls-removal-homeless-people-before-royal-wedding.

Shields, David. *The Thing About Life Is That One Day You'll Be Dead*. Penguin, 2009.

Sibley, Eugene. *A Brief Early History of Certain Fresno County Cemeteries: As Told in Recorded Documents*. Fresno, 2018.

———. "List for Memorial Mausoleum Interments at Ararat Armenia Cemetery." *Fresno County Public Library*, https://www.fresnogenealogy.org/graves/memorialmausoleum/. Accessed 9 Apr. 2018.

———. Personal interview. 15 Jul. 2016.

———. "A Short History of Fresno County Owned Cemeteries for Indigents: Paupers and Potters Fields." *Fresno County Genealogical Society's Ash Tree Echo*, vol. 50, no. 3, Jul./Aug. 2015.

Siegler, Kirk. "Fresno Officials Dismantle Homeless Encampments." *NPR*, 26 Sep. 2013, https://www.kcur.org/2013-09-26/fresno-officials-dismantle-homeless -encampments.

Sisson Quinn, Jill. "Big Night." *New England Review*, vol. 36, no. 1, 2015, https://www .nereview.com/vol-36-no-1-2015/jill-sisson-quinn-big-night/.

Six Feet Under. Created by Allan Ball, Actual Size Films and the Greenblatt/Janollari Studio, 2001–2005.

"Sleep in the Park." *Social Bite*, https://www.social-bite.co.uk/who-we-are/the -movement/. Accessed 14 Mar. 2019.

Sloane, David Charles. *Is the Cemetery Dead?* U of Chicago P, 2018.

———. *The Last Great Necessity: Cemeteries in American History*. John Hopkins UP, 1991.

Smith, Marie. Personal interview. 13 Feb. 2019.

Snow, Kimberly. Personal interview. 23 Jul. 2024.

Solnit, Rebecca. *The Mother of All Questions*. Haymarket, 2017.

Solomon, Sheldon, et al. *The Worm at the Core: On the Role of Death in Life*. Random House, 2015.

Song, John, et al. "Dying on the Streets: Homeless Persons' Concerns and Desires About End of Life Care." *Journal of General Internal Medicine*, vol. 22, no. 4, 2007, pp. 435–441.

———. "Experiences with and Attitudes Toward Death and Dying Among Home-less Persons." *Journal of General Internal Medicine*, vol. 22, no. 4, 2007, pp. 427–434.

Sottile, Leah. "When Death Is a Fascination." *Atlantic*, 13 Aug. 2015, https://www .theatlantic.com/health/archive/2015/08/death-obsessed/400880/.

Spary, Sara, and Jasmine Gray. "People Who Are Dying, Sick or in Poor Men-tal Health Are Spiraling into Debt." *Huffington Post*, 20 Jun. 2018, https://www .huffingtonpost.co.uk/entry/people-who-are-sick-dying-or-in-poor-mental -health-are-spiralling-into-debt_uk_5b28d6a4e4b0a4dc9920611b.

Speer, Jessie. *Right to the Tent City: The Struggle over Urban Space in Fresno, Califor-nia*. 2014. Syracuse University, master's thesis.

Srivastava, Ranjana. "Dying at Home Might Sound Preferable. But I've Seen the Reality." *Guardian*, 1 May 2017, https://www.theguardian.com/commentisfree/ 2017/may/01/dying-at-home-terminally-ill-hospital.

St. Francis House, Boston. https://www.stfrancishouse.org/about/. Accessed 25 Feb. 2019.

St. Luke's Hospice. *A Model to Support End of Life Care for the Homeless*. St. Luke's Hospice, 2018.

Stajduhar, Kelli I., et al. "Caregiving at the Margins: An Ethnographic Exploration of Family Caregivers Experiences Providing Care for Structurally Vulnerable Populations at the End-of-Life." *Palliative Medicine*, 2020, pp. 1–8, https://doi.org/10.1177/0269216320917875.

"Statistics." *National Funeral Directors Association*, https://www.nfda.org/news/statistics. Accessed 5 Dec. 2019.

Steimle, Susie. "Headshots for the Homeless: Photographer Helps Clients See New Self Worth." *CBS SF Bay Area*, 12 Feb. 2020, https://homelessness.ucsf.edu/our-impact/research-areas/aging.

———. "UCSF Researchers Focus on 'Aging into Homelessness' in Bay Area." *CBS SF Bay Area*, 4 Nov. 2019, https://homelessness.ucsf.edu/our-impact/research-areas/aging.

Steinbeck, John. *The Grapes of Wrath*. Penguin Classics, 1939.

Stephenson, Wesley. "Do the Dead Outnumber the Living?" *BBC News*, 4 Feb. 2012, https://www.bbc.com/news/magazine-16870579.

Stroh, Perlita. "Life on the Streets 'a Killer': New Hospice Offers End-of-Life Care to the Homeless." *CBC News*, 2 Jul. 2018, https://www.cbc.ca/news/health/journey-home-hospice-toronto-homeless-end-of-life-care-1.4715540.

Sussman, Tamara. "To Die Well, We Must Talk About Death Before the End of Life." *PBS Newshour*, 27 Oct. 2019, https://www.pbs.org/newshour/health/to-die-well-we-must-talk-about-death-before-the-end-of-life.

Swain, Kelley. "A Place to Write, a Place to Heal." *Lancet*, vol. 388, no. 10045, 2016, https://www.thelancet.com/pdfs/journals/lancet/PIIS0140-6736(16)31282-X.pdf.

Sweeney, Erica. "Good Practice: Medical Respite Programs Offer Homeless Patients a Place to Go." *Rewire.News*, 20 Dec. 2018, https://www.rewire.news/article/2018/12/20/medical-respite-homeless-patients/.

TalkDeath. "The Death Positive Movement: What Is It?" *TalkDeath*, 9 Jun. 2015, https://www.talkdeath.com/death-positive-movement/.

Tarzian, Anita J., et al. "Attitudes, Experiences, and Beliefs Affecting End-of-Life Decision-Making Among Homeless Individuals." *Journal of Palliative Medicine*, vol. 8, no. 1, 2005, pp. 36–48.

"They're like Puzzles: Inside NC's Effort to Identify Nameless Dead." *WRAL.com*, 7 Oct. 2013, https://www.wral.com/-they-re-like-puzzles-inside-nc-s-effort-to-identify-nameless-dead/12916155/.

Thomas, Pat, and Leslie Harker. *I Miss You: A First Look at Death*. Baron's, 2001.

Thompson, Derek. "Your Brain on Poverty: Why Poor People Seem to Make Bad Decisions." *Atlantic*, 22 Nov. 2013, https://www.theatlantic.com/business/archive/2013/11/your-brain-on-poverty-why-poor-people-seem-to-make-bad-decisions/281780/.

Thoong Chong, Mok, et al. "Assessing Health Conditions and Medication Use Among the Homeless Community in Long Beach, California." *Journal of Research in Pharmacy Practice*, vol. 3, no. 2, Apr.–Jun. 2014, pp. 56–61, https://doi.org/10.4103/2279-042x.137073.

Thorpe, Deborah, et al. "Meeting the Challenge of Providing Hospice and Palliative Care for the Homeless (TH115)." *Journal of Pain and Symptom Management*, vol. 63, no. 5, May 2022.

To, Matthew J., et al. "Foot Conditions Among Homeless Persons: A Systematic Review." *PLoS One*, vol. 11, no. 12, 2016, https://doi.org/10.1371/journal.pone.0167463.

Tobias, Manuela, and Matt Levin. "California Just Counted Its Homeless—a Tally Sure to Be Inaccurate, and Politically Weaponized." *Fresno Bee*, 30 Jan. 2020, https://www.fresnobee.com/news/local/article239607353.html.

Topping, Alexandra. "'People Care for Five Minutes': Homeless Man's Death Is Wake-Up Call Says Charity." *Guardian*, 15 Feb. 2018, https://www.theguardian.com/society/2018/feb/15/man-found-dead-london-tube-station-former-model-homeless-charity.

Tradii, Laura, and Martin Robert. "Do We Deny Death? II. Critiques of the Death-Denial Thesis." *Mortality*, vol. 24, no. 4, 2017, pp. 377–388.

Trujillo, Taelar. Personal interview. 23 Jul. 2024.

Turner, Nicola, and Glenys Caswell. "Moral Ambiguity in Media Reports of Dying Alone." *Mortality*, vol. 25, no. 3, 2019, pp. 266–281.

Twigg, Julia, et al., editors. *Body Work in Health and Social Care: Critical Themes, New Agendas*. Wiley-Blackwell, 2011.

"UCLA Medical Center Pilots Strategies for Having End-of-Life Conversations with Homeless Community in Santa Monica." *Coalition for Compassionate Care of California*, 26 Jul. 2015, https://www.coalitionccc.org/2015/07/pilot-program-at-ucla-medical-center-tracks-advance-directives-among-santa-monicas-homeless-community/.

"The US Congress Joint Economic Committee on 'Deaths of Despair.'" *Population and Development Review*, vol. 45, no. 4, 2019, pp. 939–943.

Utecht, Tom. "A Good Death: Thoughtful Planning Eases the Family's Anguish." *Fresno Bee*, 7 Oct. 2016, https://www.fresnobee.com/opinion/readers-opinion/article106231512.html.

"Vagrancy Act 1824." *legislation.gov.uk*, https://www.legislation.gov.uk/ukpga/Geo4/5/83/section/4. Accessed 22 Mar. 2019.

VanTol, Victoria. "How to Use Respectful, Instead of Degrading, Language Around Homelessness." *Invisible People*, 18 Jun. 2020, https://www.invisiblepeople.tv/how-to-use-respectful-instead-of-degrading-language-around-homelessness/.

Venable Moore, Catherine. "The Book of the Dead." *The Best American Essays 2017*, edited by Leslie Jamison, Houghton Mifflin Harcourt, 2017, pp. 128–159.

Wadsworth, John. *Art of Dying*, vol. 1, 21 Nov. 2016, https://www.artofdying.net/.

Waldman, Elisha. "What We Get Wrong About Dying: A Pediatric Oncologist Describes the Lessons of His Practice." *Nautilus*, 28 Dec. 2017, http://nautil.us/issue/55/trust/what-we-get-wrong-about-dying.

Walker, Alissa, and Emma Alpern. "How We Talk About Homelessness Is Finally Changing." *Curbed*, 11 Jun. 2020, https://archive.curbed.com/2020/6/11/21273455/homeless-people-definition-copy-editing.

Walker, Nicole. "The Braided Essay as Social Justice Action." *Creative Nonfiction*, no. 64, 2017, https://www.creativenonfiction.org/online-reading/braided-essay-social-justice-action.

"Walking Tours in Manchester." *Invisible Cities*, https://www.invisible-cities.org/cities/manchester. Accessed 25 Jul. 2020.

Waters, Michael. "No One Really Knows What to Do with All of America's Unclaimed Corpses." *Atlantic*, 12 Feb. 2019, https://www.theatlantic.com/health/archive/2019/02/unclaimed-bodies-problem/582625/.

Watts, Bobby. Personal interview. 15 Apr. 2017.

"We Need to Change How We Bury the Dead." *Vox Media*, 24 Aug. 2017, https://www.facebook.com/Vox/videos/751224188398519/.

Webb, Wendy Ann. "Hungry, Homeless and Heading for Heaven. Exploring End-of-Life Preferences of Homeless People in the UK." *European Association for Palliative Care*, 10 Oct. 2018, https://www.eapcnet.wordpress.com/2018/10/10/hungry-homeless-and-heading-for-heaven-exploring-end-of-life-preferences-of-homeless-people-in-the-uk/.

———. "When Dying at Home Is Not an Option: Exploration of Hostel Staff Views on Palliative Care for Homeless People." *International Journal of Palliative Nursing*, vol. 21, no. 5, 2015, 236–244.

"Welcome to Death Cafe." *Death Cafe*, https://www.deathcafe.com. Accessed 17 Jan. 2018.

"Welcome to the Fresno County Sheriff's Office Website." *Fresno County Sheriff's Office*, https://www.fresnosheriff.org/. Accessed 24 Jul. 2020.

"We're All Gonna Live Forever! The Stories We Tell About Conquering Death." *Hidden Brain*. NPR, 23 Sep. 2019, https://www.npr.org/2019/09/23/763474019/were-all-gonna-live-forever-the-stories-we-tell-about-conquering-death.

Westervelt, Eric. "Sprawling Homeless Camps—Modern 'Hoovervilles'—Vex California." *NPR*, 13 Jan. 2020, https://www.npr.org/2020/01/13/795439405/sprawling-homeless-camps-modern-hoovervilles-vex-california.

"What Is a Pauper's Funeral? Public Health Funerals Explained." *Funeral Guide*, 9 Jan. 2020, https://www.funeralzone.co.uk/help-resources/arranging-a-funeral/what-is-a-paupers-funeral-public-health-funerals-explained.

"What We Do." *Poverello House*, https://www.poverellohouse.org/what-we-do/shelter. Accessed 25 Jul. 2020.

"When Remains Unclaimed, NC's Dead Scattered at Sea." *WRAL.com*, 8 Aug. 2014, https://www.wral.com/when-remains-unclaimed-nc-s-dead-scattered-at-sea/13876971/.

"Who We Are." *C4 Innovations*, https://www.c4innovates.com/who-we-are/. Accessed 25 Jul. 2020.

"Who We Are." *Rosie's Place*, https://www.rosiesplace.org/who_we_are. Accessed 25 Jul. 2020.

Wilde, Caleb. *Confessions of a Funeral Director: How the Business of Death Saved My Life*. HarperOne, 2017.

Wills, Garry. *Lincoln at Gettysburg: The Words That Remade America*. Simon and Schuster, 1992.

Wilson, Albert. Personal interview. 23 Jul. 2024.

Woods, Douglas. Personal interview. 23 Jul. 2024.

Woolf, Virginia. *Killing the Angel in the House*. Penguin, 1995.

Wyatt, Karen. "Why Some People Don't Die in Peace." *Huffington Post*, 18 Jan. 2018, https://www.huffpost.com/entry/why-some-people-dont-die-in-peace_b_5a53ec06e4b0ee59d41c0d48?fbclid=IwAROI6kYecD-CQ3B8kxaumyA4y_u5qmQ3H8pV9nOXs59Z7m8B-QFWvDfmKYA.

Yalom, Irvin D. *Staring at the Sun: Overcoming the Dread of Death*. Piatkus, 2008.

"You're Going to Die with Ned Buskirk." *YouTube*, uploaded by Death Hangout, 26 Mar. 2017, https://www.youtube.com/watch?v=H59-PcQ1BKg.

Yuknavitch, Lidia. *The Misfit's Manifesto*. Simon and Schuster, 2017.

INDEX

Page numbers in italics refer to figures and tables.

AMY SHEA holds an MFA and a doctorate in creative writing from the University of Glasgow. Her essays have appeared in *The Missouri Review*, *Portland Review*, *The Massachusetts Review*, the *Journal of Sociology of Health and Illness*, and others. She is the writing program director for Mount Tamalpais College, a college for the incarcerated people of San Quentin Rehabilitation Center in California.